D0053682

Stampf

James Shepherd Pike

Courtesy of Mr. Ned Lamb and Calais Free Library

James Shepherd Pike

James Shepherd Pike

Republicanism and the
American Negro,
1850-1882

Robert Franklin Durden

Durham, N. C.
Duke University Press
1957

Copyright, 1957, Duke University Press

Cambridge University Press, London, N.W. 1, England

Library of Congress Catalog Number 57-6284

Printed in the United States of America

By the Seeman Printery, Inc., Durham, N. C.

To
Professor Jeter Allen Isely
1913-1954

Preface

THE ORIGINAL question which prompted this study was
this: How did James S. Pike come to write *The Prostrate
State: South Carolina under Negro Government?* The book,
published in 1873, is a classic indictment of Radical Reconstruction and the Negro's role in it. Indeed, in his allegations
and implications about the Negro, not merely the Negro voter
and office-holder but the race, Pike goes as far as any "Conservative," white-supremacy Southerner of that era could possibly have wished.

Yet Pike was a Republican from Maine. He had first become famous as one of Horace Greeley's fire-eating antislavery
writers on the New York *Tribune.* When it came to attacking
slavery, slaveholders, and "Doughface" Northern Democrats
in the 1850's, Pike managed to be even more extreme than
Editor Greeley. After the Republicans won the presidential
election of 1860, Pike realized a long-sought goal by securing
a diplomatic appointment as President Lincoln's minister to
the Netherlands. He watched the entire Civil War from there,
seeing men and events, both in Europe and the United States,
in an unusual, Radical Republican light. Returning to this
country in 1866, he sympathized with and supported the Radical program but finally bolted the Republican party, behind
his friend Greeley, to join the Liberal Republican movement
of 1872.

An obvious purpose which Pike had in his writings about
Reconstruction in South Carolina was to continue the attack of
the disappointed Liberal Republicans on the Grant administration and its Southern supporters. But a more fundamental
clue to Pike's position, in the 1850's no less than in the 1870's,

is to be found in his constant antipathy towards the Negro race.

Research in the large collection of his papers which are now in the Free Library of his home town, Calais, Maine, warrants these conclusions: (1) that Pike had been ardently free soil partially because he thought Western soil should be white man's soil; (2) that he advocated disunion, along Garrisonian lines, partly because he despaired in the mid-1850's of living alongside arrogant slaveholders and their repulsive property; (3) that he temporarily urged peaceful secession in the winter of 1860-61 with one eye cocked toward getting rid of a "mass of barbarism" and the other on the necessity of Republican refusal to compromise; and (4) that during the dark days of the war in 1863-64 he would have been satisfied to settle for a compromise peace if it meant that only a Gulf coast or Deep South "negro pen" would be lost to the Federal government. In this context, Pike's 1873 book made only too much sense, for he had, long before his visit to South Carolina, shared many of the racial notions which are generally regarded by historians as having been motivating factors only among Southern whites.

A question about which I have thought much is this: How typical were Pike's racial ideas among his Northern contemporaries? In many ways he was an unusual and admirable person, as I have tried to suggest in the following pages. But because of his particular time and place in our history, his ideas are important and not a private, personal matter of no significance. To the extent that they were representative or "typical," I suggest that the Civil War and Reconstruction eras take on a new dimension of tragedy. If our Civil War victors, or any considerable portion of them, shared and were partially motivated by racial considerations similar to those of the vanquished, then truly the Fates had made high tragedy of our great national bloodletting.

The late Jeter A. Isely of Princeton University was responsible, in several ways, for my writing this book. He first mentioned Pike as a subject worthy of investigation and, subsequently, his advice and criticism were valuable, his diligence and co-operation far in excess of the limits set by the teacher's duty. He suggested many of the revisions and additions which I have made but which his untimely death on September 30, 1954, prevented his seeing.

My friend and fellow student at Princeton, Mr. John Hemphill, read and criticized portions of my manuscript, and the members of a seminar conducted by Professor Robert R. Palmer made useful suggestions concerning the fourth chapter. The staff of the Princeton University Library was consistently helpful, and particularly so Mrs. Margaret Thompson, Mr. Alexander Clark, and Mr. Malcolm Young. Miss Edith Beckett and Mr. Shirley A. Bradish, librarian and trustee respectively of the Calais, Maine, Free Library, extended many courtesies and warm hospitality in providing easy access to the Pike MSS. In Washington, D. C., Mr. Thomas Riggs of the Manuscripts Division of the Library of Congress and Mr. Alex Mavro of the National Archives were especially helpful to me. Other individuals who have been kind enough to read and criticize chapters or who otherwise encouraged me are Professors Harold Davis of Bradford Junior College; William B. Hamilton, William T. Laprade, Harold Parker, and Robert H. Woody of Duke University; Wesley F. Craven and Howard Horsford of Princeton University; and Mr. Richard B. Harwell of the Virginia State Library. Ann Oller Durden helped with the index.

Portions of this book, in somewhat different form, have appeared in the *Journal of Negro History,* the *South Carolina Historical Magazine,* the *Lincoln Herald,* and the *New England Quarterly.*

I am indebted to the Duke University Research Council for its generous grants in aid of both research and publication.

Duke University   Robert F. Durden
March, 1956

Contents

James Shepherd Pike

I . *The Maine Years*

1811-1850

W AY DOWN EAST in Maine, the small town of Calais today enjoys a quiet prosperity, drawing sustenance from a few small industries, agriculture, and tourists. In the first half of the nineteenth century conditions were different, and Calais boomed. Located on the St. Croix River directly opposite the Canadian town of St. Stephen and close to the Atlantic, the Yankee community hit its most exciting stride in the days of the sailing vessels. Shipbuilding and lumbering were then the central activities that enriched a few enterprising individuals and occupied many others. The population jumped from about one hundred persons in 1800 to almost five thousand in 1850. Calais thus participated in the general expansion and exploitation of natural resources that accompanied the opening of this scenic frontier area.[1]

One of Calais' most prominent sons in the nineteenth century was James Shepherd Pike. He became famous in the 1850's as an ardent champion of the antislavery crusade and a leading Republican writer for Horace Greeley's *Tribune*. Before he appeared on the national scene, Pike had accumulated a modest fortune and abundant political experience in the Maine village where he was born on September 8, 1811. His father, William Pike, drowned in 1818 in a small boat on the

---

[1] Harold Davis, *An International Community on the St. Croix* (Orono, Maine, 1950), is a fine regional history of the colorful Canadian-American valley and its towns. The above is based largely on Davis, especially pp. 114-33, 309, and on personal observation.

St. Croix. Mrs. Hannah Shepherd Pike was left with four small sons, of whom James was the second, and two other children by William Pike's first marriage. Not much is known of Mrs. Pike except that she took in boarders to support her family. One small clue does suggest that she possessed ability: in the early 1830's she became president of the "Calais Ladies Jews Society," which apparently aimed at missionary work among the Hebrews.[2]

One of the family boarders in the 1820's was a parson-schoolmaster. Young James had received only occasional, inadequate schooling up to that time, but the parson launched in a big room of Mrs. Pike's house "a school of higher pretensions than any we had had before and the larger boys from both sides of the river went to him." Sadly enough, the parson proved to be a "puffy man" and James became, in his own words, "rowdy." His formal schooling ended abruptly when the schoolmaster expelled him. He was on his own.[3]

His future promise did not reveal itself quickly. The young boy, unhampered by crotchety schoolteachers, ran errands, took care of the cow, picked berries, shot pigeons, and made "camps in the bushes" with other footloose Huck Finns of the community. Then about 1826 or 1827 his commercial life began when he clerked in a series of stores. This continued for six or seven years, and during this time he developed commercial acumen and acquired the love of reading which he kept throughout life. He subscribed to newspapers and borrowed books from friends or from the local literary club. With perhaps a touch of romantic nostalgia he later remembered that he had "read Walter Scott's poems by candle light after I had shut the store and retired by myself into the back counting room." And even in his early twenties politics began to interest him; at the age of twenty-three he joined with several other

[2] For family background see "Pike Genealogy," Notebook in Pike MSS, Calais Free Library, Calais, Maine. Also I. C. Knowlton, *Annals of Calais, Maine and St. Stephen, New Brunswick* (Calais, 1875), p. 206.

[3] Memoir of his early life from 1818 to 1856, Pike MSS.

local Whigs in 1834 to launch the *Boundary Gazette,* which survived only briefly.[4]

Pike helped launch another weekly paper in 1836 and accepted a one-year term as editor. The "Prospectus" for the Calais *Gazette and Advertiser,* curiously mixing humility and pugnacity, announced that "If a Whig paper is wanted here, it will be supported, unless our claims to support are forfeited by want of industry or ability." The paper lived, precariously, for a few years, but Editor Pike found his newspaper duties galling, especially so since the Whigs won no victories over the triumphant Jacksonian Democrats. After a year he quit the job. "Amid the constant pressure of private affairs," he confessed, "and the absence of strong party feeling (which of all things is most efficacious in sustaining a political paper) we have trudged along to the end of our journey. Here we rest."[5]

Land speculation offered quick profits to those who could scrape together the necessary capital. The enterprising young Whig sold his interest in a general store to his older half-brother and plunged into the flourishing speculation. Economic conditions in northeastern Maine closely paralleled those of the other frontier areas of the United States where newly opened land led to extensive speculation along with the over-expansion of banking and other credit facilities.[6] Pike's speculative operations were in the valuable timber lands of northern Maine, around the upper reaches of the St. Croix, as well as in "crown lands" which were being sold across the river in the Canadian province of New Brunswick. Within about a year's time, in 1835-36, he and his associates bought and sold various

[4] *Ibid.* The 1830's brought a rash of newspapers, mostly short-lived, to the Calais area. See Davis, *International Community,* pp. 375-76.

[5] *Gazette and Advertiser,* Aug. 16, 1836, for the "Prospectus" and Aug. 29, 1837, for the valedictory.

[6] For the Calais area, see Davis, *International Community,* pp. 114-33; for the same conditions elsewhere, see Frederick J. Turner, *The United States, 1830-1850: The Nation and Its Sections* (New York, 1935), pp. 228, 289-95. Roy M. Robbins, *Our Landed Heritage: The Public Domain, 1776-1936* (Princeton, 1942), pp. 59-71, treats the same problem.

townships and timber tracts, with his year's profit from these operations amounting to $7,500.[7]

And true to the general picture of frontier economics in the frenzied mid-1830's, the young capitalist joined forces with another Calais entrepreneur, as well as with two Boston businessmen, and launched the St. Croix River Bank in 1836. This, together with the other new bank opened in the same year and the oldest bank, which had been established in 1831-32, gave three banks to the small community of about two thousand residents. Cashier Pike later recalled that the bank "never had over $15,000 actual capital" for in "those days of kite flying, the most cautious man who was in business, sometimes found his name on notes and drafts known as 'accommodation paper,' where it ought not to have been." Aside from the feverish economic activity that encouraged these banking operations, President Jackson's veto in 1832 of the bill re-chartering the second United States Bank, and his subsequent removal of Federal deposits, had opened the door to the "wildcat" banking that spread across the country in the 1830's. But just as Pike and Calais had briefly floated on top of the prosperity wave, they were soon forced by the panic of 1837 to retrench drastically.[8]

Despite the hard times, Pike managed to remain solvent. In his brief reminiscences of this period he alludes to "growing losses" and threatening bankruptcy; but the fact that the panic of 1837 and the subsequent depression did not economically wreck him is indicated by his mentioning that in 1838 he began "some little ventures in the navigation line with some ready means I kept command of." In fact, by 1842-43 his personal economic outlook was indeed bright. He successfully and hon-orably extricated himself from the bank and its debts, and he operated "under a full head of prosperous business." His ac-

[7] Memoir, Pike MSS.

[8] "Biographical Notices of People of Calais and Vicinity," Pike MSS; Memoir, Pike MSS.

tivities now centered around another store which he had built, his new steamboat wharf built on piles ("the first in Calais"), and his investments in sailing vessels. By the end of 1846, when he acquired a business partner, he records that he had "accumulated some 18 or 19,000 dollars and felt rich and willing to lay down hard work."[9]

At thirty-five Pike virtually did "lay down hard work." He retained the property which he had acquired and judiciously multiplied his accumulated capital by investment in securities, but for the remainder of his life his primary interests were politics and journalism rather than business. His fortune was never great; it was always adequate. Undoubtedly he might have amassed a great deal more wealth, but the explanation for his choice seems to lie in the fact that he simply enjoyed politics and writing. Too, he admitted in his memoir that the "years of reverses" in the early 1830's and after the 1837 panic had "entered into my soul." Why not participate in politics, the great American pastime?

As early as 1834, when he was only twenty-three, Pike "eagerly engaged" in politics. The newspaper which he helped launch in that same year was staunchly Whig, and Whig he remained until the advent of Republicanism. Generally speaking, the New England Whigs represented the conservative, well-to-do classes. Pike, the ambitious young entrepreneur and politician, followed the example of most of his friends in adhering to the party of Webster and Clay. The intense fight over President Jackson's fiscal policies furnished the new Whig coalition with one of its chief rallying points. But banks were not popular in Maine, and Jacksonian 'Democracy' there won repeated triumphs over the business-minded Whigs. During Pike's brief editorship his paper scoffed when farmers, hard

[9] Memoir, Pike MSS. His first wife, Mrs. Charlotte Grosvenor Pike, whom he had married in 1837, died in 1847. Pike's mother took care of the daughter, Mary Caroline, who was born in 1841. He married Miss Elizabeth Ellicott of Avondale, Pennsylvania, in June, 1855. Salmon P. Chase had pursued her also; there are several coyly flirtatious letters from Chase to Miss Lizzie Ellicott in the Pike MSS. Chase became a friend of Pike's also.

hit by the panic of 1837, held a mass meeting about bank loans to enable farmers to obtain seed. "Bank accommodations for *Farmers*," the Whig organ exclaimed. "Who ever heard of such a thing. Why, the true farmer is the most independent man on the face of the earth, and asks no loan of money. . . ."[10]

The actual issues between the Whigs and the Democrats tended to become lost in a maze of other matters, such as the "executive usurpation" of "King Andrew I." Yet Pike as a young Whig politician broached the economic subject, although concentrating on other and less sensitive matters in his denunciation of the Democrats. In 1838 he prepared the party manifesto for the Whigs of his district, and he denied that his party was friendly to the United States Bank or to Nicholas Biddle, its controversial head. Nor should any voter "be scared or humbugged," he declared, by the apparition of Federalism. "Although the ear of the country is stunned with the declarations of exclusive democracy on the part of the supporters of the administration," he protested, "we yet undertake to dispute the right of the Loco Foco party to be considered the democratic party of the country." The Democrats, by bringing on the 1837 panic and the subsequent depression, had prostrated the "mercantile interest" and paralyzed "productive industry." The Whigs, on the other hand, were acknowledged supporters of "a Banking system, a credit system, and a paper currency." But lest there be any doubts, the Whig spokesman insisted that any national currency had to rest upon "a sure and solid basis." If it did that, the policy would certainly secure "equal advantages to all." Although the Whigs lost in this campaign, the Calais paper reported that Pike's address was "not a clap trap production."[11]

The Calais Whigs also were beginning to feel abolitionist

[10] *Gazette and Advertiser*, June 6, 1837. See E. Malcolm Carroll, *Origins of the Whig Party* (Durham, N. C., 1925), pp. 58-70; Louis C. Hatch, *Maine: A History* (New York, 1919), pp. 1, 216 ff.

[11] "Address to the Cherryfield Convention," July 31, 1838 (Calais, 1838). This pamphlet is the earliest extensive evidence of Pike's political ideas. *Gazette and Advertiser*, Aug. 8, 1838.

pressures. A local debating and reading club to which **Pike** belonged, the Calais Young Men's Society, took up the abolition question, with its cluster of related topics such as free speech and the right of petition, in 1838. And at near-by Machias, Maine, a local preacher called for an abolitionist meeting to stir up a "holy excitement" among Downeasters.[12] By the early 1840's the Maine abolitionists began to name their own candidates, and the Calais Young Men's Society debated the question of whether or not a distinct political organization of the abolitionists of the country would hasten their ultimate success. Pike, already sympathetic with the antislavery cause, attended antislavery conventions where slavery, the Mexican War, and the annexation of Texas were resolutely condemned. In 1849 he toured Maine in a futile effort to amalgamate the lethargic Whigs with the Free Soilers. Although he considered the Maine Whigs "asleep or dead up to their navel[s]," bolting his party was something which Pike carefully avoided until the Whig organization finally sank in the angry sea of slavery controversy during the 1850's.[13]

Except for the famed log-cabin campaign of 1840, Maine Whiggery faced a stronger foe in the Democracy. On three successive occasions in the 1840's the Calais businessman had this unpleasant knowledge driven home to him. In 1844 he stood as the Whig candidate for state senator from his county but, as he puts it, was "defeated as the Whig candidates were in the habit of being." Again in 1846 Pike's office-holding aspirations were crushed when he ran as the Whig candidate for Congress; the district's Whig party was still a "hopeless minority." Finally in 1850, in his last try for elective office, his Democratic rival for the district Congressional seat forced Whig candidate Pike into second place.[14]

[12] *Gazette and Advertiser*, Jan. 3, March 7, 1838.

[13] *Calais Advertiser*, July 14, Dec. 8, 1841; *ibid.*, July 8, 1846; Pike's "Journal of a Political Tour through Maine, August 1849," Pike MSS.

[14] Memoir, Pike MSS. See Hatch, *Maine*, II, 309-46, for state background; Turner, *United States*, pp. 65-75, relates Maine to New England and both to national politics.

Disappointed in politics, he had already found another outlet for his abilities and ambitions. Pike made his first visit to Washington in the winter of 1844, and while there he wrote political letters for the *Boston Courier*, a strongly Whig paper. After that, a winter visit to Washington became his regular routine for the next thirty-seven years, and his political interests became inextricably involved with his newspaper work. Having so frequently met defeat at the polls, he gradually relinquished hopes of winning an election. That does not mean that he despaired of securing an appointive position. This dream he nourished until Abraham Lincoln's election in 1860 made fulfilment possible. In 1849, however, the zealous Maine Whig failed to receive a diplomatic appointment from the new Whig president, General Zachary Taylor; Pike recorded merely that in 1849 he "wanted to go abroad but could not accomplish it." In 1852 his energetic participation in behalf of General Winfield Scott, the Whig nominee, clearly placed Pike in line for a political plum. But to the despair of the disintegrating Whig party, the Democrats led by Franklin Pierce took control for another four years.[15] Pike had to wait eight more years before his dream of occupying a foreign mission materialized. But in the interval he became, for his own generation at least, a famous man.

Pike had the good fortune to launch his national journalistic career at a time when newspaper reporters and correspondents were just coming to the fore as members of an influential profession. The introduction of the telegraph in the 1830's stimulated the newspaper world by making possible an immediate coverage which had been hitherto impossible. Since newspapers and politics in that era were thoroughly intermeshed, Washington proved to be a fortunate assignment for

[15] Memoir, Pike MSS. Pike wrote a brief campaign biography of General Scott but had only a week's notice in which to prepare it; thus the General's biographer is justified in describing it as the product of "some hack writer whose talents failed to equal his industry." See Charles S. W. Elliott, *Winfield Scott; The Soldier and the Man* (New York, 1937), p. 642.

Correspondent Pike. In the "high-minded, strident, election-conscious journalism" of the pre-Civil War decades, the Calais native had few peers.[16]

Unfettered by any responsibility to attempt impartiality or comprehensiveness, Pike filled his newsletters with pungent and highly partisan prose. The editor of the *Boston Courier* until 1848, Joseph T. Buckingham, shared the Downeaster's antislavery or "conscience" Whiggery, and he may have helped to make a top-caliber newspaperman out of Pike.[17] But his experience on Calais papers in the 1830's plus his Whig career and antislavery beliefs, were Pike's chief assets in the new role he had selected.

Crowing over Zachary Taylor's recent election to the Presidency, Pike announced from Washington early in 1849 that the "great team of Democracy is unyoked, and its load is in the gutter." Bitter debate raged in Congress over the arrangements to be made for territories newly acquired from Mexico. Pike noted, concerning Mississippi's Senator Henry Foote, that "a few splendid passages of *silence* would improve this gentleman's reputation." Senator Henry Wilson of Massachusetts, on the other hand, thrilled him with a "powerful, manly" speech on the slavery question and struck a "true Northern *tone*" with his plea that the Union be dissolved rather than allow human slavery to be spread over another inch of territory.[18]

For a lighter note during a lull in the bitter session, Pike once reported that Senate discussion of the army appropriation bill brought out no subject more interesting than that of Colt pistols. "When we came away, Mr. Rusk of Texas was ex-

[16] Bernard A. Weisberger, *Reporters for the Union* (Boston, 1953), p. 17, describes prewar journalism; for the new, professional role of newspaper correspondents, see *ibid.*, pp. 42-73.

[17] For Buckingham, who published James Russell Lowell's *Biglow Papers*, see Frank L. Mott, *American Journalism: A History of Newspapers in the United States through 260 Years: 1690 to 1950* (New York, 1950), p. 262.

[18] *Boston Courier*, Feb. 2, 19, and 22, 1849. Pike initialed all his letters "J. S. P." All citations are to the semiweekly edition of the *Courier*.

plaining the infinite felicity and promptitude with which a revolver would turn live Mexicans into dead ones. Thereupon that grave body voted a hundred or two thousand dollars of the sovereign people's money for the purchase of an indefinite number thereof, to be put into the belts of Anglo Saxons, in order, as Mr. Benton would say, that funerals might follow. Well, if the Mexicans and Indians must have daylight let into them, it is perhaps best to have the thing done in the most thorough and skillful manner."[19]

He poked fun at the office seekers who swarmed over the capital, not mentioning that he himself suffered the disappointment that inevitably came to many of the patronage-starved Whigs. In the *Courier*, Pike suggested that reasonable Whigs would wait patiently until the next administration could get around to considering their claims. "Let this reflection animate and sustain the hopes of every good Whig who wants an office and don't get it as soon as he thinks he ought to have it."[20]

Pike's articles became ominously grave when he returned to Washington early in 1850. Debate began on Henry Clay's compromise proposals in late January, 1850, and Pike's inner hostility to anything less than the Wilmot Proviso's specific exclusion of slavery from the new territories made the whole business of sectional bargaining and compromising distasteful to him. Nor did he bother to hide his disgust when Massachusetts' Daniel Webster proclaimed his acceptance of the compromise scheme. The *Courier*, no longer edited by Joseph Buckingham, defended the influential senator and found itself increasingly embarrassed by its Washington correspondent's vehement denunciation of the whole pro-compromise wing of

[19] *Boston Courier*, March 8, 1849.

[20] *Boston Courier*, March 5, 1849. Later Pike reported that the Secretary of the Treasury had issued a "ukase" that he would not knowingly appoint any man to office who was bodily present in Washington. Pike explained that a recent suicide of a despairing office seeker in the East Room of the White House might have alarmed the Secretary about his safety. Some such frustrated gentleman "might do the same thing in the office of the Secretary, and forget to take the precaution to point the pistol towards his *own* head" (*ibid.*, April 26, 1849).

the Whig party. Long editorials defending Webster's position followed on the heels of Pike's fiery assaults. The editor admitted in a note appended to one of these Washington stories that "Our Washington correspondent is a forcible, perspicacious and eloquent writer. He is so highly independent, and his signature is so well known, that it is clearly enough understood that he speaks for himself. . . ."[21] Such artful dodging would not do, however, and the editor, harassed by "business obligations," shortly terminated Pike's association with the Boston paper. He explained in a private letter: "We have now a real job to do in sustaining Dan, and it is impossible to get ahead if we pull down with one hand what we build up with the other. People are quoting your letters against us. . . . Small causes we don't mind, but this is cutting our own throat."[22]

In that same month of April, 1850, Horace Greeley invited Pike to write for the *Tribune*. "J. S. P." soon became famous throughout the Northern states. He helped to make the *Tribune's* Washington coverage "the best showcase for high-minded reporting" in the nation and to earn Greeley's paper the record of having "the most brilliant staff any American newspaper had yet assembled."[23]

[21] *Boston Courier,* April 11, 1850.

[22] S. Kettell to Pike, April 15, 1850, in Pike's *First Blows of the Civil War* (New York, 1879), p. 26. *First Blows* is discussed below, pp. 227-229. Many of Pike's 1850 letters to the *Courier,* which were also occasionally printed in the *Boston Atlas* and the *Portland Advertiser,* are printed in *First Blows.*

[23] Weisberger, *Reporters,* pp. 50-51; Mott, *American Journalism,* pp. 270-71.

II. *The Making*
of a Radical Republican

CONSERVATIVE Bostonians might recoil from Pike's attack on the "God-like Daniel," but Horace Greeley and other antislavery Whigs welcomed assistance from the forceful Maine writer. "Will you write me some letters?" the crusading editor asked. "You are writing such abominably bad ones for the *Boston Courier* that I fancy you are putting all your unreason into these, and can give me some of the pure juice. Try!"[1]

Thus was Pike's great opportunity offered. Greeley's *Tribune* in the 1850's became much more than just a New York newspaper. It was a "sectional oracle" in the antislavery movement, the movement which gave a cohesiveness to the Republicans that the Whigs had never had.[2] Pike's association with the *Tribune* and the men who ran it, especially Greeley and Charles A. Dana, became increasingly intimate after 1850. The Downeaster was soon an associate editor, writing many unsigned editorials in addition to his Washington letters. Pike's articles, interpretative and individualistic, were much like the columns of our twentieth-century political analysts, and his Washington despatches invariably carried his "J. S. P." at the bottom. The *Tribune* editor considered the initialing of articles as beneficial both to the paper and to the ego

---

[1] Greeley to Pike, April 24, 1850, Pike MSS; also in *First Blows*, p. 41. Greeley and Pike were probably friends by the late 1840's when both were much in Washington.

[2] Jeter A. Isely, *Horace Greeley and the Republican Party, 1853-1861* (Princeton, 1947), p. 3.

of the correspondent.[3] Famed and incomparably colorful
though he was, Greeley by no means dominated his brilliant
staff. There were ten associate editors by 1854, and Charles
A. Dana served as managing editor. The "Tribune Association" had been organized in 1849. Greeley owned consider-
ably less than half of the paper, while Pike and others on the
staff were allowed to buy shares of the valuable stock. These
business arrangements, together with Greeley's loose concept
of his function as editor, made for a dazzling and stimulating
variety in the paper's contents.[4]

Pike's relationship with Greeley lasted until the influential
editor's death in 1872. On the whole they agreed on a great
many more points than they differed. Both were strong champions of antislavery long before the Republican party appeared
on the scene to serve as the instrument of fusion for the various
Northern groups which opposed the spread of the South's peculiar institution. Both adhered to many of the Whig economic policies relating to issues like the tariff and governmental encouragement of the country's industrial development.

Yet despite their essential similarity in aims, Pike and
Greeley differed on many tactical matters. The correspondent tended to be more extreme in his attacks on slavery
than the editor; more than this, Pike stubbornly flirted
with Northern disunionism, such as the Garrisonian abolitionists advocated, and this became especially embarrassing in the
late 1850's when the Republicans faced the political necessity
of winning Northern moderates to their cause. Greeley steered
clear of the abolitionists. Differences among the *Tribune's*
talented staff, however, were commonplace and added interest
to the lively paper. And as far as the Democrats or slave-

---

[3] Glyndon G. Van Deusen, *Horace Greeley: Nineteenth Century Crusader* (Philadelphia, 1953), p. 132. Pike wrote his initialed articles as a "special" Washington
correspondent, while James E. Harvey served as the *Tribune's* "regular" correspondent in
the 1850's and signed his articles as "Index" (Isely, *Greeley*, p. 8).

[4] Van Deusen, *Greeley*, p. 132.

holders were concerned, the antislavery spokesmen on the *Tribune* closed ranks for attack.[5]

To illustrate Pike's position with regard to slavery and the crucial question of its extension into the territories, nothing serves more admirably than the Kansas imbroglio that began festering in 1854. The slavery controversy, along with other factors, had already dangerously weakened the bonds of existing political parties. Senator Stephen A. Douglas unwittingly made a major contribution to the formation of the Republican party when he introduced his Kansas-Nebraska Bill early in 1854. Railways, not slavery, occupied the Illinois Democrat's primary attention when he introduced his bill, but the explicit repeal of the Missouri Compromise of 1820, which had barred slavery north of 36° 30′ in the Louisiana Purchase, again opened wide the slavery question. The resulting dismay, confusion, and fear, both in the North and in the South, lasted until war began in April, 1861. Compromise on the issue of whether or not slavery should go into the territories became impossible as extremists, North and South, increasingly pushed aside the moderates and talk of compromise became a target for the heaviest political attack from both Calhounite Democrats and Radical Republicans. As the special Washington correspondent for the *Tribune* and an associate of rising leaders such as William H. Seward, Salmon P. Chase, and William Pitt Fessenden, Pike established his reputation as one of the Northern extremists.[6]

[5] *First Blows, passim;* unpublished Dana and Greeley letters during the 1850's in the Pike MSS. See also, Isely, *Greeley,* pp. 8, 123. Although the old Whig dream of a central bank was not an issue in the 1850's, it should be noted that Greeley approved the New York State system of "free banking" which later served as a general model for the National Banking Act of 1863. Pike, on the other hand, after his unpleasant experience with land speculation and wildcat banking in the late 1830's, became a convert to the subtreasury system of the Democrats. This economic difference between the editor and his associate became clear during discussion of the 1857 panic but was of no significance at the time. Greeley made this clear when he announced in the *Tribune,* "We do not mean to be diverted from the great issue of Freedom against slavery by any quarrel about Banks or Tariffs" (Isely, *Greeley,* pp. 219-22).

[6] For Douglas and the Kansas-Nebraska Act, see Frank H. Hodder, "The Genesis of the Kansas-Nebraska Act," *Proceedings of Wisconsin State Historical Society, 1912*

The principal theme of Pike's angry response to the 1854 repeal of the Missouri Compromise was that the "whole North" had to unite in maintaining its rights, for the "south has united to assail them." Ignoring the Western origin of the hated Kansas-Nebraska Bill, the Maine journalist charged that a "solid phalanx of aggression rears its black head everywhere south of Mason and Dixon's line, banded for the propagation of Slavery all over the continent." This being the case, the duty of "every independent man, of every workingman in the North," plainly required that old party lines be obliterated and a new, Northern antislavery coalition be effected.[7]

Such appeals as this were directed not only against the despised Democrats. They were also aimed at the quickly growing Know-Nothings, or Native Americans, who wished to escape the dangerous sectionalism of the slavery question by concentrating their attack on "foreign" immigrants, especially Catholic ones. Men like Pike and Greeley, along with a host of others, preferred antislavery to nativism as the ideological cement for the new political coalition which would replace the battered and dying Whig party; and they fought strenuously and successfully in the mid-1850's to lure many of the powerful Know-Nothings into the antislavery party. Pike's aversion to Irish and French Catholics was rooted in his unhappy political experiences as a Whig in the 1830's and 1840's, when the Democrats invariably secured support from these immigrant groups. His intellectual and political hostility to "papists" did not, however, suffice to carry him into the new nativist party. His antislavery principles were stronger. And unlike many of his Northern contemporaries, he was ready in 1854 to launch a frankly sectional political party.[8]

(Madison, 1913), pp. 69-86; George F. Milton, *The Eve of Conflict: Stephen A. Douglas and the Needless War* (Boston, 1934), pp. 98-128. On the beginnings of the Republican party, see Nevins, *Ordeal of the Union* (New York, 1947), II, 311-46; Isely, *Greeley*, pp. 83-111.

[7] *Tribune* editorial, Feb. 25, 1854. Pike's authorship is shown by internal evidence and the editorial's inclusion in his scrapbooks, Pike MSS.

[8] For the Know-Nothings, see Ray A. Billington, *The Protestant Crusade, 1800-1860*

Pike's clarion call for an antislavery party involved a great deal of vituperation and partisan name-calling, in the accepted fashion of the day. But at the core of all the furor over the violation of the 1820 Missouri compact lay a readiness to resort to almost any means in order to secure a positive Federal prohibition of slavery in the territories, a prohibition such as had been envisaged by the Wilmot Proviso of 1846-48. In 1854, rather than see the Douglas bill embodying popular sovereignty pass the House, the *Tribune* correspondent declared in a despatch from Washington that it would be better that "confusion should ensue—better that discord should reign in the National Councils—better that Congress should break up in wild disorder—nay, better that the Capitol itself should blaze by the torch of the incendiary . . . than that this perfidy and wrong should be finally accomplished."[9]

As former Southern Whigs joined ranks with Southern Democrats to support the Kansas-Nebraska Act, the Maine journalist assailed all "Northern traitors" who had betrayed their section. Northern Democrats, especially Stephen A. Douglas, were "enemies to their country and enemies to their race." They had trampled on Christian doctrine by not positively barring slavery and should be "vomited forth" from the Northern free states. But, after all, perhaps "some such gigantic outrage upon the living sentiment of the North as the repeal of the Missouri Compromise was necessary to arouse and consolidate the hosts of freedom in the Free States."[10]

(New York, 1938), pp. 380-430. Greeley too was ready by 1854 for a new antislavery party to replace the Whigs but modified his position until after the fall elections. See Isely, *Greeley*, pp. 82 ff., where the process whereby Know-Nothings were brought into the Republican party is made clear. Pike's brother, Frederick A. Pike, joined the nativists in the 1850's prior to becoming a Republican (Memoir, Pike MSS).

[9] *Tribune*, May 18, 1854; omitted from *First Blows*, p. 232. As noted below in chap. ix and as will be clear from notes in the remainder of this chapter, Pike omitted his exhortations to extreme action and his disunionist threats from his published collection of 1879. This constituted the only major distortion of his later compilation.

[10] *Tribune*, May 24, 1854; *First Blows*, pp. 235-37. For Pike's political contacts with congressmen at this time, see *ibid.*, pp. 224, 226, 229, 233-34. Representative Elihu B. Washburne from Illinois, who later became a prominent Republican senator, wrote Pike that his only hope was the *Tribune*. "It is the terror of all the traitorous

"Bleeding Kansas" soon guaranteed, as Pike had wished, that nobody in the North or South would forget the Kansas-Nebraska "outrage." During the interval between the initial anti-Nebraska eruption and the Presidential election of 1856, the new Republican party became an organized and powerful antislavery coalition which fused together, among others, Northern "conscience" Whigs, free-soil Democrats, and anti-slavery Know-Nothings. The Maine political correspondent played an active role in this development; he kept in close contact with Greeley and Dana in New York, with Fessenden and other Maine Republicans, and with Western antislavery leaders like Governor Salmon P. Chase of Ohio. But he stubbornly clung to an extreme position with regard to slavery and the Union which proved embarrassing to some of his Republican friends.

Manifestations of this in 1856 were particularly inexpedient. The election in the fall promised to afford the new antislavery party its first major test. The Kansas controversy furnished most of the emotional excitement in the election year. Pike, for example, declared that there had been enough argument and logic about Kansas. What the North wanted was *"preachers,* with tongues of fire, and a leader holy, rapt, and mystical as a seraph." Where was "the Master" who should seize the "great harp of liberty" and rouse all Northerners?[11]

Such rhetorical nonsense was a commonplace of the tumultous decade in all parts of the country. But after the hot-headed South Carolinian, Preston Brooks, assaulted Senator Charles Sumner in late May, 1856, Pike went too far even for Greeley. The Washington correspondent proclaimed in the *Tribune* that unless "the Northern and Southern civiliza-

---

scandals here. It should now be devoted to the exposure of this ungodly infamy. The rascals stand about the hotels trembling when the newsboys come in with the *Tribune"* (*ibid.,* p. 233). Isely, *Greeley,* pp. 64-69, shows that Pike was several steps ahead of the editor.

[11] *Tribune,* datelined from Washington, April 24, 1856; omitted from *First Blows,* pp. 322-24, although the printed portion of the article is in the same vein.

tions can be harmonized, become positively assimilated, a long union of the two is impossible." In other words, if the Southern states did not abolish slavery the Northern states should separate from them. On the more immediate level, however, every Northern man who came to Congress had to be ready and trained to accept a duel and to defend himself or else to be humiliated by the slaveholders.[12]

Greeley immediately sent word by Dana that such disunionism would harm the Republican cause. Dana advised Pike to send such extreme letters, if he must write them, to New England papers, where they would not lose votes for the Republican candidate as they would if the *Tribune's* vast Northwestern audience read them.[13] The willful Washington correspondent refused to heed this advice, and a few days later he came forth with a strong restatement of his notions. "Personally, I have no doubt that the Free and Slave States ought to separate," he wrote in his article; otherwise constant fighting and arguing appeared inevitable. But he admitted that the idea of separation was "not now palatable" and "not generally shared by our people." For that reason Northerners must send more and better warriors to Congress. Freedom's principles were not enough to assure her triumph in the end. "Persuasion and argument are good," he concluded, "but there always comes a time when steel and gunpowder are better." He thought that time had now come for the United States, since a "collision is at hand."[14] Greeley himself immediately wrote the obdurate associate editor and urged him to stay away from such speculation. "My objection to your Disunion articles is not that I am for or against Disunion; or do or don't believe it is coming," the editor explained, "but that I know its proposition from our side would injure the Republican cause and drive back thousands into Union saving." He believed that if

---

[12] *Tribune,* datelined May 28, 1856; cf. *First Blows*, pp. 342-43.
[13] Dana to Pike, May 30, 1856, Pike MSS.
[14] *Tribune,* June 3, 1856.

New York City voters were given a choice of disunion with Kansas as a free-soil state or union with Kansas as a slave state, the latter choice would prevail by a majority of thirty thousand in the city and would also carry the state. "Now if you really want Disunion," Greeley continued, "keep still and let events ripen. I don't want it; for I believe the same spirit and resolution on our part which are required to dissolve the Union would suffice to rule it, rescuing it from the rule of the Slavedrivers." He concluded that rather than disunion, he preferred "the ascendancy of Liberty" with the slave states remaining in the fold. But "if they choose to go, let them go."[15]

Even this personal plea from Greeley failed to convince Pike to keep quiet, but the remainder of his disunion letters were kept out of print, presumably on the orders of Greeley and Dana. The latter wrote in late July that Pike's *Tribune* stock dividend was being sent along with "$300 for your disunion letters." Dana added: "Ah, if we had only been as big fools as you and printed those letters, how they would now be coming back to curse us! It's lucky for the world there's brains somewhere."[16] Not until after James Buchanan had defeated John C. Frémont in the fall elections did Pike's articles advocating separation reappear in the *Tribune*. Pike opposed Frémont as the Republican candidate, since he preferred Supreme Court Justice John C. McLean. Consequently, he retired to his Maine home and took little interest in the presidential election. In Maine, however, he contributed "liberally" to the local Republican campaign chest; the results there were already more satisfactory than most of the old Whig efforts.[17]

[15] Greeley to Pike, June 5, 1856, Pike MSS. Dana also sent another protest telling Pike not to waste his breath on "the issues of fifteen years or even of five years hence; there's enough on hand for to-day" (Dana to Pike, June 5, 1856, Pike MSS). For an explanation of Greeley's complex attitude, see Isely, *Greeley*, pp. 151 ff.

[16] Dana to Pike, July 24, 1856, Pike MSS; passage omitted from *First Blows*, p. 346.

[17] Memoir, Pike MSS. Greeley's dislike of McLean was one factor that led to his favoring Frémont. In late May, 1856, the editor had written that Pike's legs seemed to be traveling in opposite directions. "I distrust that which has got on to disunion more

The party's strong showing in 1856 heartened most Republicans, including Pike. The antislavery presidential candidate carried all save five of the free states. The sprint for 1860 began as soon as Congress convened in December, 1856, and the *Tribune's* zealous Washington correspondent plunged into the midst of the increasingly tense political battle. His friend Dana had suggested earlier that there was no point in Pike's returning to the capital. "Your sort of disunion speculations might just as well be written in a country town where living is cheap & printing inexpensive," Dana explained. "You ought to join that set of old philosophers who sought truth by contemplation of absolute things, and in order to avoid external disturbance, fixed their gaze steadily on their own navels. However, if you will come around to our side & help hang the southern fools, I dare say you can get into the Union-saving church again. How would you like a foreign mission?"[18] As for membership in the "Union-saving church," the Downeaster as yet felt no interest in the political program of moderation and conciliation which Dana and Greeley preferred. Pike wielded a potent pen in disposing of the "Southern fools" and their "doughface" associates in the North; but he continued to embarrass his colleagues by espousing an extreme position with regard to the incompatibility of the free North and slave South.

The Dred Scott decision in March, 1857, proved a pivotal point both in the triumph of the Republican party and in the fatal disruption of the Democrats, which finally came in 1860 when Southern Democrats rejected Stephen A. Douglas and his popular-sovereignty doctrine. The complicated background of the famed decision which outlawed Federal control over slavery in the territories need not be elaborated here. The

---

than that which has hobbled back to McLeanism; yet the former has far more of my sympathy. When we are ready to dissolve the Union for Liberty's sake, the South will not let us do it. . . . So let us off on disunion for the present" (Greeley to Pike, May 30, 1856, Pike MSS; *First Blows*, p. 344).

[18] Dana to Pike, Oct. 5, 1856, Pike MSS; passage omitted from *First Blows*, p. 349.

important thing in reference to Pike was that he considered the decision as definitive proof that the existing Union faced inevitable disruption.[19] Republicans in general, as well as some non-Republican Northerners, joined in the widespread, deeply felt protest against the decision that so well suited the purposes of the Calhounite extremists in the South. These Southerners insisted that Congress had no power to bar slavery from the territories, as the Dred Scott decision also held, and they went further to hold that the Constitution compelled the Federal government to give the peculiar institution positive support and protection in the territories. Greeley had already realized that the Calhounite Southerners and the Douglas or popular-sovereignty wing of the Democratic party were probably headed for a disruptive clash. Encouraging this split became one of the editor's paramount tasks.[20] Pike, on the other hand, proved himself much less politically astute than Greeley and continued to put his disunionist foot forward.

"If we cannot, as a nation, agree to go back to the position of the founders of the Government, and regard Slavery as an exceptional institution, and administer the Government in the interest of universal Freedom; or, if we will not agree upon any fixed compromise in respect to the institution of Slavery," Pike proclaimed in the *Tribune,* "the longer continuance of the existing Union is a political impossibility."[21] Since this blast came when Washington political circles were merely anticipating the Dred Scott decision, the extent of Pike's disgust and anger with the proslavery judges on the Supreme Court may

[19] Allan Nevins, *Emergence of Lincoln* (New York, 1950), I, 90-118, II, 473-77, summarizes the more recent scholarship; Isely, *Greeley,* p. 226, corrects an error with regard to the *Tribune* and Pike which is made by both Charles Warren, *The Supreme Court in United States History* (Boston, 1922), III, 5-7, and Carl B. Swisher, *Roger B. Taney* (New York, 1936), pp. 488-94. Professor Isely points out that it was *Tribune* correspondent James E. Harvey and not Pike who was in contact with Justice John McLean, sole Republican then on the bench, in the spring of 1856. In the winter of 1856-57, however, long before the court's decision was announced on March 6, Pike seems to have had a good notion of what was coming. This was probably through contact with Harvey.

[20] See Isely, *Greeley,* pp. 235-54.

[21] *Tribune,* clipping datelined Dec. 18, 1856; omitted from *First Blows,* p. 354.

be easily imagined. But while pouring opprobrium on Chief Justice Taney and on the decision was indeed the ordinary Republican reaction, Greeley felt compelled to reprimand publicly his overly ardent associate in Washington.

Greeley first spanked the Northern disunionists in rather general terms, hitting at the unnecessarily extreme methods which they employed to combat slavery. But rival newspapers in New York, especially the *Times,* charged the *Tribune* with advocating unconstitutional acts and the separation of the free states from the slave. This provoked Greeley into an editorial declaration that Pike spoke only for himself and that the *Tribune* had always published correspondence with which the editor himself might not agree. Thus the editor tossed the uncomfortably hot issue back to his Washington correspondent, who would have to fend for himself.[22]

This action on the part of Greeley forced Pike to clarify his position, and the long explanation of his alleged "disunion-ism" which he soon submitted in the *Tribune's* columns must be examined in some detail. The correspondent began with the denial that he actually was a disunionist. "A 'disunionist,' in the popular and generally received acceptation of the term," he wrote, "is one who desires the dissolution of the Union. I desire no such thing, and have never expressed any such desire." He charged that the *Tribune's* editor had cast the "unhand-some imputation" of disunionism upon him in order to escape the "malignity of a mendacious rival," the *Times.* Such an un-chivalrous act on the *Tribune's* part did not become "either a generous ally or a gallant enemy." He first met the charge that he had " 'lately become' anything different" from what he always had been. At the time of the repeal of the Missouri Compromise in 1854 he had believed that the Douglas bill "would spread Slavery, nationalize Slavery, and bring the natural antagonisms of Free society and Slave society, then partially kept asunder by the buffers of compromise, into direct

[22] *Tribune,* Jan. 3, 21, 1857.

and violent collision." Then in plain words, similar to those later ones of Lincoln's about a "house divided," Pike asserted that "this Union cannot long stand, except upon the basis of fixed limitation of Slavery, and a general admission, North and South, that Slavery is an exceptional institution—a temporary evil, to be gradually ameliorated and ultimately removed." This he had firmly believed at least since 1854, so no accusation about his having changed his principles would stand up: "I am not aware that I have ever turned the course of my political opinions in any direction from a straight onward faith since I was capable of forming an opinion."

As for the alleged disunionism, Pike entered into a tortured explanation built around the premise that he should be regarded as "fighting a political battle on a forlorn hope." He saw little chance of escaping defeat at the hands of the slaveholders, but he still carried the "flag of resistance." He believed that the proslavery party was destroying the "very foundation of the Constitution," and in its place was substituting a "totally different one." Addressing the friends of slavery, he insisted: "You are violating utterly the understanding upon which the Union rests. It was made to subserve the cause of Liberty. You and your doughface allies in the North are perverting it to the pestilent uses of human servitude. This perversion of the purposes of this Government, if not arrested, must work its downfall, and should work its downfall." The slaveholders' program of indefinite or perpetual bondage meant that "an Ethiopia in the South is inevitable." But that would merely be "retribution" for the new crimes of slavery. The slaveholders held four millions of blacks now and would eventually hold ten millions. "This mass of barbarism will enforce its own expulsion from our system as a matter of necessity."

These remarks were directed to the slaveholders and their allies. To the North he declared that the Republicans had failed in 1856 to arrest the "revolution commenced by the

Nebraska bill." Many believed that the "revolution" would be arrested in the future, but he did not believe that the Republicans could accomplish it. "We are carried along, as every generation and every age is carried along," Pike suggested, "by a force which we cannot control." If the "Slave Power" continued to dominate the Federal government, the antislavery exponents would be "forced upon the refuge of separation," or else would have to choose "submission and thus exhibit a shameful desertion of our principles and our duty."

Thus, Pike held that he was no disunionist in the opprobrious sense implied by the *Tribune*. Then came a significant point in his argument, for he maintained that in actuality the possibility of the proslavery party's returning to "sound views," that is Republican views, was if anything increased by the position which he and others like him occupied. "The bold promulgation of the actual condition of our political affairs," he said, ". . . will if anything can, avert the results it is so fashionable to deplore." In other words, the best antidote for Southern threats of disunion, which had been heard so often, especially after 1850, was the Northern threat of disunion. Although he himself did not elaborate on this notion of countering Southern secessionism, it was one definite motive that lay beneath all of Pike's readiness to witness the separation of the North and South.[23]

The timing of Greeley's protest against disunionism and of Pike's long reply is of special interest because of related events which were occurring about the same time. The Republicans in the winter of 1856-57 were politically embarrassed

[23] *Tribune,* Jan. 30, 1857; in an editorial in the same issue Greeley replied that Pike's letter was a "very circular piece of logic" and a "confused" statement. For Lincoln's "house divided" speech and Seward's "irrepressible conflict" speech, both of which contained ideas related to Pike's, see Albert J. Beveridge, *Abraham Lincoln, 1809-1858* (New York, 1928), II, 573-77, 602-6, and *passim;* Frederic Bancroft, *The Life of William H. Seward* (New York, 1900), I, 461-62. Both Lincoln and Seward soon repented of their famed utterances and, indeed, their subsequent careers largely belied these early flirtations with "radicalism."

by a paucity of issues. Kansas had ceased to bleed so dramatically; public indignation about the repeal of the Missouri Compromise had worn thin; and even within the Republican party there was no unity on issues like the fugitive slave law, much less on economic subjects. Their situation was soon to be greatly helped by the Dred Scott decision, Hinton Helper's *Impending Crisis,* and the panic of 1857, but during the interval between Frémont's defeat and the Dred Scott decision the hustings lacked excitement. One consequence of this lull was that the left wing of the party, as well as some abolitionist ultras who repudiated even the Republicans, began making much noise and thereby discomfiting antislavery leaders who struggled to dissociate Republicanism from abolition and disunionism.[24]

Although Greeley realized that abolitionism was a political liability, Pike for a long time stubbornly ignored this fact. While he did not openly demand immediate emancipation in the slave states as did the Garrisonian element, his apparent reconciliation to a disruption of the existing Union gave him an important link with the extremists. Thomas Wentworth Higginson, one of the Massachusetts abolitionist fire-eaters, recognized a kindred spirit in the *Tribune's* Washington correspondent and sent encouragement. Higginson did not know whether Pike had any interest in the "Massachusetts disunion movement" but his "powerful letters in the *Tribune*" suggested that he was not "so blind as most people to the real tendencies of the time." "All the laws of nature work for disunion," the zealous minister explained; "there is a mine beneath us, and the South will cram in powder quite as fast as we can touch it off."[25]

[24] Beveridge, *Lincoln,* II, 449-54, discusses these passionately antislavery extremists, i.e., abolitionists, who demanded immediate action on the part of the North regardless of the consequences. Also, Edward Channing, *A History of the United States* (New York, 1925), VI, 180-84. The *Tribune,* Jan. 21, 1857, has a long account of the Massachusetts convention of the disunionists.

[25] Higginson to Pike, Feb. 9, 1857, Pike MSS; *First Blows,* p. 360. Higginson solicited Pike's aid in distributing abolitionist literature in Washington, but whether or not he complied is not known.

From Maine also came approval of Pike's strong stand. George F. Talbot, an ardent Maine Free Soiler now working for the Republicans, assured Pike that "your opinion is by no means a heretical or unusual one but is shared by nearly all of the intelligent thinkers in the country who are opposed to slavery." According to this distant admirer, the *Tribune's* leading position in the North arose from the fact that its readers considered it "an independent journal that will discuss political subjects upon absolute principles, without reference to the necessities of candidates or the odium of particular opinions." Pike merited high praise as an "independent and profound thinker" whose ideas were rooted in "convictions of truth" rather than in party exigencies.[26]

Either Pike's conviction weakened or the aforementioned party exigencies became more pressing, for the high-water mark of his readiness to see the Union disrupted was reached and passed in the spring of 1857. After that he eschewed pleas for such drastic measures. In fact by 1860, when Southern secessionists were threatening immediate action if the sectional antislavery party should triumph in the fall elections, Pike dismissed the slaveholders' disunionism as "so much gasconade" from the "bogus democracy." In reference to a speech by Senator Jefferson Davis, the Maine journalist declared that "nothing is meant by all the blustering and bullying on the question [of secession], except to try to intimidate the North from voting as the masses of the people are inclined to vote."[27]

Shortly after this, Georgia's imperious Robert Toombs delivered an "irritating and incendiary harangue" in the Senate. Pike reported in the *Tribune* that Toombs's speech merely

[26] George F. Talbot to Pike, Feb. 5, 1857, Pike MSS; *First Blows*, pp. 358-59. Displaying something less than candor, Pike appended a note to this and the above letter explaining that they referred to "a personal discussion in the *Tribune*, for which there is not room or appropriateness in the text" (*First Blows*, p. 360). Since most of his explicit disunionist writings are omitted from the printed work, the two letters make little sense in the printed context.

[27] *Tribune*, Jan. 31, 1860; *First Blows*, pp. 481-82.

typified a lot of nonsensical sound and fury. The national situation had truly improved since 1857, in Pike's eyes, for this was his analysis of February, 1860: "From the clearest survey we are able to make of the whole field, we have come to the conclusion that there is no nation in existence whose disorders are so trivial as our own. We know of none whose present state is so fortunate, so slightly disturbed, or whose future seems so clear. And this notwithstanding the efforts of men like Mr. Toombs, of incendiary newspapers and other agencies, to excite discord and magnify our national ailments."[28]

Thus Pike calmed any *Tribune* readers who might be apprehensive about the Southern secessionists. He also labored in 1860 to clarify for the voters the vital distinction between abolitionists and Republicans. Democratic partisans, North and South, deliberately confused this distinction between the abolitionists, who demanded immediate emancipation within the Southern states regardless of the Constitution or the consequences, and, on the other hand, the antislavery Republican party which was pledged only to halting the extension of slavery into the territories. Abolitionism repelled the Northern masses only a bit less than it did Southerners, and in 1860 Republicans again found it desirable to emphasize their moderation.

Pike, whose now forgotten disunionism had earned him favor in New England abolitionist circles, insisted in the *Tribune* that the Republicans had never proposed to use Federal power to abolish slavery. The antislavery party did not even have any "crusades to project," and was perfectly content to allow the Southern states to manage "their peculiar social evils in their own way, subject only to the public discussion, exposure, and comment which human action inevitably provokes from a free and intelligent people." Every "sensible man" in the North or South should realize that the Republi-

[28] *Tribune*, Feb. 1 [or 2?], 1860; an editorial. See also Isely, *Greeley*, pp. 300-3.

cans stayed strictly within constitutional limits.[29]   On another
occasion, however, distinctions became blurred when Pike criticized the Reverend Henry Ward Beecher.   The Downeaster
suggested that abolitionists viewed slavery "in its moral aspects
only, or mainly, and aim to shape their action so as to bring
about an extirpation of the evil everywhere, as well as to arrest
its spread."   The Republicans, on the other hand, viewed
slavery only from a political viewpoint and in reference to the
territories, not the states.   Beecher enjoyed membership in
both Republican and abolitionist camps, but in a recent sermon
about John Brown the famed preacher had suggested that the
best way of treating slavery in the states was to teach the
slaves to obey their masters and, in Pike's words, to be "good
boys generally."   Pike suggested that Beecher as a Republican
had no business saying anything whatsoever about slavery
within the states.   Yet in a moral or abolitionist sense the
Tribune correspondent considered that the Brooklyn pastor's
advice of obedience and submission would have moral validity
only after "a scheme of emancipation is put in operation."
The only form of effective moral attack on slavery, according
to Pike, was "that which invariably shows itself in clear,
stern, and uncompromising hostility to the institution, without
regard to the consideration of its minor details."   In other
words, the *Tribune's* political correspondent chastised the abolitionist preacher for suggesting that servile revolts be discouraged.[30]

Pike himself was not an avowed abolitionist but an antislavery Republican.   Yet he obviously had several goals in
mind other than preventing the spread of slavery, emancipation
being one of these semicovert aims.   If his own "uncompromising hostility" to slavery led him to ignore "minor details" such
as slave insurrections and racial warfare in the South, it is
clear that he was not especially moderate in his contemplated
methods of achieving emancipation.

[29] *Tribune,* Feb. 11, 1860; an editorial.   [30] *Tribune,* Jan. 27, 1860.

' As deep and strong as was his hatred of slavery, it was
accompanied by a strange indifference, even hostility, toward
Negroes. Clues scattered throughout the 1850's make this
clear. One example early in 1853, from his many *Tribune*
articles about the "slavocracy's" manifest destiny schemes,
indicates that his aversion to slavery as an institution sprang
partially from his racial distaste for the enslaved. To the
then frequently heard suggestion that manifest destiny would
make Cuba fall into the possession of the United States, Pike
replied that we did not want any populous territory like that
island, which was filled "with black, mixed, degraded and
ignorant, or inferior races." No one could deny that "robust
and enterprising" Americans would eventually spread into
Mexico and down into the Isthmus and elevate these areas to
the position of "independence and nationality." Despite that
inevitable expansion, we "want no more ebony additions to the
Republic." The African race already had a foothold on the
North American continent; its "fecundity" suggested that it
could never be "rooted out." If it were possible, the best solution of the African problem would be to give them all of the
West Indies and thereby rid North America of "the burden and
hindrance" of the black population. "But we fear that not only
must we allot the islands of the Caribbean Sea to them," Pike
concluded, "but a portion also of our own territory lying upon
the Gulf of Mexico."[31]

Later in the decade Pike served as chairman of the resolutions committee of the 1857 Republican state convention in
Maine. The convention unanimously adopted his report, and
this was one of the resolutions: "That the natural increase of
the white race on this continent demands the widest possible
area for its expansion, and thus requires the confinement of
the degrading character and influence of African slavery to the
narrowest limits."[32] Then in 1860, after many Republicans

[31] *Tribune*, Jan. 10, 1853; *First Blows*, pp. 162-64. For Greeley's related idea about
the Negroes' living alone in the Gulf states, see Isely, *Greeley*, pp. 298-99.
[32] Undated clipping in Pike MSS about Republican convention in Bangor, Maine, on

had espoused the demand for a Western homestead law, the *Tribune* correspondent most clearly stated his position with regard to the Negro race.

Discussions of slavery among Republicans rarely touched on the purely racial aspect of the problem; it was usually the Southern slavery apologists who insisted that the institution be considered in its racial context. In 1860 the antislavery party in many areas of the North found it politically essential to avoid the complex subject, since racial prejudice existed in the free states as well as in those which clung to slavery.[33] Pike, however, openly declared the racial beliefs which underlay so much of his own thinking at the time and for the next twenty years. There were undoubtedly many Republicans, particularly in New England, who disagreed with the opinions he expressed in an article entitled "What We Shall Do with the Negro," but there were probably equally as many who shared his outspoken prejudices.

Pike premised his argument with the assertion that the only way the Negro could be eliminated as an extremely controversial subject was to remove him from the scene, by separating the "White and Black" races. He believed that nothing could be more "certain than that a great democratic republic cannot forever submit to the anomaly of negro Slavery in its bosom." But even with the hated institution of slavery extinguished, "the ignorant and servile race will not and cannot be emancipated and raised to the enjoyment of equal civil rights with the dominant and intelligent race; they will be driven out." Such action might be a "cruel and unchristian process, but it is natural," and the only solution possible in the American situation.

The *Tribune* correspondent already anticipated some of the

June 25, 1857. The convention also adopted Pike's resolution that "the country is weary of the stereotyped alarms sought to be spread in relation to the danger of a dissolution of the federal Union. We deprecate the constant agitation of this topic. . . ."

[33] See Beveridge, *Lincoln*, II, 202-5, 673 ff.; Nevins, *Emergence*, II, 142-48; Isely, *Greeley*, p. 298.

problems he and other Republicans would later face. He declared that the peculiar difficulty of treating the abolition question, under the democratic system, arose from "the necessity of conferring political power by the act of liberation." The slavery apologists knew how vain and hopeless were ideas about the "amalgamating process" or other suggested panaceas for racial friction. The slaveholding Southerner feared "nothing but the blind forces of the enslaved mass, or the great storms of political action, breaking from prescribed boundaries, and acting with whirlwind force, threatening Slavery and society alike with sure and overwhelming destruction." The slaveholder's fierce temper, his violence, and his "impotent threats of pulling down the pillars of the political communities associated with him," all these had roots in his realization that when slavery as an institution crumbled, the "existing society" must fall with it.

But the "battles of Freedom against Slavery" were not to be viewed only from the slaveholder's viewpoint. The "white laboring classes" had to be considered. The Negro, free or slave, stood in their way also. "The slaveholder is claiming to spread the negro everywhere, and the Popular-Sovereignty man stands coolly by, and says, 'Let him do it wherever he can.' We say the Free States should say, confine the negro to the smallest possible area. Hem him in. Coop him up. Slough him off. Preserve just so much of North America as is possible to the white man, and to free institutions. We shall get none too much any way. We are likely to get far too little." The idea of separating the white and black races he considered "all important as a means of promoting the national harmony and progress; and to mitigate the urgency of the Negro question among us."

Pike admitted that his ideas were partially inspired by the political necessity of repudiating the Democratic charge that the Republicans advocated "the raising of a degraded, ignorant, and servile black population to civil and political equality with the whites." Senator Benjamin Wade, soon to become a leader among the anti-Lincoln, Radical Republican faction, had recently suggested colonizing the free colored people somewhere on the southern border; this should certainly help make it clear, according to the journalist, that the Republicans were repelled by the notion of "Negro equality in its most offensive form." But the free blacks were but "the mere twigs and branches torn from the great forest of Negro Slavery." The four millions of enslaved Negroes were the important class. The first object of the Republicans concerning them was to limit the extension of slavery by every possible means. Their "next aim" must necessarily be "to get rid of the negro population entirely, by massing it within its present limits." The Republicans could not, of course, deal with all the minor details of the question without encountering opposition that might hinder the progress of their "great conceptions and duties." But at least they should "assail the whole body of evil, so far as we can do it within constitutional limits, and leave its accidents and its fragmentary aspects, like those we have commented on, to individual action."[34]

This frank article treating the racial aspects of the slavery question is of great significance in understanding Pike's position with regard to the issue of slavery, which had served as the most convenient and yet most dangerous focus for sectionalism in the decades prior to the Civil War. One reason the *Tribune* man had joined the Northern disunionists and abolitionists in the mid-1850's was his sincere belief that the Negro

[34] *Tribune,* March 12, 1860. Concerning Senator Wade's colonization scheme, it is interesting to note that one of his constituents wrote him as follows: "You are right upon every issue which will be likely to agitate the country in this campaign. And I like this new touch of colonizing the Niggers[.] I believe practically it is a d—n humbug[.]   But it will take with the people[.]   Our creed runs into what the French call a *Cul de sac,* which I take to be a Road with the end chopped off. If we are to have no more slave states what the devil are we to do with the surplus niggers? Your plan will help us out on this point. But practically I have not much faith in it[.] You could not raise twenty five cents from a Yankee to transport a Nigger to South America..." (Dan Tilden to B. F. Wade, Wade MSS; furnished through the courtesy of Mr. Thomas Clark, Roanoke Rapids, N. C.)

could not and should not be incorporated into the American democratic system. Even in the early 1850's he had believed that the lower Gulf states would inevitably be "Africanized" and surrendered to the blacks. In the 1860-61 secession crisis this idea still lingered in his mind, and he desired emancipation in the border states, by Federal mandate if necessary, and the subsequent segregation of the blacks in a Gulf coast African belt, or as he later described it, a "negro pen." Then during the war, especially about 1863-64 when Northern armies faltered and Federal financing became difficult, he reverted to this idea of "fighting for a boundary" rather than for the preservation of the old Union. That is, he urged a compromise peace which should leave the Negroes and their arrogant masters in their own, Africanized Gulf states.

That is one half of the complex network of ideas that Pike entertained. But it is not the whole story. His earlier *rapprochement* with the Northern disunionists also meant that he regarded slavery as a great evil and domination of the Federal government by the slaveholding and "doughface" Democrats as an intolerable situation that had to be ended regardless of the costs. There must be no more compromising with the slaveholders, and Northern threats of disunionism were one effective counteragent to the more familiar Southern cries for secession. In other words, Pike's disunionism meant, on one hand, that he wanted no more compromise with slavery; on the other hand, however, it meant that if the Union should disintegrate, then there might be a good chance to get rid of the slaveholders and their Negroes by shoving them into a Southern Liberia along the Gulf coast. It appears that as long as he had the choice he preferred the Union if it could be had without compromise and with Republican domination of the Federal government; but his second choice, in 1860 and later, looked to separation from the Negro-filled states in the Deep South.

Many of these ideas were at cross purposes, but there came a showdown in the winter of 1860-61 when secession was no longer an empty, slaveholders' boast but a fast-spreading, terrible reality. Because of his own conflicting ideas, many of which were paralleled among other Republicans, Pike's course was ambiguous, to say the least. But he had worked hard in the 1860 Republican campaign. His brother, Frederick A. Pike, had been elected to the House of Representatives, and at last he himself stood on the threshold of enjoying the personal fruits of a great antislavery political victory. He rushed to Washington early in December to watch closely the action of Congress during the crucial lame-duck session, and he supplied the *Tribune* with a steady stream of articles dealing with the secession crisis. From these newsletters his position as a staunch Radical Republican gradually became clear. Above all, as it finally developed, he opposed any compromise, hoped for Republican action with regard to slavery in the territories as well as in the states, and, finally, discovered anew that he did love the Union and the Constitution.[35]

Pike wrote his first letter about the secession crisis on the day that Congress convened, December 4, 1860. His first stand, and the one to which he ultimately reverted after a great deal of twisting and turning, presented Pike the patriot and Union lover. He forgot completely that he had once been ready to see North and South separate, for he now wrote that the government had in the past always been successfully administered upon the basis of majority rule, under certain Constitutional modifications. There was no reason why the same basis should not suffice for the future. "If a government on this foundation proves to be a failure," Pike asserted, "it will be a gigantic surprise to the friends of popular rule, and a

[35] T. Harry Williams, *Lincoln and the Radicals* (Madison, Wisconsin, 1941), is the best treatment of the Republican wing which, because of their fierce hatred of slavery and the slaveholders and their root-and-branch approach to the explosive problems facing the country, earned the name of "Jacobins" from young John Hay, Lincoln's secretary. Throughout the Civil War and Reconstruction the faction was more generally dubbed as "Radical."

terrible commentary on the good sense of the American people." There was no question in his mind that the government's duty was to maintain the Union as it exists; if that were not the duty of the administrators of affairs, "then indeed is Government a farce." The causes or the "qualifying incidents" of "our existing embarrassments" had nothing to do with the secession issue. Nor was it a party question. Men had to take sides "for or against the Government, not for or against a party, or its principles or notions."[36]

This was a clear statement of determination to save the Union, and regardless of the personal circumstances which made it strange for Pike to approve this course, it was the basic policy which Lincoln ultimately adopted upon taking control of national affairs. It meant, as Pike implied in December, that slavery was to be relegated to second place and the crisis met on Constitutional lines; that the government would fight if it were necessary to preserve the Union and would ignore the slavery issue if that suited the primary purpose of saving the Union. Thus far Pike hewed a clear line, even if it was a new one for him.

But four days after writing the Union plea, he coolly declared in the *Tribune*, "We seem about to surrender the Gulf States to the Black race, and the Whites who as yet rule that race." He himself did not view the development with too much repugnance, but it was clearly the duty of the Federal government to keep control of events. There would be a "peaceable issue" of the complications threatening from the South, for there was no apparent cause for any "physical conflict in the readjustment of our political relations . . . except in the exercise of the unbridled passions of men." Let us have a "peaceful separation," he insisted, at least in "its incipient stages." It might be all right to permit a few "uneasy slave-holding States to secede from the existing Union"; but there

---

[36] *Tribune*, Dec. 6, 1860; datelined Washington, Dec. 4. Pike included none of his *Tribune* articles after June, 1860, in *First Blows*.

were serious boundary questions connected with secession. Territory or states beyond the Mississippi River, including Louisiana and Texas, would be required for the "future
development" of the United States even if the lower South
should "peaceably" separate itself.[37]

Now to surrender "the Gulf States to the Black race, and
the Whites who as yet rule that race" was an entirely different
matter from taking sides "for or against the Government," as
Pike had demanded in his first, Union-saving letter. The
"peaceable separation" mentioned in the second letter apparently implied the opposite of his original statement that it was
the government's clear duty to preserve the Union "as it
exists." Pike had fallen into an ambiguity that continued in
his thinking for the next four years, for he was clearly caught
in a web of contradictory ideas. The explanation seems to be
that Pike feared above all else in the winter of 1860-61 that
the Republicans would compromise with the seceding slaveholders in order to save the Union. The "peaceable separation," at least in the "incipient stages," actually meant that
Pike would talk about peaceful secession in order to prevent
the widespread fear of war from compelling the Republicans
to compromise. Horace Greeley advocated a much qualified
right of peaceful secession in order to allow Southern Unionist
sentiment to strengthen and organize itself.[38] But Pike did not
concern himself with the Southern Unionists. Still the right
of peaceful secession gained recognition in 1860-61 from many
Northern quarters. The Massachusetts abolitionists, for example, appeared to be generally strong for a peaceable dissolution
of the Union, and many Republican newspapers in the fall and
winter of 1860 seemed to advocate the right of peaceful secession. Professor David M. Potter has pointed out that all this
ostensible willingness to separate from the South was essentially

[37] *Tribune*, Dec. 10, 1860; datelined Dec. 8.
[38] See Isely, *Greeley*, pp. 305-12; Van Deusen, *Greeley*, pp. 260-69.

a roundabout way of expressing a reluctance to compromise.[39] It seems to have been precisely this in Pike's case, but it was also another expression of his second choice: namely, that if the United States could somehow manage to get rid of the Negroes and some of their haughty masters then that too would be satisfactory provided the Africanized zone were limited to the Deep South and east of the Mississippi.

The second choice was strictly second, however. A few days after writing that "peaceable separation" might occur, the *Tribune* correspondent reverted to his patriotic role of Union-saving. "This Government is an engine of commanding power," he proclaimed on December 18, two days before South Carolina seceded; "and when its legislative and executive branches are in harmony, as they soon will be, if the secessionists execute their threats, it will show itself abundantly able to cope with all its difficulties, and take the country triumphantly through all its perils." All the current talk of civil war was "idle and childish," since the "overshadowing power of the Federal Government" could make itself felt nationally by its control of fleets and armies and its "command" of peace or war. The Southern "revolutionists," in the meantime, had chosen their own foolish course and would pursue it "until they get the discipline they seem so much to need." As for compromising the questions at issue, there seemed to be no prospect of that "except by a seemingly impossible surrender on the part of the Republicans." The only way out of current difficulties, Pike insisted, lay in allowing events to "accelerate themselves, as fast as they will, and bring us to the end of our journey through a series of fresh and inevitable experiences." As menacingly vague as this statement was, the Downeaster hurriedly added that he saw "no chance for a war of any kind growing out of existing complications, not even one between the sections." The explanation he offered for this optimistic

[39] David M. Potter, *Lincoln and His Party in the Secession Crisis* (New Haven, 1942), pp. 51-57; hereinafter cited as Potter, *Secession Crisis*.

analysis was that the North possessed such disproportionate strength that the South would not dare secede or fight. "The national government may have to *show* its teeth, but it is not at all likely that it will have to *use* them."[40]

The burden of Pike's articles which appeared during the week that South Carolina seceded was the purely partisan assertion that apprehension of civil war was dwindling in Washington. Peculation in the Department of the Interior, according to Pike, was the "universal topic in political circles," and a *Tribune* editorial declared that South Carolina's secession had not "seriously disturbed" the country but the fraud in the Department of the Interior had "astonished and electrified it." The compromise committees in Congress were functioning by this time. Pike reported that their sole object lay in appeasing the "revolutionists." Most of his emphasis in explaining the opposition to compromise dealt with his belief that the secessionists did not want to be appeased; but he admitted that the Republicans were strongly opposed to concessions which were claimed under threats of disunion.[41]

As the compromise talk increased with the scope of the crisis, Pike became increasingly militant and began making veiled allusions to emancipation. On December 28 he declared that the "revolutionists" did not really want to secede at all; they desired a new constitution and a new union "constructed for the nationalization and perpetuation of Slavery." But if they did secede (and South Carolina already had), Pike recalled Senator Benjamin Wade's assertion that an act of secession would bring forth an edict of emancipation. Another interpretation which he gave to the purpose of the secessionists had an interesting twist. He viewed the familiar Southern boast about cotton's being king as "only a modest way" of saying

[40] *Tribune*, Dec. 18, 1860. Another despatch from "J. S. P." in the same issue declared that the "time has fully come for men of Mr. Wade's stamp." A *Tribune* editorial of the same day lauded Senator Wade's stout rejection of any compromise as a "calm, luminous, and authoritative statement of the principles and purposes of the Republican party...."

[41] *Tribune*, Dec. 21, 25, 1860.

that "the Negro is King." "It is now simply a question of whether he shall be deposed, and the White Man take his place," he declared.[42]

In January and February of the secession crisis the disunion movement spread from South Carolina to the Gulf states, and the Confederacy was being organized in Montgomery. In Washington, Senator John J. Crittenden and others labored diligently to achieve a compromise; they got no substantial help from Southern secessionists or from the Republicans.[43] The *Tribune's* correspondent, in the meantime, lashed out at any mention of compromise and demanded, even as the border states hesitated, that the Federal government make military preparations and take "positive" action. Since secession, according to him, indicated that the Southerners really wanted to spread and to secure slavery, it was clear that secession meant war. Emancipation loomed as the best Federal weapon against the seceders, for "if the Free States are driven into war," they would surely strike at the root of the conflict. "Stern necessity rules in war. . . ." The administration of President Buchanan he violently excoriated, declaring that "imbecile hands" had the levers of control and "eunuchs" led affairs. "What is needed here is wine, and bark, and iron, and sulphur, and steel," he suggested. "Such another pack of Miss Nancies [as Buchanan, *et al.*] to oppose treason and bullying, the world never saw."[44]

Despite his own militancy, he yet insisted that if the free states stood firm the whole "disunion stampede will end in the utter humiliation and ruin of its authors and abettors." A small matter like the departure of the "filibustering senators" from the South merely meant that the country would soon get "some healthy legislation." He only hoped that "they will

[42] *Tribune*, Dec. 28, 31, 1860; Jan. 1, 1861. On January 1 he also published an article showing Northern merchants why secession would be of "vast advantage" to them.
[43] Potter, *Lincoln*, pp. 57 ff.; Nevins, *Emergence*, II, 385-413.
[44] *Tribune*, Jan. 4, 5, 11, 12, 13, 1861.

have gone before Congress is crowded to a vote on the Compromise." The great danger lay in a "demoralization of the
Northern position on the Slavery question." He did not
specify what he meant by the "permanent settlement" that
lay just ahead, but, at any rate it "would be a great misfortune
to have anything occur now to interrupt that settlement."[45]

By late January Pike had moved to the position that all
of the slave-holding border states, except Delaware perhaps,
would secede and that the government might as well accept that
fact. He suggested in the *Tribune* on January 31 that the
only effectual "weapons with which to battle Secession" in
states like Maryland and Missouri were emancipation and compensation. Two and a half months before the war had even
begun the Downeaster foreshadowed the critical issue which
would soon divide President Lincoln and the Radical Republicans. While Senator Seward and the President-elect concentrated on protecting and strengthening the strained ties which
held Kentucky, Missouri, and Maryland in the Union, Pike
suggested the very policy which would have been most likely
to have driven those states straight into the arms of the Confederates. He reasoned that if "the Secession epidemic reaches
the extreme border States, and the whole aspect of affairs
becomes threatening, high reasons of State may compel prompt
and radical measures of emancipation wherever it can be safely
attempted." Instincts of self-preservation and "demands of
imperative duty" might well require immediate abrogation of
slavery in the states "by whatever power can accomplish the
object." The common view among "thinking men" in Washington was that revolution had to be met by revolution, he
reported, and the fact could not be disguised that slavery constituted "the root and fountain of our disorders."[46]

---

[45] *Tribune,* Jan. 13, 17, 22, 1861.

[46] *Tribune,* Jan. 31, 1861. A *Tribune* editorial in this same issue reintroduced Pike's
idea that "peaceable secession" of the Gulf states might well be permitted but that
the border states or the trans-Mississippi region could not be allowed to secede; nobody had any objection to "getting rid of South Carolina." Whether or not Pike wrote

The *Tribune* correspondent had moved to the advanced position that secession would be answered by emancipation, but Republican moderates, led chiefly by Lincoln's future Secretary of State, William H. Seward, concentrated on encouraging the Unionist elements within the border states. Seward encouraged compromise and conciliation, so the radicals within his own party turned their most powerful attacks against him. This split of the radicals and moderates within the party, with the two groups tending to polarize respectively around Salmon P. Chase and Seward, found Pike in the vanguard of the wing which was soon labeled as the Radical Republicans. The *Tribune* man's animosity to Seward went back at least to 1858, and probably earlier. One reason for it was the eminent New York senator's tendency to compromise with the Democrats and to play down the slavery issue. Pike also shared Greeley's particular aversion to Seward, which had developed out of the editor's personal disappointments in New York state politics. Seward-haters were becoming, for diverse reasons, Radical Republicans in the first months of 1861.[47]

Pike's last contributions to the *Tribune* during the secession crisis were primarily assaults on the Seward-Weed compromise propositions or, as he put it, the appallingly dangerous "Gospel according to Albany."[48] Pike declared that the compromisers threatened "to lose us the hard-won fruits of a victory won in behalf of civilization and humanity, and to reinaugurate the Slave Power in the Union, and enthrone it on the enduring basis of the Constitution itself." In February, as Seward's

---

this editorial is not clear, but, during the war, he reverted to the thesis of the editorial that it was "A War of Boundaries."

[47] For the split in the Republican party, see Potter, *Lincoln*, pp. 20-44; Nevins, *Emergence*, II, 438-39, 444-46. For Greeley's fight with Seward, and with the senator's alter ego, Thurlow Weed, see Isely, *Greeley*, pp. 318 ff. For Pike's hostility to Seward, see *First Blows*, pp. 297 ff., 441-42, also Pike's letters of 1859-60 to William Pitt Fessenden, in the James S. Pike Papers, Library of Congress; hereinafter cited as JSP Papers. For Pike's thinly disguised glee when Seward lost the Republican nomination of 1860, see *Tribune*, May 20, June 1, 1860.

[48] For Seward's important activities in January and February, 1861, see Potter, *Lincoln*, pp. 280-314.

moderating influence in Washington increased, the Downeaster openly expressed his doubts as to Abraham Lincoln's policy. Would the President-elect follow the Weed-Seward "compromisers" or would he follow what Pike considered the "main body" of Republicans?   Not seeing (or not caring?) that Seward concentrated on retaining the border states, Pike stated his fear that the Lincoln administration would not be "anything above average hight [sic] of public sentiment in regard to present emergency" and would probably therefore be in favor of a weak, conciliatory program.   Then on March 1 the *Tribune* correspondent groaned that opponents of the Republicans in Washington taunted them with being under leaders (like Seward) who wished to "bind the party who have elevated them, hand and foot, and hand it over to its enemies."   "Thank God," Pike exclaimed, "the time approaches when this uncertainty, the existence of which is a damning disgrace, will soon be removed."   The day following Lincoln's inauguration he happily expressed the belief that the "back of compromise" had been broken.

Looking back on the anxious months when it appeared that the wretched secessionists might be lured back into the Union by compromise, Pike declared that it made him "blush to think there was ever any ground afforded for the hope that such a scandalous enterprise was possible."   Now that there were to be no concessions he demanded full exercise of the "legitimate powers of the Government in the direct line" of Republican principles; that is, he urged an emancipation policy.   As for the border states, the Radical merely remarked that they could do as they liked about the emancipation program.   They could take it or leave it.[49]

Pike had clearly disapproved of the drift and tone of the policy Lincoln and Seward had chosen toward the border states. Not until September, 1862, did the troubled President catch up

[49] *Tribune,* Feb. 15, 18, 23, March 1, 5, 7, 1861. *Tribune* editorial attacks on Seward were appearing during this same time; see Isely, *Greeley,* pp. 327-31.

with the Radical demand for an emancipation program. Even then Lincoln's cautious approach to the gigantic problem of slavery in the states lacked the directness and scope that Pike and many of the other Radicals would have preferred. When that step came, Pike could only look on and object from Europe, for he succeeded in obtaining the diplomatic post which he ardently sought in March, 1861.

Like many other former Whigs who had become Republicans, Pike regarded the 1860 victory as the first political rainfall after the dry, patronageless administrations of the Democrats, Pierce and Buchanan. Henry Adams later recalled that even before the "traitors" had flown in 1861, the "vultures" had descended on Washington in swarms and had torn "the carrion of political patronage into fragments and gobbets of fat and lean, on the very steps of the White House"[50] Although the problem of dividing the spoils did harass Lincoln as much as did the secession crisis, young Henry Adams himself took a job as his father's private secretary in the United States ministry in London. Pike too deserved well of his party. He had fought strenuous Republican battles in Maine as well as in the *Tribune*. In the Maine elections of 1858 and 1860 he had particularly exerted himself and with marked success, as evidenced by his younger brother's election to Congress.[51]

[50] *Education of Henry Adams* (New York, 1931), p. 109. For detailed discussion, see Harry J. Carman and Reinhard H. Luthin, *Lincoln and the Patronage* (New York, 1943).

[51] See his speech on slavery in the *Machias* [Maine] *Republican*, Aug. 31, 1858. In the spring of 1859 Republican Governor Lot M. Morrill appointed Pike as his special commissioner to investigate election frauds in Maine's northern "French District." Pike obliged with a scathing attack on the Democrats for their New England "Lecomptonism" (clippings from the *Kennebec Journal, Bangor Whig and Courier, Portland Advertiser,* and *Eastern Argus,* March-April, 1859, Pike MSS). Then in 1860 Pike jubilantly reported to Senator Fessenden, "We have blown them sky high all over this District. There never was such a triumph." Referring to the last-minute sending of $500 into the "French plantation" area of Aroostook County, the happy Republican testified that the "operation on the French to which I referred was a success . . ." (Pike to Fessenden, Sept. 10, 1860, JSP Papers). Other items in this Pike-Fessenden correspondence suggest that the Maine Republicans were not only well organized but well financed. Concerning the Rhode Island elections, Dana wrote Pike as follows after a visit into Connecticut and Rhode Island: "Sprague [Rhode Island industrialist and Republican politician] is spending $100,000 mainly in buying voters. The current price

In March, 1861, the *Tribune* correspondent who aspired to become a diplomat had the backing of prominent Maine Republicans as well as of many of the most influential senators and congressmen. He made his application for the Belgian mission to Secretary of State Seward and submitted a memorandum to President Lincoln. The Maine Congressional delegation and Vice President Hannibal Hamlin, another Downeaster, gave him full support. Among others whom he felt "at liberty" to offer as references to President Lincoln were Senators Benjamin Wade, Thomas Corwin, Charles Sumner, Henry Wilson, Preston King, Zachariah Chandler, and a host of congressmen which included Anson Burlingame, Owen Lovejoy, and Lewis Tappan.[52] The Belgian mission, however, went to Henry S. Sanford, who had diplomatic experience as well as a closer personal relationship to Seward than Pike could claim.[53]

Pike received, instead of Brussels, The Hague. And despite his poor personal relations with the Secretary of State, it is not strange that he did become a diplomat. In the first place, Lincoln's diplomatic appointments were, on the whole, awarded on a strictly partisan, patronage basis. The Cabinet included such figures as the former Democrat, Gideon Welles, and Lincoln had even made futile overtures to one or two Southern Unionists about a Cabinet post. The diplomatic and consular posts, however, were delivered to the staunch Republican faithful regardless of the war threat. An unusually large number of newspapermen who had contributed to the Republi-

---

is $25. The Spragues regard the election in a mode of advertising their business, and charge the bribery to expense" (Dana to Pike, March 26, 1860, Pike MSS).

[52] Pike to Seward, March 12, 1861, and "Mr. Pike's card to the President in reference to the Belgian Mission," March 13, 1861, in the Department of State Papers, National Archives, Washington, D. C.; hereinafter cited as DoS Papers.

[53] Sanford's appointment papers, DoS Papers. Sanford also had the backing of powerful New York City merchants like John A. Stewart, J. J. Astor, Jr., and Wm. H. Russell. It is interesting to note that one astute New York Republican had suggested as early as February that Sanford be sent immediately to Europe to propagandize for the Republicans. He expected the party to pass a strong protective tariff, and although he considered it wise and prudent, he knew that no measure would so damage the North in England, or would so "quickly reconcile even the abolitionists [in England] to recognize the South" (J. B. Davis to Seward, Feb. 11, 1860 [1861?], *ibid.*).

can triumph were given diplomatic appointments. Murat Halstead of the *Cincinnati Commercial* growled that the appointments were a "disgrace to journalism" and that the public had a "right to suspect the qualifications of men who are continually eager to forsake their legitimate and chosen profession for an office."[54]

Seward later wrote Pike that he personally had secured his appointment to The Hague. If this was true, the Secretary of State probably had two good reasons for favoring his political enemy. One was that Pike enjoyed a close relationship with Salmon P. Chase, whom Lincoln had appointed Secretary of the Treasury. Just as the Chase party and the Sewardites disagreed about administration policy concerning slavery and preserving the Union, they also intensely distrusted each other about the distribution of the patronage. Shortly after the inauguration, Dana and other New York Republicans visited Lincoln to assert their fear that "the power of the Federal administration would be put into the control of the rival [Seward-Weed] faction. . . ." This pro-Chase delegation secured the President's promise that one side should not "gobble up everything." Lincoln told them to make out a list of the places and men they wanted and he would endeavor to apply the "rule of give and take."[55] Thus the Chase men did get well looked after, for Lincoln had every reason to try to heal the dangerous divisions in his party. Whether Chase himself exerted any personal pressure in Pike's behalf is not known, but he may well have spoken with Seward or with Lincoln about his good friend from Calais.[56]

[54] *Cincinnati Commercial*, April 2, 1861, as quoted in Robert S. Harper, *Lincoln and the Press* (New York, 1951), p. 76; see also the long list of newspapermen appointees, *ibid.*

[55] Charles A. Dana, *Recollections of the Civil War* (New York, 1898), pp. 2-4. See also Carman and Luthin, *Lincoln*, pp. 10, 79. An interesting coincidence as well as revealing clue to the ambitions of Chase is found in an 1853 letter of his to Miss Lizzie Ellicott, in which Chase says that he shares her longing to visit Europe: "But, never mind; when I am elected President Mr. Pike shall have a diplomatic appointment, and you shall enjoy old world sights for me" (Chase to Miss Ellicott [who became Mrs. Pike], April 7, 1853, Pike MSS).

[56] Aside from the published Chase letters in *First Blows*, the Pikes also received two

In addition to Pike's strong position with the Chase faction, Seward probably had another reason for approving his appointment: he must have been happy to see "J. S. P." transferred to the other side of the Atlantic Ocean. Regardless of Pike's personal feud with the Secretary of State, Seward and Lincoln were probably aware that the Downeaster's ideas on border-state policy and on the slavery issue differed drastically from their own. Pike had possessed a powerful, venomous pen in the fight with the Democrats and had established a leading reputation as a hater of slavery, slaveholders, and "dough-faces." The *Tribune* ranked as the leading Republican paper in the country and exerted a tremendous influence in New England as well as in the Western states. If the most famous political correspondent of that paper had already urged emancipation in early 1861, might it not be just as well to send the redoubtable Radical out of the country?

There were a striking number of the more extreme Republicans, like Pike, in the ranks of Lincoln's diplomatic appointees. Cassius Clay, for example, became the American envoy to Russia; and though he was from Kentucky, and one of the few border-state residents to share the diplomatic spoils, he hated and fought slavery with a vehemence that outraged his fellow Southerners.[57] Carl Schurz, Anson Burlingame, and George G. Fogg were among the numerous diplomatic appointees who had distinguished themselves by fierce, fire-eating denunciations of the South's peculiar institution. And while it is clear that Lincoln and Seward used the patronage in an

interesting letters from the Ohioan in Jan., 1861, when he was nervously wondering and worrying about his Cabinet post, which Lincoln had not yet proffered. See Chase to Pike, Jan. 10, and Chase to Mrs. Pike, Jan. 27, 1861, Pike MSS. Pike himself was under pressure during these months from Maine acquaintances who desired appointments as postmasters, customs collectors, etc. Count Adam Gurowski, a former *Tribune* colleague, requested Pike to influence Chase about a job for Gurowski; he later became a foremost Radical spokesman and already in the spring of 1861 he was complaining that "Seward is conceited & ignorant" (Gurowski to Pike, [spring?] 1861, Pike MSS).

[57] On one occasion an overzealous Negro friend, wishing to express appreciation for Clay's liberality, gave the following toast: "To the health of Cassius M. Clay—Liberator. Though he has a white skin, he has a very black heart" (C. M. Clay, *The Life of Cassius M. Clay*, Cincinnati, 1886, I, 209).

attempt to close the breach in the party, there is also a good possibility that they were exporting antislavery extremists who could do much harm in the United States and, on the other hand, much good among influential liberal and humanitarian circles in Europe. Lincoln's policy from the first was to ignore the slavery question as far as possible and concentrate on preserving the Union. Not until his preliminary emancipation proclamation of September, 1862, did he yield to the Radical pressure for a war against slavery, as well as for the Union. In the crucial interval between the Confederate attack on Fort Sumter in April, 1861, and the adoption of the emancipation program, his advanced antislavery diplomatic representatives not only pressed Lincoln and Seward for an avowed policy of emancipation, but they also represented the Federal cause in a manner most likely to win the favor of Europeans— that is, as a contest between freedom and bondage, between modern civilization and barbaric feudalism. Whether or not Lincoln and Seward fully realized the multiple advantages of many of their diplomatic appointments is not clear. At any rate, in despatching James Shepherd Pike to The Hague they certainly placed one articulate Radical in a position where he could do little domestic damage in the United States and, at the same time, could inform Europeans that the North waged a humanitarian crusade as well as a constitutional struggle against a "treasonable" minority.[58]

Radical or not, the Downeaster at last was about to realize his ambition of visiting Europe as a diplomat. The fact that he knew no foreign languages and had not the first jot of diplomatic training probably bothered him very little. All the other Republican envoys were in the same boat, and anyhow, to

[58] William B. Reed, a Pennsylvania Democrat who had occupied a diplomatic post under Buchanan, first made the point about the ambiguous nature of many of Lincoln's appointments in an anonymous criticism of administration diplomacy entitled *A Review of Mr. Seward's Diplomacy* (n. p., 1862) and also in his *Paper Containing a Statement and Vindication of Certain Political Opinions* (n. p., 1862), both of which are available in the Library of Congress. See also Jay Monaghan, *Diplomat in Carpet Slippers: Abraham Lincoln Deals with Foreign Affairs* (New York, 1945), pp. 68-69.

be an American diplomat in the nineteenth century presumably called for little other than political influence. He and Mrs. Pike made their preparations in New York to sail in late April. In Washington his friend and former *Tribune* colleague, James E. Harvey, who had received the Portuguese mission, took care of the matter of collecting the commission and other papers for Pike. Harvey owed his appointment primarily to Seward, for the adroit newspaperman acted as one of the Secretary of State's intermediaries in the confidential negotiations with the Confederates that were carried on during the crisis about supplying Fort Sumter. Harvey, as well as any man, knew the inside story during those crucial days in early April when an "irrepressible" civil war needed only the smallest spark to bring it into flaming life. Sometime during this last crisis prior to open war he informed Pike: "In a week you will hear the first guns South—perhaps at Sumter to begin with. This is private."[59]

The Confederate guns roared, as Harvey predicted, on April 12. The long and bloody Civil War had begun. From far away Maine came word that patriotic feeling ran at fever pitch. "We had quite a Union demonstration here yesterday," wrote a Calais relative; "all the stars & stripes were thrown out early in the day with the exception of the Democratic when about 11 o'clock they were requested to send up the stars, but refused, when a crowd gathered & threatened to cut down the staff, they then caved in. . . . There is in Port between 50 & 60 sail of vessels & with but one or two exceptions [all] had the American Flag flying. At noon, 34 guns, & both Bells Rung,

[59] James E. Harvey to Pike, [April? 1861,] Pike MSS. Harvey's statement, though interesting, adds no new knowledge about the decision to send supplies to Major Anderson; for Harvey's minor role in the Sumter imbroglio, see James G. Randall, *Lincoln the President: Springfield to Gettysburg* (New York, 1945), II, 343; also his article, "When War Came in 1861," *Abraham Lincoln Quarterly*, I (March, 1940), 3-42. Another interpretation is offered by Charles W. Ramsdell, "Lincoln and Fort Sumter," *Journal of Southern History*, III (Aug., 1937), 259-88. For Harvey's relationship to Seward, see Carman and Luthin, *Lincoln*, pp. 91-92.

so you see we are all right here, & Endorse the Policy of the Government."[60]   But Pike had little time for patriotic rejoicing. He sailed on April 27.   Ahead lay five years of diplomacy and European life.

[60] Sam Pike to Pike, April 20, 1861, Pike MSS.

III. *American Diplomacy*
at The Hague

THERE ARE advantages in approaching the Civil War diplomacy of the United States through a less important minister such at Pike at The Hague. In the first place, a few outstanding events like the *Trent* affair, the threat of Anglo-French intervention in the fall of 1862, or Napoleon III's Mexican adventure have largely overshadowed other aspects of wartime foreign relations. Many scarcely known Lincoln-Seward policies and foreign problems are brought into a clearer focus when there is no competing glare from the major crises. The understandable concentration of diplomatic historians on England and France has left the United States' wartime relations with other European powers relatively ignored.

In addition to this, Pike himself furnishes an interesting angle. He was in most matters, domestic and foreign, closer to the Radical Republicans than he was to Lincoln and Seward. Just as the Radicals at home came to disagree violently with Lincoln and to despise Seward, Pike obeyed many of his instructions with misgiving and disobeyed some with alacrity. Pike affords, in short, an unique perspective on Civil War diplomacy and on the men in Washington who shaped it. Nor did the minister to Holland confine himself or his observations to affairs at The Hague.

During his five years abroad, Pike utilized to the utmost his opportunity for seeing Europe and Europeans. He spent a surprising amount of time in London and Paris, and on occasion toured western Germany, Switzerland, and northern Italy. He did a good bit of ordinary wide-eyed sightseeing, as his notebooks reveal, but he also met and talked with many Europeans, especially Englishmen. John Bright, Thomas Carlyle, and Lord Brougham, the ancient Whig champion and ex-chancellor, were among his London acquaintances. Pike conversed frequently with them on topics ranging from the American war to the London weather.

He read both English and French newspapers and gave Seward clear, balanced reports on many political developments in that turbulent decade of Europe's history. But his home post was The Hague. In the mid-nineteenth century American envoys to The Hague found their ministerial accommodations democratically unpretentious, to say the least.

Pike arrived at The Hague on the first of June, 1861.[1] He and his wife took rooms in a boardinghouse since the government furnished no official residence. In fact the government furnished little or nothing, and when Pike discovered this situation, he smoldered. He declared to Seward that the legation library barely deserved the name. He found no United States history or map, and there was not even a "Stars and Stripes" to display on appropriate occasions. The government provided no money to pay rent for permanent offices, and State Department regulations clearly forbade the use of contingent funds for such purposes. "One small book case and a chest less than 18 inches square in an upper seven by nine room in a Hotel, was the official legacy bequeathed to me by my predecessor," Pike groaned. Public documents, some in unopened crates, were stored in a garret in a remote part of town. "So long as the Government pursues its present plan of furnishing no place in which to store its treasures of this character, I would suggest a suspension of the shipments," Pike pertly concluded.[2]

---

[1] Henry C. Murphy, Pike's Democratic predecessor, to Seward, June 8, 1861, DoS Papers.

[2] Pike to Seward, No. 9, July 16, 1861, *ibid.*

The documents kept coming. Pike cooled down. It is unlikely that he blushingly remembered having written an article for the *Tribune* a decade earlier in which he devastatingly ridiculed the expenditures of American diplomats abroad. At that time, 1852, many of the envoys were Southern Whigs and conservative Northerners, and their propensity for living abroad in sybaritic luxury had then both amused and outraged *Tribune*-correspondent Pike.[3]

Perhaps Pike just came to accept the situation as he found it in 1861, for he filed no more scorching complaints. After all, he could not expect too much in Holland if the London legation found itself in much the same straits. Benjamin Moran, a crotchety diarist and American legation secretary in London, found inventory-taking nothing but literally dirty work. Moran discovered that the "books are mainly kept over the stable, are soiled, dusty & damp, and altogether in a sad state." As Pike had done at first, Moran railed at Washington's utter indifference "to the comfort of Legations."[4]

Regardless of his own inconvenience, Pike had other things to worry about in the summer of 1861. Secretary Seward's foreign policy was a bow with many strings, and Pike soon discovered that even at The Hague one might be kept occupied in negotiations that related directly to the awesome conflict at home.

Seward's diplomacy throughout the Civil War, and especially in 1861, is complex and often downright baffling on first approach. A good example is his abortive but significant attempt to negotiate separate treaties with the maritime powers that had ratified the Declaration of Paris in 1856. According to the brief, far-reaching Declaration, the ratifying powers agreed that privateering was abolished; that the neutral flag covers enemy goods with the exception of contraband of war; that neutral goods, except contraband, are not liable to capture

---

[3] *Tribune*, Dec. 22, 1852; Pike, *First Blows*, pp. 156-57.
[4] Sarah A. Wallace and Frances E. Gillespie, eds., *The Journal of Benjamin Moran, 1857-1865* (Chicago, 1948), I, 797. Hereinafter cited as *Moran Journal*.

under the enemy's flag; and, lastly, that blockades must be effective in order to be binding.[5]

William L. Marcy, Secretary of State under President Pierce, had informed the negotiating powers that the United States, which had long advocated doctrines similar to those embodied in the Declaration of Paris, could not accede to the pact unless a fifth article were added which would exempt all private property at sea, except contraband, from capture. In other words, without such protection the United States would not forego the right to send out privateers, which had earlier in her history proved the most effective maritime weapon.[6]

Seward reopened this question on April 24, 1861, when he instructed the representatives of the United States abroad to negotiate conventions for American adherence to the Declaration of Paris, with Marcy's proposed amendment if possible but without it if necessary.[7] Seward's move takes on significance when it is remembered that Jefferson Davis had proclaimed one week earlier, on April 17, that the Confederacy proposed to send out privateers. But the greatest complicating twist was given to the whole matter when Foreign Secretary Lord Russell, the same 'Finality John' of Reform Bill fame, announced on May 6 that Great Britain intended to recognize the belligerent status of the Confederacy and to maintain a policy of strict neutrality in the American war.

The crucial negotiations connected with this phase of Seward's program were conducted in London and Paris, and have been scrupulously studied by Professor E. D. Adams in his *Great Britain and the American Civil War*. The conversations and written communications concerning the matter were

[5] John B. Moore, *A Digest of International Law* (Washington, 1906), VII, 562.

[6] Sir Francis Piggott, *The Declaration of Paris* (London, 1919), pp. 142-49, 393-404; summarized in Ephraim D. Adams, *Great Britain and the American Civil War* (London, 1925), I, 140-41. Hereinafter cited as Adams, *Great Britain*.

[7] Seward to United States ministers in Great Britain, France, Russia, Prussia, Austria, Belgium, Italy, Denmark, April 24, 1861, in U. S. Department of State, *Papers Relating to Foreign Affairs 1861* (Washington, 1862), pp. 18-20; hereinafter cited as *Foreign Papers*. The proposal to the Netherlands was not made until May 10, 1861.

protracted and tortuous.   After several months had passed,
Charles Francis Adams, the American envoy to Britain, prepared for signing a maritime convention only to discover that
Her Majesty's government insisted on an added clause.   This
newly inserted amendment stated emphatically that Britain
"did not intend thereby to undertake any engagement which
shall have any bearing, direct or indirect, on the internal differences now prevailing in the United States."[8]

Both the British and French ministers clearly foresaw
dangerous potentialities in the fact that they had recognized
the belligerent status of the Confederacy while the United
States had not.   Lincoln and Seward had already referred to
Southern privateers as pirates, and Lord Russell recognized
that a convention with the United States could be interpreted
as forcing Britain, or any other signatory European power, to
accept Seward's view.

The upshot was that Adams refused to accept the qualifying clause and asked for instructions from Washington.   Seward
bluntly refused to sign any such article which would completely
undermine his and Lincoln's interpretation of the war as simply
a domestic uprising.   And the futile negotiations ended on a
note of recrimination and suspicion, causing European powers
to regard Seward, whom Britons already considered bellicose,
with even more of a jaundiced eye.[9]

Pike's role in these negotiations, while secondary because
of the Dutch tendency to take cues from Britain in maritime
matters, illustrates an interesting aspect of Seward's diplomatic
and political problems.   The Hague minister disagreed with
Seward over the propriety and wisdom of the negotiations and
counseled with important friends in the United States Senate
whose distrust of Seward came to be one of the most critical
of President Lincoln's many political problems.

Pike failed to realize that Seward stubbornly persisted in

[8] Adams, *Great Britain*, I, 141-45.
[9] *Ibid.*

the vain attempts to procure the Declaration of Paris conventions primarily because the Secretary of State still hoped to convince the maritime powers that they should not, indeed could not, recognize Southern belligerency. This question of belligerency determined most of Seward's policy throughout the first six months of the American conflict. Obstinately determined that no such status existed, Seward returned repeatedly throughout the war to press foreign powers into recalling their proclamations of neutrality.[10]

Pike, however, considered that the granting of belligerent status had so changed the situation that it would be futile and unnecessarily irritating to proceed further. To the Secretary of State himself Pike wrote, asking if the government did not desire to modify its instructions. "On reflection," Pike explained, "I am in doubt whether our government knew of the position, or anticipated it, of England & France in regard to 'belligerent rights' of the revolting States, at the time the recent instructions were issued."[11] This failed to shake the resolute Secretary of State's determined policy, but Pike did not rest with his official inquiry.

He wrote privately to his close friend and fellow Downeaster, Senator William Pitt Fessenden, an influential Republican associated with the Radicals in Congress. Hardly had he arrived at The Hague before Pike requested Fessenden's opinion of Seward's circular instructions concerning the Declaration of Paris. "And I confess," Pike wrote, "I am [at] a loss to see what we are to gain by accepting the Paris propositions. It looks to me to be an inopportune time to do it, and we are already twitted about it in the French papers." Pike wondered

[10] *Ibid.*, I, 169. Professor Adams does not agree with Charles Francis Adams, Jr., and others who have interpreted Seward's proffer to accede to the Declaration of Paris as a "trap" in which to catch unsuspecting European governments with regard to the Civil War. Yet he admits that Seward probably "foresaw an advantage through expected aid in repressing privateering, but primarily he hoped to persuade the maritime Powers not to recognize Southern belligerency." The question of Seward's motivation is discussed lengthily in *ibid.*, I, 144-71. Cf. Frederic Bancroft, *The Life of William H. Seward* (New York, 1900), II, 189; hereinafter cited as Bancroft, *Seward.*

[11] Pike to Seward, No. 4, June 16, 1861, DoS Papers.

if the Senate was "of a temper" to confirm such treaties if they were concluded, and he ended with the following observation, which would have understandably shocked the Secretary of State if he had seen the letter: ". . . I have such a strong misgiving about the Senate's ratifying such a treaty that I do not feel like entering upon active negociations [sic] till I see whether my suspicions be well founded."[12]

A bit later Pike asked Fessenden if Lincoln's Cabinet had thoroughly considered the Paris Declaration matter. Pike suggested that Fessenden consult Salmon P. Chase, now Secretary of the Treasury, and send the information on to him at The Hague. Apparently feeling some misgivings about his own actions, Pike confessed: "I don't know how much of this that I am writing to you I should communicate, and I do it in strict confidence, & should not do it to any body but you or Mr. Chase. I am not administering the Govt. and have no responsibility for its acts and in such a case as this of direct instruction, can fairly hold no other position than that of executing my instructions." Nevertheless, Pike thought that the case had "serious, national bearings, & may easily take on an aspect to complicate us with any party with which we might make a treaty."[13]

Pike, as well as some of the Radicals at home, doubted the efficacy of Seward's persisting in the negotiations after it had become clear that Europe could not be shaken from its stand on belligerency and neutrality. Senator Fessenden confessed his disapproval of the negotiations to Pike, and declared United States adherence to be out of the question. But "there is nothing too mean to be suspected" of Seward, Fessenden added.[14] Count Adam Gurowski, already an extreme Radical and temporarily employed in the State Department itself, publicly assailed Seward for blundering into the abortive negotiations. Gurowski asserted that he had warned President Lin-

[12] Pike to Fessenden, June 7, 1861, JSP Papers.
[13] Pike to Fessenden, July 19, 1861, ibid.
[14] Fessenden to Pike, June 30, 1861, Pike MSS.

coln that the United States stood to gain nothing by a "too hasty accession" to the Declaration, that the action would not prevent belligerent recognition and would only chain the hands of the United States "in case of any war with England."[15] To Pike, Gurowski insisted that the United States sadly lacked leadership, for neither "pighead Lincoln" nor any of the Cabinet measured up to the crisis. Gurowski scorned the "crew of noninities [*sic*] at the helm."[16]

In Pike's case, it is not the criticism of Seward's policy which is striking but his method of making known his doubts and opinions. This was not the last occasion on which he wrote confidentially to Fessenden, either criticizing Seward and his policies or else seeking specific information about the attitude of Congress. It was Fessenden and other Radicals who later brought on the famed Cabinet crisis of December, 1862, which ended with Lincoln's pocketing letters of resignation from both Seward and Chase and sagely remarking that now he could ride on, since "I have got a pumpkin in each end of my bag."[17]

Despite the letters to Fessenden, Pike apparently obeyed his instructions regardless of the private opinions which he held. He submitted Seward's proposition to the Dutch government and found that they would agree to a convention embodying the Declaration of Paris as it stood as well as to the Marcy amendment. The Dutch foreign minister made it clear, however, that Holland could act only with Britain and France; he suggested that the United States might try to secure a general congress of the powers to consider the subject.[18] Seward's plans for the treaties collapsed, as mentioned earlier, when Britain and France insisted that any step they might take with regard to maritime warfare could not be interpreted

---

[15] Count Adam Gurowski, *Diary* (Boston, 1862), I, 29; entry for April, 1861.

[16] Gurowski to Pike, Washington, August 30, 1861, Pike MSS.

[17] Randall, *Lincoln the President*, II, 241-49; hereinafter cited as Randall, *Lincoln*. Francis Fessenden, *Life and Public Services of William Pitt Fessenden* (New York, 1907), I, 231-53.

[18] Pike to Seward, No. 10, July 30, 1861, DoS Papers.

as affecting their neutrality in the Civil War. Pike's role in the negotiations furnishes an interesting glimpse of the off-stage political and diplomatic maneuvering of Lincoln's harassed administration.

Another of Seward's somewhat mystifying and little-known projects was the suggestion he made on May 14, 1861, a month after the attack on Fort Sumter, that some of the European powers join the United States in a naval demonstration against Japan. Antiforeign incidents in that recently "opened" land furnished Seward with the reason, or excuse, for this overture to Europe, and he invited Britain, France, Russia, Prussia, and the Netherlands to join the contemplated expedition.[19]

Pike found the Dutch government again in agreement with Seward on both the need for some such action and the suggested method. Yet nothing came of the plan at that time because of the preoccupation of both the United States and Europe with more urgent matters.[20] The subject is mentioned as another illustration of Seward's persistent efforts to tie the European powers to the United States while, at the same time, making it more difficult for them to indulge in any friendly attitudes or acts concerning the Confederacy.[21]

Preventing the recognition of the Confederacy by European powers and exerting every effort to have these same powers withdraw their acknowledgment of Southern belligerency— these were the foremost objects of Seward's diplomacy during the opening months of the Civil War. But if Seward concentrated on preventing recognition, the Confederates were just as assiduously seeking that same diplomatic boon. To the Southerners, European recognition would guarantee the success

---

[19] Adams, *Great Britain*, I, 126.

[20] Pike to Seward, No. 8, July 12, 1861, DoS Papers.

[21] Tyler Dennett, "Seward's Far Eastern Policy," *American Historical Review*, XXVIII (Oct., 1922), 48-49. Dennett sees Seward's proposed action against Japan not as another aberration, comparable to the well-known memorandum of April 1, 1861, in which the Secretary of State suggested to Lincoln that a foreign war with France or Spain or both might be employed to reunite the country; but as a consistent step in the Far Eastern policy which Seward developed, especially after the war.

of their cause, and they quickly initiated an energetic diplomatic offensive in Europe.[22]

Aside from their commissioners and agents in Europe, the Confederates launched a flank attack partially aimed at the goal of recognition when they sent out Raphael Semmes, the "Rebel Raider," on his career as a destroyer of Northern commerce. Curiously enough, Pike's duties at The Hague became linked with the cruise of Semmes's first ship, the *Sumter*. The *Sumter's* visit to a Dutch colonial port led ultimately to Dutch recognition of Confederate belligerency. But in order to understand Minister Pike's tasks in the staid capital of the far-flung Dutch empire, it is necessary to look briefly at the Caribbean, and the colorful career of Raphael Semmes.

In his memoirs Semmes records that on the bright afternoon of July 16, 1861, his ship, the C.S.N. *Sumter*, approached the small port of St. Anne's on the Dutch island of Curaçao. The sea was a "deep indigo-blue" and the barren little island with its rocky, black shore seemed surrounded by "perpendicularly deep" waters. Semmes discovered that entering this tranquil Dutch haven was not as easy as it appeared. Under pressure from a zealous United States consul ("doughty little Consul" in Semmes's version), Curaçao's Dutch governor refused to allow the *Sumter* to enter port.

The scholarly Semmes immediately penned an indignant note to the governor in which he suggested "that there must be some mistake here." He pointed out that the *Sumter* was a ship-of-war "duly commissioned by the government of the Confederate States, which States have been recognized, as belligerents . . . by all the leading Powers of Europe. . . ." Admitting that captured prizes might justly be prohibited from the port, Semmes inquired if the Dutch government would follow the practice of admitting United States cruisers while

[22] For the early phases of Confederate diplomacy in Europe, see Frank L. Owsley, *King Cotton Diplomacy* (Chicago, 1931), pp. 52-87; hereinafter cited as Owsley, *King Cotton*.

banning those of the Confederacy. If so, he insisted, Holland would be departing from her neutrality in the war and not only ignoring the Confederate States but "aiding and abetting their enemy." "If this be the position which Holland has assumed," Semmes concluded, ". . . I pray your Excellency to be kind enough to say as much to me in writing."[23]

The hard-pressed Dutch governor quickly summoned his council. While the transplanted but still ponderous burghers gravely debated the matter the *Sumter's* messenger sipped "delightful mint juleps" and waited. In the meantime, Semmes, according to his own account, became impatient on board ship and ordered a gunnery practice.

Semmes relates, probably with more than a touch of exaggeration, that the shells from the gunnery practice burst "like a clap of rather sharp, ragged thunder" beyond but still "in close proximity" to the council chamber where the Dutchmen sat debating. "Sundry heads were seen immediately to pop out of the windows of the chamber, and then to be withdrawn very suddenly, as though the owners of them feared that another shell was coming. . . ."

In a few minutes the messenger returned. The Dutchmen had decided to admit the *Sumter*. "The quays were crowded with a motley gathering of the townspeople, men, women, and children, to see us pass, and sailors waved their hats to us, from the shipping in the port. Running through the town into a land-locked basin, . . . the *Sumter* let go her anchor, hoisted out her boats, and spread her awnings,—and we were once more in port."[24] Semmes had gained a vital opportunity to refuel, but he also scored a point diplomatically.

[23] Admiral Raphael Semmes, *Memoirs of Service Afloat, during the War between the States* (Baltimore, 1869), pp. 151-53. The report of this incident to Confederate Secretary of the Navy, Stephen Mallory, as well as Semmes's note to the Dutch governor, may be found in *Official Records of the Union and Confederate Navies in the War of the Rebellion* (Washington, 1894), Ser. I, Vol. I, pp. 621-22, 631.

[24] *Ibid.*, pp. 153-54. The gunnery-practice incident is not included in the earlier version of his memoirs which Semmes published as *The Cruise of the Alabama and the Sumter* (New York, 1864); in Pike's subsequent conversations at The Hague there

Semmes's primary mission was the destruction of Northern vessels, and he achieved some success in this line.[25] But he seems in addition to have worked consciously either for the recognition of the Confederacy by a European power or else for some concession which might furnish the South a diplomatic lever. According to Britain's proclamation of neutrality of May 6, 1861, which became official on May 14, "public vessels" (i. e., warships) of both North and South could enter her ports and take on supplies, but neither privateers nor captured prizes could enter. The other maritime powers, including the Dutch, were expected to follow Britain's lead, although not necessarily to imitate the unusually severe restrictions on prizes.[26]

Semmes, who was well informed in international law, had studied carefully the various aspects of recognition before sailing. He hoped to obtain concessions from other European nations, or from a South American state, on the grounds that Britain's proclamation discriminated against the Confederacy. That is, since Southern coasts were blockaded while those of the United States were not, any port-closing order was actually regarded as working the greater hardship on the Confederacy. And, at any rate, Semmes could not lose at Curaçao since Holland had not accorded belligerent status to the South. Aside from the coal he needed, Semmes apparently strove to obtain for the Confederacy those very goals connected with recognition which Pike and Seward fought desperately to prevent.[27]

When Seward learned that the "privateering" and "pirati-

---

seems to be no mention of the incident or of its bearing on the Dutch governor's and council's decision. But it is a good story.

[25] The *Sumter* burned seven out of the eighteen Northern vessels she captured in seven months' time. See Harpur A. Gosnell, ed., *Rebel Raider: Being an Account of Raphael Semmes' Cruise in the C. S. A. Sumter* (Chapel Hill, 1948); George W. Dalzell, *The Flight from the Flag* (Chapel Hill, 1940), pp. 30-63.

[26] For the matter of prizes and their disposition, see Dalzell, *The Flight from the Flag*, pp. 22-23.

[27] W. Adolphe Roberts, *Semmes of the Alabama* (New York, 1938), pp. 55-56. Owsley, *King Cotton*, ignores this aspect of Semmes's naval activity.

cal" *Sumter* had enjoyed Dutch hospitality, he despatched an indignant protest for Pike to pass on to the Dutch government. Seward's proclivity for challenging Britain in his early despatches is well known.[28] That he should take a peremptory tone with Holland is not surprising. He informed Pike that the United States would later consider the subject of damages for "so great a violation" of its rights. But in the meantime "you will ask the government of the Netherlands for any explanation of the transaction it may be able or see fit to give." And furthermore, Seward explained, the United States expected the Netherlands, in case the reports from Curaçao proved correct, both to disown the action of the colonial authorities and to "adopt efficient means to prevent a recurrence of such proceedings hereafter."[29]

Before this message even arrived, Pike learned unofficially of Semmes's activities. Pike informed Foreign Minister van Zuylen that the United States would regard the incident with "equal regret and surprise" if it proved to be true. To Seward, Pike suggested soothingly that The Hague's order excluding privateers probably had failed to reach Curaçao. Pike, of course, viewed the *Sumter* as a "privateer" despite her commission from the Richmond government. The Dutch messenger ship might be delaying its visit to "avoid the heats of summer."[30]

Soon Pike received Seward's explicit demands and returned for another interview with van Zuylen. The Dutch minister casually mentioned on this occasion that the *Sumter* might not have been a privateer at all but a ship-of-war of the "so-called Confederate States." This idea nettled Pike into asserting that if Semmes were furnished shelter and supplies on this ground, it would be substantially "a recognition of the southern confederacy, and that in my judgment such an act would be

[28] Adams, *Great Britain*, I, 125-27.
[29] Seward to Pike, No. 15, August 15, 1861, *Foreign Papers* 1861, p. 342.
[30] Pike to Seward, No. 14, August 28, 1861, *ibid*, p. 343.

regarded by the United States as an unfriendly, and even hostile act, which might lead to the gravest consequences." Hitting his stride, the Yankee diplomat warned that "if there were to be exhibited a disposition anywhere to take advantage of our present situation, I believed it would be found that such a course could not be taken with impunity now, nor without leading to alienation and bitterness in the future."[31]

At this point Baron van Zuylen hastily assured Pike of the Netherlands' friendly purposes and asked for time to consider the facts and gain additional information.[32] The Dutch position, as it subsequently emerged, at first evaded the issue by claiming that the *Sumter* gained entrance into their port as a vessel in distress. The Curaçao authorities apparently submitted this handy explanation of distress, though Semmes's letter to the island's governor had insisted on admission to the port for different reasons.[33]

More important than this distress dodge, however, was the question about the status of the *Sumter*: piratical privateer, as Pike and Seward insisted, or war vessel of a belligerent power? Holland remained one of the few maritime powers that had not followed Britain's lead in according belligerent rights to the Confederacy. The *Sumter* case necessitated a change in her policy.

Pike argued strenuously against Holland's admitting the vessel-of-war character of Semmes's ship and thus conferring belligerency rights on the Confederacy. He threatened: the government of the Netherlands might "make an enemy of the United States, through the consequences growing out of that act." He cajoled: "The Dutch government has been wiser [than the British and French]. In . . . refusing all countenance to the authors of such a hateful rebellion, the Netherlands will

---

[31] Pike to Seward, No. 15, September 4, 1861, *Foreign Papers* 1861, p. 344.

[32] *Ibid.*

[33] Semmes mentions acquiring a new fore-topmast at St. Anne's in his report to Secretary of Navy Mallory, but his communication to the governor of Curaçao has no reference to this. See above, p. 61.

do an act which will be viewed with the liveliest satisfaction by the United States, and will set an example well worthy the respect and consideration of other nations."

Pike cleverly introduced the slavery question by maintaining that the rebels fought only "to perpetuate and extend African slavery," the clear implication being that the United States was waging an antislavery crusade. He urged the Dutch government to escape the "practical difficulty" with which Semmes had confronted them by ordering their colonial authorities to "regard *all* armed vessels bearing the so-called confederate flag as *privateers*." Unless a vessel claiming to be a ship-of-war exhibited some *prima facie* evidence of being such, that is in size or "other external symbols and aspects," Pike argued that the Dutch authorities should merely claim the right to decline all investigation and to "*assume* her unlawful character!" Since Pike considered that the Confederacy's "piratical craft" could not meet the external qualifications he had suggested for determining the status of a vessel, he thought he was indicating a neat solution to the Dutch dilemma.[34]

Pike's claims notwithstanding, the logic of the case worked against him. Baron van Zuylen pointed, as Lord Russell had earlier, to the fact that the United States might talk of the secessionists as rebels and pirates, but Confederate prisoners were not treated as traitors and pirates should be; that is, captured Southerners were not executed. The Dutch government considered that it had no alternative but to recognize Confederate belligerency. In the specific matter of Raphael Semmes's *Sumter*, the Dutch clung to the distress angle while also maintaining that the ship was classified as a vessel-of-war. In addition to Semmes's declarations and official papers, the Dutch foreign minister cited a sketch of the *Sumter* in *Harper's Weekly*. The drawing carried the caption "The 'Sumter,' A

---

[34] These arguments of Pike's and of the Dutch government are found in several despatches from Pike to Seward and notes exchanged by Pike and van Zuylen, the Dutch minister, in *Foreign Papers 1861*, pp. 344-48.

Rebel Ship of War," and to van Zuylen this tell-tale caption apparently clinched the argument.[35]

Thus, three months after the *Sumter's* visit to Curaçao, Pike suffered a diplomatic defeat. Semmes, at least indirectly, had gained Dutch recognition of Southern belligerency. Pike rushed forth with strong protests when the Dutch decision became known. Echoing Seward, Pike declared that the United States was "one whole undivided nation, especially so far as foreign nations are concerned. . . ." Holland's taking a different view must cause "very deep regret" to President Lincoln and the Northern public.[36]

Seward reacted even more violently than Pike to the Dutch stand. Far from merely regretting the Dutch action, the Secretary of State talked of providing "for the protection of our rights in some other way." According to Seward in his despatch of October 17, 1861, the matter of the "piratical vessels" neither required nor admitted of debate; and if the Netherlands government failed to prohibit these vessels from its Continental and colonial ports "its proceedings in this respect will be deemed unfriendly and injurious to the United States."

Seward ordered Pike to inform Foreign Minister van Zuylen that the United States "unreservedly claim to determine for themselves absolutely the character of the Sumter, she being a vessel, fitted out, owned, armed, sailed, and directed by American citizens who owe allegiance to the United States. . . ." If the Dutch failed either to give the necessary orders or else to explain, Seward concluded, "it will become necessary to

[35] *Ibid.*, pp. 348, 350-51. For the *Harper's Weekly* sketch, see issue of June 22, 1861, p. 398.

[36] Pike to van Zuylen, Sept. 23, 25, 1861, *ibid.*, 350-51. The question of the viability of the United States-Netherlands treaty of 1782 arose during these negotiations, but the Dutch government viewed the treaty as obsolete in 1861. Since the Unted States tacitly agreed to this view in 1861 and officially admitted as much in 1873, the question seems unimportant and is not treated in this study. See J. C. Westermann, *The Netherlands and the United States: Their Relations in the Beginning of the Nineteenth Century* (The Hague, 1935), pp. 390-93; Ernst J. Kiehl, *Ons Verdrag met Amerika* (The Hague, 1863), pp. 146-50.

consider what means we can take to protect, in the ports of the Netherlands, national rights which cannot be surrendered or compromised."[37]

Seward's obvious anger sprang from two chief causes, aside from his chronic but understandable aversion to any whisper of the word "recognition" in whatever context. First, reports had arrived from Surinam (Dutch Guiana) that the *Sumter* had once more enjoyed Dutch hospitality. On this second occasion the "piratical craft" had been at the port of Paramaribo from August 19 to 31, 1861.

And the second cause of Seward's outburst lay in the fact that the Dutch government, at the same time it admitted Southern belligerency, had also promised virtually to close its ports to both the United States and the Confederacy. By such a step, contrary to British and French practice, the Dutch government actually meant to favor the United States. The blockaded South depended more than did the United States on neutral ports.[38] Despite this promise, however, here was Semmes back in Dutch waters. For these reasons, then, when Seward wrote his despatch of October 17, 1861, which threatened "protection of our rights in some other way," his uncertainty and annoyance were compounded with his usual reaction to "recognition" talk. The Secretary of State became bellicose, at least on paper.

Pike needed no additional pushing from Washington. He too had heard of Semmes's exasperating second visit to Dutch territory. Even before Seward's virtual ultimatum arrived, Pike wrote the Dutch foreign minister that the "reappearance of the Sumter in a port of the Netherlands, after so brief an interval, seems to disclose a deliberate purpose on the part of the persons engaged in rebellion against the United States government to practice upon the presumed indifference, the expected favor, or the fancied weakness of the Dutch govern-

---

[37] Seward to Pike, No. 26, Oct. 17, 1861, *Foreign Papers 1861*, pp. 366-67.

[38] Seward to Pike, No. 24, Oct. 4, 1861, *ibid.*, p. 358; Pike to Seward, No. 18, Sept. 25, 1861, *ibid.*, pp. 350-51.

ment." Pike could see no reason for the *Sumter's* confining
its visits so largely to one nation's ports, "especially one so
scantily supplied with them as Holland."[39]

This note, like Seward's angry despatch, represents strong
talk for diplomacy in that era. Pike's tone is especially strange
in view of his simultaneous admission to Seward that the intentions of the Dutch were friendly, that the Dutch desired to
avoid all difficulty with the United States, and that he (Pike)
believed that orders impeding the operations of the Southerners
had already been issued.[40] Despite his hopeful estimate to
Seward, Pike had addressed a stern note to van Zuylen. One
reason might have been that such a tone and attitude suited
Seward's whole policy in the *Sumter* affair. And if Pike had
not already spoken sternly, Seward's despatch of October 17
would have required an equally if not more rigorous stand
when it arrived.

At any rate, the Dutch government produced an order
prohibiting from its ports not only privateers but also war
vessels belonging to both belligerents in America. This was
as Pike had predicted to Seward. Specifically the Dutch permitted belligerent war vessels to remain in their ports for only
forty-eight hours (Pike erroneously reported twenty-four) and
to purchase not more than twenty-four hours' coal supply.
This arrangement gratified Pike, since the United States stood
to suffer least from it. He basked in the reflection that the
Netherlands now conceded more to the United States than did
either Britain or France. If these other maritime powers should
adopt the same restrictions, Pike predicted an end "to rebel
operations by steam" in the Caribbean and South Atlantic.[41]

When Pike informed his British colleague at The Hague,
Sir Andrew Buchanan, about the port-closing order of the
Netherlands, the Briton expressed great surprise. He declared

[39] Pike to Seward, No. 20, Oct. 9, 1861, *Foreign Papers 1861*, pp. 359-60. The
note to van Zuylen is enclosed.

[40] *Ibid.*

[41] Pike to Seward, No. 22, Oct. 12, 1861, *ibid.*, p. 361.

that neither Britain nor the United States would follow the Dutch example in similar circumstances. He reminded Pike of a Crimean War incident when Russia wanted Swedish ports closed to both belligerents but England refused to allow this on the grounds that it would be unneutral conduct.

Pike reported this sobering comment to Seward. And in doing so, Pike appended a standard complaint against England during the Civil War: "You see herein [by the British minister's remarks] how thoroughly English officials (and it seems to me all others) are imbued with the idea that the rights of a mere belligerent are the same as the rights of a nation, in cases like the one under consideration." In other words, Pike and most other Americans—North and South—could never forgive Britain for remaining neutral during the Civil War.[42]

Regardless of the British minister's opinion, Seward and other American diplomats abroad were pleased with the Dutch action. Seward directed Pike to express the United States' satistion to the Dutch government. At the same time Pike should file the usual caveat concerning belligerent recognition. "Felicitate the government of the Netherlands," Seward purred, "as we felicitate ourselves on the renewed auguries of good and cordial relations between friends too old to be alienated thoughtlessly, or from mere impatience." The closing portion of Seward's message must have pleased Pike, the diplomatic novice: "I am directed by the President to express his approval of the diligence and discretion you have practiced in this important transaction."[43]

Charles Francis Adams in London congratulated Pike on "persuading the government of Holland of the expediency of putting a check on the piratical experiments of vessels like the Sumter." Nevertheless, Adams added sagaciously that as a general thing the United States would have to rely upon

[42] Pike to Seward, No. 23, Oct. 16, 1861, *Foreign Papers 1861*, p. 362.
[43] Seward to Pike, No. 31, Nov. 11, 1861; No. 33, Nov. 23, 1861, *ibid.*, pp. 370-71.

its own energies rather than the co-operation of European authorities in the West Indies. From Madrid also came Carl Schurz's word of praise for the Dutch arrangements which Pike had secured.[44]

Not everybody shared in the general happiness, however. In America, Count Gurowski growled his displeasure: "The little cheese-eater, the Hollander, was the first to raise a fuss against the United States concerning the piratical flag. This is not to be forgotten."[45] In Holland, Pike's strong protest about the *Sumter's* second visit to a Netherlands' port had grated on Dutch ears. Foreign Minister van Zuylen mentioned in a note to the American envoy that certain of Pike's expressions had "caused an unpleasant impression on the King's government" and did not correspond with the manner in which the Dutch government had striven to settle the matter nor with its desire to find a solution "perfectly in harmony with its sentiments of friendship towards the United States. . . ." The Dutch official declared his astonishment at the "feeling of distrust" which seemed to permeate Pike's inquiry about the *Sumter's* return to Dutch waters.[46]

If Pike smarted under these raps from the Dutch government, there is no record of it. Perhaps the commendation from Lincoln and Seward, as well as from his colleagues abroad, sufficed to offset the scolding. His triumph with regard to the Dutch port-closing order did not last too long. A change in the Dutch government brought a new foreign minister forward, and by early 1862 the Dutch had abandoned their port-closing order by which the United States was meant to benefit.[47]

[44] Adams to Pike, Oct. 24, 1861; Schurz to Pike, Oct. 30, 1861, Pike MSS.

[45] Gurowski, *Diary*, I, 122.

[46] Van Zuylen to Pike, Oct. 15, 1861, *Foreign Papers 1861*, p. 364. This reprimand to Pike appears in the published documents, although there is no record of Seward's taking any account of it. In fact, most of the *Sumter*-affair correspondence which shows Seward's tendency to threaten is published. Bancroft, *Seward*, II, 502, mentions that much of this type of thing was meant for "the reading public at home."

[47] Pike to Seward, No. 32, Jan. 1, 1862, DoS Papers; No. 43, March 16, 1862, *Foreign Papers 1862*, Pt. 2, p. 599; No. 44, April 2, 1862, *ibid.*, p. 600.

Pike's negotiations in the *Sumter* matter constituted his first important diplomatic assignment. His initial handling of the question suggested that he might have preferred a conciliatory approach similar to that employed by Charles Francis Adams in treating with the British about a parallel case.[48] After prodding from Seward, however, Pike imitated his superior's boldness.

Seward's *Sumter* correspondence reveals his outspoken, threatening manner in handling some, not all, of the diplomatic questions which arose out of the Civil War. In the case of Pike at Holland, the tendency on Seward's part obviously was less dangerous than it was in London, where Charles Francis Adams ably presented a modified Seward to the British government.[49] Pike had found it expedient in negotiating about the *Sumter* to follow the Secretary of State's lead. But this does not mean that Pike had become reconciled to Seward's general policies.

The slavery issue and the Lincoln-Seward approach to Northern war aims brought Pike into clear disagreement with Washington. From the first, Pike veered from the Lincoln administration's official view that the United States fought the Confederacy simply to preserve the Union. The Maine diplomat's attitude and statements serve admirably to focus this important aspect of Northern diplomacy. Aside from potent domestic pressures for and against an antislavery policy, could the North afford to fight merely for the Union's preservation and still hope to keep Europe neutral and possibly friendly to the Federal government? To this question, Lincoln and Seward long gave an affirmative answer. Pike's beliefs and observations led him to dissent, firmly and openly.

[48] See the Adams-Seward-Russell correspondence, *ibid.*, pp. 137-51.
[49] Bancroft, *Seward*, II, 505.

IV. *Slavery and Europe*

PIKE presented some startling observations in his first important conversation with Baron van Zuylen van Nyevelt, the Dutch foreign minister. He strongly hinted at an emancipation policy as early as June, 1861, and this was certainly no part of Lincoln's or Seward's much avowed purpose of preserving the Union, at any cost and regardless of the South's peculiar institution. Yet the fact was that Minister Pike in far-away Holland spoke much from the first about slavery and considered the subject of the greatest importance.

Most Europeans were thoroughly mystified by American affairs in 1861, and Baron van Zuylen was probably no exception. Explaining to him the "character of the rebellion," Pike declared it to be "merely a war in behalf of African slavery," for "if we had no slavery we should have no war and no rebellion." The United States intended to crush the rebellion of the seceding states, he continued; and "whenever it chose to employ them" the United States government "possessed extraordinary means of ending the rebellion," although it preferred more moderate means if possible. To avoid any ambiguity Pike added: "The union of the States could be restored whenever the government saw fit to render the institutions of the several States homogeneous. For when they were once made free States there would be no wish to separate and no tendency to separation."[1]

[1] Pike to Seward, No. 2, June 12, 1861, *Foreign Papers 1861*, p. 335, reporting a conversation with the Dutch foreign minister.

At the same time that Pike put the American conflict in this clear light, President Lincoln, as is well known, strove to keep slavery out of the picture. Border state pressure, widespread Northern aversion to abolitionism, and the terms of Lincoln's electoral mandate, all combined, during the first year and a half of Lincoln's administration, to set the President firmly against the slightest threatening allusion to slavery. And Seward mapped out his diplomatic policies in accordance with Lincoln's interpretation of the war.

Seward categorically ordered Charles Francis Adams at London to abstain from any debate about "opposing moral principles which may be supposed to lie at the foundation" of the American war. William L. Dayton in Paris received even more explicit instructions; Seward explained to him that the "condition of slavery" in the states would remain unchanged and subject to the same laws and administration regardless of the war's outcome.[2] In other words, Seward demanded that the United States' representatives abroad avoid imputing abolitionist motives to the government.

Although Seward apparently failed to prepare specific instructions for Pike on this point, that is no reason for assuming that the minister to The Hague enjoyed exemption from the general prohibition of antislavery discussion. There is every reason, in fact, for crediting Pike with a knowledge of the Lincoln administration's indisputable policy of ignoring slavery in 1861. For one thing, he did not sail from the United States to take up his diplomatic duties until late April, 1861. He had ample opportunity before leaving the country to become familiar at first hand with the program of the administration. Seward also issued circular despatches of a general nature to the United States foreign posts, and he sent Pike copies of some despatches sent to other legations which clarified

[2] Seward to Adams, April 10, 1861, *ibid.*, p. 60; Seward to Dayton, April 22, 1861, *ibid.*, p. 182.

the general position of the government and the State Department.[3]

The fact of the matter was that Pike simply considered Lincoln's and Seward's slavery policy to be mistaken, especially as far as Europe was concerned. And he let this fact be known. First to receive his analysis of European opinion and his plea for an attack on slavery was his friend from Maine, Senator Fessenden. Pike had barely reached The Hague before he informed Fessenden that a consideration of American affairs "from this point of view" made him believe that the "shortest way out is to overturn slavery & then the Union will reconstitute itself."[4] Shortly afterwards he declared to the Maine senator that the war in America could "be made respectable" in the eyes of the world or posterity only by making it "a war for the destruction of the race of slaveholders on our continent." They were the criminals, Pike judged, "& they should be the victims." He added that by punishing the victims he referred not to personal slaughter but to the overthrow of the institution "that has spawned these infernal rebels."[5]

The diplomat confessed to a realization that the government could not speak out at home, but he knew of "nothing to restrain me from speaking *to* it, or to others." Pike avowed that everywhere he went he preached "that there is nothing in our difficulties but *the nigger* and that when the Govt. *chooses* it can end the contest, simply by destroying slavery, and that it will do it, whenever it has to choose between doing that or submitting to dismemberment."[6] Pike admitted, with characteristic candor, that the only thing the North had to do concerning the Negro was "*to make the most of him for our own purposes.*" The Republicans must not be so "utterly unwise" as to become divided on the issue. At the same time, they had

---

[3] Seward to Pike, No. 2, July 8, 1861, DoS Papers.

[4] Pike to Fessenden, June 7, 1861, JSP Papers.

[5] Pike to Fessenden, June 22, 1861, *ibid.*

[6] *Ibid.* Pike elaborated on these ideas in his Notebook, No. 5, pp. 4-5, 11-12. All italics are in the original.

to remember that the party had embarked on an "anti-slavery errand." In short, the Republicans had to accomplish their goal without "going so fast as to stumble." Meanwhile, he would explain and proclaim in Europe the Republican anti-slavery position.[7]

If he had revealed these attitudes and actions only to Fessenden, who approved of them, Pike might be considered indiscreet, if not dishonest, in the discharge of his duties. But he actually did "speak *to*" Lincoln and Seward; in fact Pike set forth his objections to their policy in clear, forthright fashion. Interestingly enough, few of his criticisms and suggestions appear in the published *Foreign Papers*. Consequently they have been heretofore overlooked or disregarded despite the fact that he was one of the first American diplomats to emphasize the great need in Europe of a stronger stand with regard to slavery.

On September 11, 1861, Pike made explicit in a despatch to Seward the opinion which he had earlier implied. "You will permit me to remark," Pike wrote, "that if the struggle in America were to be treated here merely as an effort on one side to preserve the Union, and on the other to break it, there would not be much more sympathy felt for one side than the other." To win any European favor, he found that he had to set forth "the real objects of the secessionists" and express the government's true opinions of these objects. Following this course, he innocently confessed, "may involve some departure from the technical theory of the rebellion held by the Government."[8] This candid admission from Pike elicited no comment from the Secretary of State.

Soon news reached Europe of General John C. Frémont's famous military order freeing the enemy-owned slaves of Missouri. Before he learned of Lincon's counteraction, Pike wrote optimistically to Seward. He noted that Federal mili-

[7] Pike to Fessenden, Dec. 28, 1861, in *New England Quarterly*, XXI, 534.
[8] Pike to Seward, No. 16, Sept. 11, 1861, DoS Papers.

tary reversals had been leading European opinion to the conviction that dismemberment of the Union was inevitable. Yet "since the appearance of Genl. Fremont's proclamation" the notion of inescapable disunion had received a partial check. "Any action of the Government that looks to emancipation as a result of the war," he reported, "is seen to involve such a scope of eventualities, that speculation in regard to results is at once checked." He firmly believed, in short, that any evidence of an antislavery intent on the government's part would quickly be rewarded by "European interests, activities, and sympathies. . . ."[9]

The contemporary Dutch scene furnished Pike with one good reason for emphasizing European antislavery sentiment. In the first month of his diplomatic career he observed that Dutch speakers and writers, in and out of the legislative chambers, constantly agitated for the removal of slavery where it yet survived in some of the Dutch colonies.[10] The antislavery movement in Holland came to fruition in June, 1862, when the Dutch government, galvanized by a recent Liberal party electoral victory, decreed the emancipation of about 36,000 slaves in the Dutch colonies. The bill became operative on July 1, 1863, and provided for compensation to the owners (300 florins or about $120 per slave) as well as supervision by government agents for ten years.[11] With such events transpiring right around him Pike could hardly fail to appreciate the crucial role of slavery in presenting the American war to Europe.

Nor were Dutchmen alone among Europeans in their hatred of slavery. Elsewhere on the Continent American diplomats began to realize the dangerous lacuna in the North's program which resulted from the silence about slavery. Aside from Pike, Carl Schurz in Spain also warned Seward and Lincoln in

[9] Pike to Seward, No. 17, Sept. 18, 1861, *ibid.*

[10] Pike to Seward, No. 6, June 22, 1861, *ibid.*

[11] Pike to Seward, No. 55, July 23, 1862, *Foreign Papers 1862*, Pt. 2, p. 613. For the Dutch political background, see Petrus J. Blok, *History of the People of the Netherlands* (New York, 1912), V, 476-80; George Edmundson, *History of Holland* (Cambridge, 1922), pp. 411-18.

September, 1861, that they had best not ignore the potentialities of European humanitarian, liberal sympathies. In the
same fashion as Pike, Schurz explained the great difficulty
of making foreigners understand why "the free and prosperous
North" should fight for the privilege of associating with the
"imperious and troublesome Slave States." Schurz saw but
two ways for averting "the overwhelming perplexities" which
a "rupture with foreign powers" would inflict upon the United
States: one was a "great and decisive military success speedily
accomplished"; and the other, governmental "measures and
manifestations" which would place the war "upon a higher
moral basis, and therefore give us the control of public opinion
in Europe."[12] Schurz feared that a quick victory was not
forthcoming; he demanded in its stead some antislavery gesture. Like his colleague at The Hague, Schurz regarded
Seward's foreign policy with critical impatience; he considered
the antislavery policy so vital that he resigned his diplomatic
post and returned from Spain early in 1862 in order, among
other things, to consult with and advise President Lincoln.[13]

From other Americans in Europe, Pike learned of their
dissatisfaction with the government's slavery stand. Minister
George P. Marsh in Turin, Italy, confided his belief that at
first the United States had received credit in Europe for antislavery intentions. But with the government's abandonment
of all "principle," the current had set in favor of the South,
and "unless we soon place ourselves in a position to appeal to
some other principle than that of mere legal right, we shall
find ourselves altogether friendless." Marsh lamented to
Pike that he sadly feared that both government and people

[12] Schurz to Seward, Sept. 14, 1861, in *The Reminiscences of Carl Schurz* (New
York, 1907), II, 285-86. Although historians have overlooked Pike's keen interest
and recommendations concerning antislavery action as a diplomatic necessity, Schurz's
part is better known, probably because of his autobiography. In E. D. Adams, *Great
Britain*, II, 91-94, for example, Schurz is mentioned in this connection, but his ideas
were not as "rarely" presented to Lincoln as Adams suggests.

[13] Schurz, *Reminiscences*, II, 302-5.

"are prepared to sacrifice honor and conscience for the sake of a new compromise with the rebels."[14]

Pike received frantic declarations from Cassius M. Clay, Lincoln's Kentuckian in Russia. Clay trumpeted that he still stood for " 'Liberty or death' in all the rebel slave states." Clay argued that the North could never subdue the South as long as she had 4,000,000 slaves doing her work. "The North will weary of the fight; and the conservatives force a dishonored peace! The South will even at last turn her slaves loose, and arm them against us!—thus instead of having 4,000,000 of natural allies—there will be superadded to our want of vital principle, 4,000,000 of efficient enemies! in a place well fitted for defence of such enemies. Wendell Phil[l]ips is right."[15] Clay, like Schurz, returned to America and felt called upon to convince Lincoln of the necessity and righteousness of an antislavery war.

Pike meanwhile devoted himself to a threefold task with regard to slavery: convincing every European he encountered that the Lincoln government actually was antislavery, arguing the antislavery case in despatches to Seward, and privately informing Senator Fessenden and other personal friends of his views and actions. In 1862 other Americans in Europe joined Pike and Schurz in their open plea for a change in policy. In London Charles Francis Adams heard rumors that Southern partisans were privately hinting that the South would launch a plan of gradual emancipation after the Confederacy won its independence. The rumors were misleading,[16] but Adams wrote in February, 1862, urging Seward to secure some sort of declaration against slavery which would counteract the pro-Southern gossip and, at the same time, attach the

---

[14] Marsh to Pike, Sept. 14, Nov. 21, 1861, Pike MSS.

[15] Clay to Pike, Aug. 27, 1861, *ibid.*

[16] Such talk came solely from English friends of the South and greatly embarrassed Southern diplomatic and propaganda agents in London. The Confederate government responded angrily to any hint of freeing the slaves until it resorted to the desperate and futile attempt of 1865 to exchange emancipation for English and French recognition. See Owsley, *King Cotton*, pp. 550 ff.

large body of English antislavery sentiment to the Northern
cause. John L. Motley in Vienna also began to advise Seward
that United States policy in Europe demanded action in the
slavery matter.[17]

By this time it must have been clear to Lincoln and Seward
that, at least as far as Europe was concerned, a move or gesture
toward emancipation was most desirable. Minister Pike, who
kept an eye on events and opinions in England and France as
well as Holland, had clearly said as much several months
before the clamor from other representatives abroad became
general. Indeed, from the very beginning of his mission Pike
followed his own diplomatic course in imputing antislavery purposes to the North. Pike had clearly admitted this to Seward
in his unpublished despatch of September 11, 1861.[18]

Pike's admission brought no rebuke or cautioning word
from Secretary Seward. If Seward's phrases may be interpreted in any sense other than purely ceremonial, Lincoln
either saw or heard many of Pike's despatches, and Lincoln
must certainly have been aware of the minister to Holland's
great concern about European antislavery sentiment. The
only messages which Pike received from the President via
Seward, however, conveyed the information that "The President is gratified. . .," "I am directed by the President to
express his approval . . .," or similar statements.[19] This does
not mean that Lincoln conferred these blessings in direct reference to Pike's personal antislavery campaign, but if Lincoln or
Seward felt any disapproval it remained unexpressed.

Contemporary critics of the administration, however,
pounced on Pike's case as the boldest attempt at "anti-slavery
agitation." William B. Reed, a Pennsylvania Democrat and
pamphleteer who early attacked Lincoln's foreign appointees
and policies, called attention to each of Pike's antislavery state-

---

[17] E. D. Adams, *Great Britain*, II, 98.

[18] Cited above, p. 76.

[19] Seward to Pike, No. 12, July 26, 1861, *Foreign Papers 1861*, p. 341; Seward to Pike, No. 31, Nov. 11, 1861, *ibid.*, p. 370.

ments in the published despatches which appeared late in 1861. But this critic damned Pike and Seward for doing just what the Radicals attacked Seward and Lincoln for not doing—that is, taking an antislavery stand.[20]

Could it have been that the President and Seward realized, perhaps inwardly hoped, that such staunch members of the antislavery church as James Pike, Cassius Clay, and Carl Schurz, among others, would find it impossible to refrain from giving the antislavery interpretation of the war? Since they would be outspokenly antislavery anyhow, would not Europe provide a safer audience than the embattled, disunited citizenry at home? If Pike and the others could not be prevented from spreading doctrines in Europe which border state residents would shudder to hear in America, then what could be done except to shield the sensitive Kentuckians and Missourians against the harsh facts as long as possible? The argument from silence is a dangerously circuitous one. Yet Seward's failure to warn Pike away from the touchy subject of slavery in 1861 suggests the possibility that the Secretary of State as well as Lincoln may have realized that they were reaping some of the advantages of an antislavery position abroad months before the government at home moved decisively toward emancipation.

Seward wrote a curious letter to Pike in December, 1861, which may relate to this theory. Seward noted that the European states had put themselves into an "embarrassing" position *vis à vis* the United States government, by which he referred to their proclamations of neutrality which had conferred belligerent status on the Confederacy. The reason for this unfortunate state of affairs was simply that Europe had misunderstood the sentiments, the character, and the purposes of the United States. But this fact, the Secretary of State reasoned, ought not to surprise us however much we might

[20] Reed, *Review,* pp. 22-26.

regret it; for it "required some months to enable us to understand ourselves."[21]

Nor should the fact be overlooked that Lincoln and Seward
had filled the diplomatic posts with a striking number of well-
known antislavery champions.[22] The general character of the
diplomatic appointments takes on added significance when considered in relation with Lincoln's cautious, halting approach
towards emancipation. It is clear that domestic circumstances
long made a cautious policy toward slavery inevitable. But
as the war dragged on, foreign pressures, joined with other
domestic developments, made emancipation an increasingly
necessary measure.

The lengthy story of how Lincoln arrived at his preliminary emancipation proclamation of September 22, 1862, needs
no repetition at this point.[23] By mid-1862 Congressional and
military action directed against slavery had assumed such pro-
portions that Lincoln, conservative though he might be, had
no alternative but to consider a drastic executive move. The
border states had remained persistently unresponsive to the
President's cherished plans for compensated emancipation on
the state level. At the same time, more and more Northern
voices, in and out of Congress, joined in the clamorous demand
for emancipation. The arguments and pleas from Pike and
others in Europe merged with this formidable domestic situation; and the combination of forces impelled Lincoln towards
his proclamation.[24]

[21] Seward to Pike, No. 36, Dec. 11, 1861, DoS Papers.

[22] See above, p. 48.

[23] The best account is that of Randall, *Lincoln*, II, 126-80. Carl Sandburg, *Abraham Lincoln: The War Years* (New York, 1939), I, 555-90, is vivid despite the complexity of the problem.

[24] There is fairly general agreement among scholars (Randall, *Civil War*, p. 487; Bancroft, *Seward*, II, 317-48; Monaghan, *Diplomat*, *passim*) that Lincoln considered the European aspects of the slavery question of great importance. An important exception, however, is E. D. Adams, *Great Britain*, II, 91-94. Adams states that there is little basis for believing that Lincoln sought to correct foreign views of the war by his Eman-cipation Proclamation. This assertion is based on what seems to be an erroneous inter-pretation of Secretary Seward's influence, which in the case of emancipation was exerted in behalf of caution ranging almost to disapproval (Bancroft, *Seward*, II, 328 ff.).

The beneficial effects of the Emancipation Proclamation in Europe did not manifest themselves immediately. In fact, the initial reaction to Lincoln's preliminary announcement of September 22, 1862, keenly disappointed many Americans in Europe, including Pike. The most serious threat of Anglo-French "mediation" or intervention in the American conflict came in the fall of 1862, partially after emancipation news reached Europe.[25] Pike looked on helplessly and raged at what he considered the barbarous cynicism of European statesmen who would act to help the slave-tainted Confederacy.

Under the cloud of depression and fear caused by the intervention crisis, Pike contradicted his earlier arguments and warned Seward in mid-October, 1862, not to expect the Emancipation Proclamation to convert any of Europe's ruling classes to sympathy with the North. He insisted that the case of the United States in Europe was now a very clear one in which "democracy everywhere supports the federal government; antidemocracy everywhere opposes it." Thus the proclamation would not change the attitude of Europe's aristocratic governments regardless of how much the war was "intrinsically ennobled by making it one for widening the area of freedom."[26] A month later Pike observed bitterly that the "civilization of Europe is not ripe for any forcible righting of the wrong of Slavery." Except among a small group of "philanthropists," he thought that Lincoln's antislavery gesture had fallen "dead."[27]

But for all Pike's gloomy forebodings, Lincoln's emancipation policy slowly made itself felt in Europe. Lord Russell might point to inconsistencies in Lincoln's proclamation. These did not prevent English working people from flocking to a

Also it should be pointed out again that the foreign aspects of the slavery question had been preached to Lincoln and Seward both earlier and more frequently than Adams realized.

[25] Adams, *Great Britain*, II, 47 ff.; Owsley, *King Cotton*, pp. 361 ff.

[26] Pike to Seward, No. 63, Oct. 15, 1862, *Foreign Papers 1862*, Pt. 2, pp. 622-23.

[27] Pike to Seward, No. 66, Nov. 19, 1862, DoS Papers.

whole series of pro-Northern demonstrations and meetings which began late in 1862 and continued throughout the remainder of the war.[28] Richard Cobden wrote his friend, Senator Charles Sumner, that these amazing demonstrations of sympathy for the United States "closed the mouths of those who have been advocating the side of the South."[29]

Frenchmen also responded to Lincoln's bid for support. John Bigelow, then the Parisian consul, declared the French to be unanimously for emancipation, and he predicted that "our cause will now daily grow in grace here as it grows in age." His prophecy proved true. Within a few months one Confederate agent in Paris ruefully admitted that Southern slavery loomed as the "real *bête noire* of the French imagination."[30]

By the last day of 1862 Pike himself was ready to admit that the Emancipation Proclamation was finally having an effect on European opinion. He reported that the antislavery position gave the government "a substantial foothold in European circles." So long as the question had been between a government and a revolt, Pike again explained, "the instincts of even the liberal masses had a tendency to side with the rebellion; revolts being instinctively regarded as merely protests against some form of oppression." But now he rejoiced that everybody could grasp the significance of a war in which "emancipation is written on one banner and slavery on the other." The United States might not have any strength with European "political organizations" but at least it was now strong in all public assemblies and in the press. Still, Pike regretted the course Lincoln and Seward had elected to follow earlier in the war, and he could not resist one last parting shot: "If we could have begun where we now stand, our position in Europe

---

[28] Adams, *Great Britain*, II, 90 ff.; Randall, *Lincoln*, II, 177-78.

[29] Bancroft, *Seward*, II, 341. Max Beloff, "Great Britain and the American Civil War," *History*, XXXVII (Feb. 1952), 40-48, points out that the pro-Northern sentiment of English workers and radicals was "anti-aristocratic rather than pro-negro."

[30] *Ibid.*, pp. 340, 342.

would at this moment be well nigh impregnable in the field of discussion."[31]

As a matter of fact, Pike secretly felt that Lincoln's concession to the antislavery cause fell far short of being what it should. Pike had hoped for something more positive, far reaching, and perhaps dramatic. Instead, Lincoln's September proclamation threatened to declare free only those slaves residing in rebellious areas on January 1, 1863. Pike, along with the Radicals at home, pressed for a stirring moral declaration. They got a military measure. Pike revealed his real feelings when he wrote to Fessenden early in 1863: "As to emancipation, the way we are managing it, I do not see how any good is to come of it.—The paltering policy is no policy."[32] The emancipation program failed to earn his genuine approval, and so did Lincoln's schemes for colonizing the American Negroes. Since Pike also played a part, heretofore overlooked, in this phase of President Lincoln's program, a word of explanation is in order.

From the standpoint of importance at the time, at least in President Lincoln's own mind and policy, the colonization projects rank above the now hallowed Emancipation Proclamation. Yet not a great deal is known about the scope and nature of the colonization plans, and even less is heard of them. There seem to be two obvious reasons, among others, for this neglect. First, the plans were abortive, and history slights failures. And second, the racial ideas and approach back of the colonization attempt do not fit the popular stereotype of the "Great Emancipator" and his policies.

Professor J. G. Randall, the eminent Lincoln authority, points out that, relatively speaking and with a view to Lincoln's principal concept for solving the Negro-slavery problem, the famous proclamation is of "minor importance." Lincoln saw the edict as "a war measure of limited scope, of doubtful

[31] Pike to Seward, No. 70, Dec. 31, 1862, *Foreign Papers 1863*, pp. 803-4.
[32] Pike to Fessenden, Jan. 13, 1863, JSP Papers.

legality, and of inadequate effect."[33]   The President's own thoughtfully developed "blueprint for freedom" looked toward gradual emancipation by the slave states with the Federal government co-operating in the vital matters of compensation to the slaveowners and the foreign colonization of the freed Negroes.[34]   Throughout 1862-63, therefore, colonization of the Negroes was a much-discussed topic in Washington. And to the Dutch the idea appeared most attractive.

The first move on the part of the Dutch government to procure a new source of colonial labor came in July, 1862. The abolition of slavery in the Dutch colonies having occurred in 1862-63, The Hague government considered it desirable to introduce additional free labor into the colony of Surinam (Dutch Guiana) in South America. The minister of the Netherlands in Washington had earlier inquired of Secretary Seward if some of the "people of color" who "have acquired or are acquiring" their freedom might not be interested in emigrating. The emigrants should "engage" to dispose of their labor to a planter for a fixed period of "say, for example, 5 years" and would be protected by Dutch law. The minister vaguely referred to "some advantages connected with their emigration to a country so fertile and extensive" as Surinam.[35]

Seward had no authority in the emigration matter at this early date, July, 1862, when Lincoln had just begun secretly to move towards emancipation. The Secretary of State referred the Dutch minister to Secretary of the Interior Caleb Smith, who was authorized to handle contracts for Negro emigration to the West Indies. Seward did seize the occasion, however, to point out that the demand for Negro laborers in the United States army and navy alone sufficed "to outweigh any inducement to their emigration abroad likely to be offered by foreign

---

[33] Randall, *Lincoln*, II, 141.

[34] *Ibid.*, II, 141-50.

[35] Van Limburg to Seward, July 19, 1862, *Foreign Papers 1862*, II, 634.

countries."[36]   Seward thus dampened the whole idea for the time being.   But on the very day that Seward wrote his answer to the Dutch minister, Lincoln for the first time broached the subject of his proclamation to the Cabinet.[37]

The preliminary emancipation proclamation of September, 1862, made it expedient that the administration quickly present a positive answer of some sort to post-emancipation questions. What was to be done with the slaves after they had gained freedom?   Lincoln continued to regard colonization as the solution, and on September 24 he conferred with his Cabinet on the subject.   Attorney-General Edward Bates submitted an interesting memorandum in which he strongly backed Lincoln's ideas.[38]   Within a week's time and apparently on the President's order, with Cabinet approval, Secretary Seward began attempts to obtain emigration treaties with European colonial powers.

The ensuing negotiations between the Dutch government and the United States continued into 1864.   This was much later than the foreign negotiations are generally believed to have lasted, and the project reached a surprisingly advanced stage.[39]   Minister Pike himself did not approve.   He nevertheless succeeded in producing the treaty which Lincoln and Seward had ordered.   The ultimate rejection of the treaty by the government of the United States made Pike's efforts futile, but this outcome gratified him.

Pike's orders from Seward were to inquire if the Dutch government felt any interest in a convention or treaty relative

[36] Seward to Van Limburg, July 22, 1862, *ibid.*

[37] Randall, *Lincoln*, II, 155.

[38] This document is contained in *The Diary of Edward Bates, 1859-1866*, ed. by Howard K. Beale (Washington, 1933), pp. 262-64.

[39] One of the better early studies is Charles H. Wesley, "Lincoln's Plan for Colonizing the Emancipated Negroes," *Journal of Negro History*, IV (1919), 7-21, yet it is misleading and incomplete with regard to the foreign negotiations.   The fact that Great Britain rejected Seward's overtures has misled historians into thinking that all of the proposals met the same fate; for example, see N. Andrew N. Cleven, "Some Plans for Colonizing Liberated Negro Slaves in Hispanic America," *ibid.*, XI (1926), 35-49; Bancroft, *Seward*, II, 346-47.

to the voluntary emigration of American Negroes to the Netherlands' tropical colonies. Among the principles which Seward suggested for inclusion in the treaty was that any agents sent over to solicit emigrants be appointed by the Dutch government, while any party of emigrants which so desired might be "attended" by an American citizen approved by the government of the United States. The latter could supervise both the voyage and the preliminary establishment of the emigrants.

The newcomers should be furnished a place to live and either land for their own cultivation "or else with employment on hire, with provision for their wants, and compensation adequate to their support and maintenance, clothing and medicines and an education of the children in the simple elements of knowledge. . . ." The provision for these needs of the emigrants should continue for a term of five years. Moreover the emigrants and their posterity should "forever remain free" and "specially enjoy liberty of conscience and the right to acquire, hold, and transmit property, and all other privileges of person common to inhabitants of the country in which they reside." Seward proposed that the duration of the treaty be ten years with the customary one-year-notice termination privilege.[40]

Pike found the Dutch government in the autumn of 1862 still interested in obtaining Negro laborers from America. Colonial labor shortages had inspired emigration proposals from them in July, 1862, and the shortages continued. Rebuffed by Seward then, the Dutch now seized at the chance which Pike made known to them. Action on Seward's suggestion took time, however, and arrangements were not completed until the spring of 1863. As part of their preparations the Dutch States-General passed two ordinances relating to emigration which King William III decreed on March 19, 1863.

[40] Seward to Pike, No. 73, Oct. 8, 1862, DoS Papers. This is the same as Seward to Adams, Sept. 30, 1862, *Foreign Papers 1862*, Pt. 1, pp. 202-4.

The first of these dealt with the regulation of laboring conditions in Surinam and established certain standards for the type of depots at which the emigrants would be collected, the vessels in which they would sail, and for the conduct of the shipmasters and others toward the emigrants. The indenture form contained in the first ordinance specified a work week of six days and an eight-hour day, as well as free lodging and medical service. But it contained no reference to the wage rate or to the number of years for which the indenture might be made.

The second law passed by the Dutch to facilitate emigration to Surinam set forth the rewards to be given to those enterprising individuals who organized emigrant expeditions, that is the agents, and to those who engaged themselves by the indenture contracts for a certain number of years. The Dutch offered only forty guilders (about $16.00) as a premium for a "male person from 16 to 40" from this country. On the other hand, a male in the same age bracket from China was worth 125 guilders (about $50.00) and one from British India worth 100 guilders (about $40.00). For a married Negro couple from the United States the Dutch would pay only sixty guilders ($24.00), whereas married couples from China or British India rated 200 ($80.00) and 150 ($60.00) guilders respectively. The Dutch apparently expected the Lincoln government's emancipation and colonization policies to flood the market with easily obtained Negro labor.

Interestingly enough, some eager colonial official at The Hague realized the importance of advertising the proposition. The result was a blue-bound, twenty-four page booklet which translated the emigration ordinances into English. This English version, probably intended for distribution in the United States, never found its audience on this side of the Atlantic, and the little pamphlet today lies buried in the National Archives in Washington.[41]

[41] "I. Ordinance, concerning The Control on the Introduction of Free Labourers in

The ordinances contained many elaborations on Seward's original suggestion. Minister Pike also had one or two Dutch alterations to report to Washington. One change desired by the Dutch consisted in eliminating the appointment of the recruiting agents by the Dutch government; instead they would merely require that the agents be of "good reputation" and have the confidence of the Netherlands government. Moreover, since The Hague would take all proper measures to prevent any abuses and to have its consuls alerted, the Dutch thought it would be both inconvenient and unnecessary to follow Seward's idea of having an American citizen in charge of the emigrants during their voyage and settlement. The Dutch would, in this fashion, release both their own government and that of the United States from any ultimate responsibility in the much desired Negro emigration which was envisaged.[42] Pike thus transmitted the Dutch suggestions and notified Seward that The Hague government was ready to sign a treaty.

Seward, and apparently Lincoln, continued to regard the negotiations optimistically. Late in July, 1863, Seward transmitted a 'full power' to Pike and along with it a convention draft such "as would probably be approved by the Senate and ratified by the President." Pike predicted prompt affirmation of the treaty by the Dutch. He tentatively accepted

---

to Surinam. II. Ordinance, concerning The Offer of Premiums by the Government on the Introduction of Free Labourers in to Surinam." The pamphlet accompanies Pike to Seward, No. 91, June 26, 1863, DoS Papers. See H. T. Colenbrander, *Koloniale Geschiedenis* (The Hague, 1925), II, 33-34, for colonial background. L. C. A. Knowles, *The Economic Development of the British Overseas Empire* (London, 1928), p. 183, states that the British government in India did not allow the Indian coolies to emigrate to Surinam until 1872.

[42] P. Van der Maesen de Somburg to Pike, June 11, 1863, in Pike to Seward, No. 91, June 26, 1863, DoS Papers. This was an important point; Lincoln had to do some last-minute planning to dissociate the government officially from the disastrous Haitian colonization attempt of 1863-64. See Walter L. Fleming, "Deportation and Colonization: An Attempted Solution of the Race Problem," in *Studies in Southern History and Politics* (New York, 1914), pp. 3-30; hereinafter cited as Fleming, "Deportation and Colonization." Also John G. Nicolay and John Hay, *Abraham Lincoln: A History* (New York, 1890), VI, 354-356.

several minor modifications of Seward's draft. And finally in December, 1863, Minister Pike returned the completed and signed treaty for ratification by the United States.[43]

The treaty which was signed and forwarded to Seward contains only eight brief articles. The matter of the recruiting agents was settled by allowing either the Dutch government or the governor of Surinam to "authorize in writing any person, who may be desirous of engaging in the United States persons of African extraction to emigrate to Surinam." While Seward appears to have won a half-victory with regard to these agents, the treaty contains no provision for supervision of the emigrant parties by an American citizen, which Seward had earlier suggested. One short section declared that the emigrants should be received on "seaworthy vessels, which shall afford them healthful and convenient accommodations as to space, air, food, water and other necessaries."

With regard to their accommodations in Surinam, the treaty merely called for "comfortable dwellings" or "homes" (i.e., rooms) with other inhabitants. The emigrants should be provided either with land for their own cultivation or else with employment, presumably agricultural, by others. They should enjoy "all civil rights held by native residents in the colony," and in no case should be "reduced to slavery or involuntary servitude, except for crime." The ten-year duration, with the one-year-notice clause for termination after ten years, went into the treaty as Seward had originally suggested. Thus, after negotiations which stretched over fourteen months, Pike supplied the Secretary of State and Lincoln with the desired treaty. The next move was theirs.[44]

Oblivion awaited the treaty in this country. By early

[43] Seward to Pike, July 31, 1863; Pike to Seward, No. 98, Aug. 26, 1863; No. 103, Oct. 8, 1863; No. 112, Dec. 2, 1863; No. 114, Dec. 19, 1863, DoS Papers.

[44] Unperfected Treaty R2, DoS Papers. The treaty is reproduced in D. Hunter Miller, ed., *Treaties and Other International Acts of the United States of America* (Washington, 1948), VIII, 856-57. Miller also includes interesting material relating to Danish and Spanish negotiations with the United States looking toward the disposal of any Africans who might be seized in the slave trade.

1864 there were many reasons why any treaty concerning Negro emigration would meet certain defeat in the Senate, even if President Lincoln and the State Department should submit it, which they chose not to do in the case of Pike's treaty. First of all, an important and vocal group of abolitionists in the North and especially in Congress had objected all along to Lincoln's plans for removing the Negroes. Congressional opposition, led by men like Senator Sumner, became stronger in 1863, and by the spring of 1864 various specific anticolonization measures appeared in Congress.

Moreover, an attempt to settle a group of over four hundred Negroes in Haiti ended in complete failure in March, 1864. When the small group of hapless survivors returned to the United States in that month, reduced about a fourth in number by disease and privation, the whole colonization idea stood discredited before the country. Finally, in July, 1864, President Lincoln signed an act repealing all of the measures relating to colonization which had accumulated since the beginning of the war.[45]

Pike, however, faced the problem of explaining the delay in final United States ratification to the Dutch. He reported in late January, 1864, that The Hague officials had repeatedly inquired when the American government would act on the treaty which Seward had suggested in the first place.[46] Answering Pike's inquiries, Seward felt "obliged to confess that it is not now expected that the treaty in regard to negro emigration will be ratified." The Secretary of State explained that the American people had advanced to "a new position" in regard to "slavery and the African class" since the time when the President, "in obedience to their prevailing wishes," had adopted the colonization idea. "Now not only their free labor

---

[45] Fleming, "Deportation and Colonization," p. 26; Randall, *Lincoln*, II, 139-41; Monaghan, *Diplomat*, pp. 253-54, 272, 276. The latter has only scattered references to the subject of colonization. For contemporary appeals from Negroes who opposed the plan, see Herbert Aptheker, ed., *A Documentary History of the Negro People in the United States* (New York, 1951), pp. 471-75.

[46] Pike to Seward, No. 121, Jan. 27, 1864, DoS Papers.

but their military service also is appreciated and accepted," Seward concluded.[47] As a matter of fact, Seward, unlike the President, seems all along to have regarded colonization as of dubious wisdom. On one occasion he remarked, "I am always for bringing men and states *into* the Union, never for taking any *out*."[48]

Pike and Seward for once agreed, at least on the subject of colonization. When he wrote formally expressing the Dutch government's regret that the treaty would not be ratified, Pike included this gratuitous opinion: "I have no doubt, however, of the good policy on our part of rejecting the treaty."[49] Even more forcibly, Pike had expressed to Fessenden his hope that Congress would "*not* ratify" the treaty which he had finally succeeded in negotiating with the Dutch. Pike confessed privately that he considered the principle on which the treaty was based a "vicious" one.[50]

The minister to The Hague had strongly and early urged an emancipation policy, and yet he opposed the colonization plan, which President Lincoln long regarded as the only available solution to the problems which would inevitably follow in the train of emancipation. One might well ask if Pike himself had any positive ideas concerning the future fate of the American Negro. The answer is that he emphatically did. And though Pike apparently failed to realize his inconsistency, it is difficult to see how his plan was any less "vicious" than Lincoln's colonization scheme; Pike's program had only the dubious, twofold merit of eliminating the Negro

[47] Seward to Pike, No. 142, Feb. 15, 1864, *Foreign Papers 1864*, Pt. 3, p. 310.

[48] Bancroft, *Seward*, II, 346. Seward has been wrongly interpreted in this connection; and the error apparently grows out of an underestimation of the importance of the colonization idea at the time and the extent to which President Lincoln believed in it. See Adams, *Great Britain*, II, 100-1, where Adams suggests that Seward grasped at colonization as another means of catering to the "material interests" of Great Britain.

[49] Pike to Seward, No. 125, March 16, 1864, *Foreign Papers 1864*, Pt. 3, p. 312. It should be noted that the published correspondence relating to the Dutch treaty deals with its rejection; the earlier, pro-treaty despatches remain unpublished.

[50] Pike to Fessenden, April 6, 1864, JSP Papers.

from the United States as well as satisfying vindictiveness toward the hated white slaveowners.

As early as 1853 Pike had hinted in the *Tribune* at a possible solution to the "race" question. At that time Manifest Destiny gasconading filled the country with covetous talk of Cuba and other Latin American territories. Pike sternly warned, "We want no more ebony additions to the Republic." He already regarded it as clearly evident that "some territory on this hemisphere" had to be allotted to the Negro. Giving the Negroes "the whole of the West India Islands" would be a happy solution. Such action could relieve the North American continent of "the burden and hindrance" of its "black population." But, Pike concluded, "we fear that not only must we allot the islands of the Caribbean Sea to them, but a portion also of our own territory lying upon the Gulf of Mexico."[51]

During his war years abroad Pike returned to this long-held idea of surrendering a part of the Deep South to the Negro. Slavery and the Negro were always much in his mind, and the pressure of the war in America merely served to focus and sharpen his thinking on the subject. At the same time that he was preaching emancipation in Europe and to his home government, Pike was privately setting forth his old solution to the Negro problem. His notebooks and confidential letters to friends furnish abundant evidence on this point.

In July, 1862, Pike wrote that his "own scheme" for settling the "slavery question" had long been "to carve out a portion of the country, embracing some states East of the Mississippi & South of the Potomac & Ohio, as few as may be, and surrender it to the blacks, and such of the whites as desire to go with them." The vast difficulty of incorporating four million slaves into "our political or social system" made it only "natural" to wish to be "rid of them." We might prefer to see them colonized in other countries, Pike admitted, and might hesitate to surrender any of our own territory, but "I

[51] *Tribune*, Jan. 10, 1853; Pike, *First Blows*, pp. 163-64.

strongly incline to the opinion that we are to have no option of this sort."[52]

As the war in America dragged on interminably, the idea of carving out a portion of the country to be set aside for Negroes became increasingly attractive to Pike. Early in 1863 he wrote a pessimistic letter to Fessenden bemoaning the North's slow progress in the war. Pike considered the Federal position to be improved in Maryland, Missouri, and Kentucky; yet the end of the war was nowhere in sight. If the Union could make sure of the country west of the Mississippi and keep its hold on western Virginia, Pike concluded, he "should have no tears to shed over the making of a negro pen of the rest of the South & withdrawing our jurisdiction over it."[53]

Aside from the curious resemblance to prewar secession talk from abolitionists like Garrison and Phillips,[54] Pike's "negro pen" plan for the Gulf states also had wartime advocates at home. In the first half of 1864, when Lincoln's colonization program had become patently impossible, various suggestions were made in Congress about setting apart sections of the South for the Negroes. Some proponents recommended South Carolina and Georgia, or the lower Mississippi valley, while another version called for each Southern state to set aside a particular area within its borders where the Negroes could go.

Senator James H. Lane of Kansas, one of the lesser lights among the Radicals, presented a bill in 1864 to set apart a large area in western Texas where the Negro should be segregated. More explicitly even than Pike, Senator Lane argued that the North both objected to the Negro as a laborer and disdained any mixture of races. The Southern whites, on the other hand, would hate their former slaves as well as reclaim

---

[52] Notebook No. 4, pp. 19-20; entry for July 14, 1862. This and all other numbered notebooks are to be found in the Pike MSS. For Pike's temporary advocacy of this policy during the secession crisis of 1860-61, see above, pp. 37 ff.

[53] Pike to Fessenden, Jan. 13, 1863, JSP Papers.

[54] Ralph Korngold, *Two Friends of Man* (Boston, 1950), pp. 163-68.

all the Southern lands once an amnesty had been declared. Senator Lane predicted that the strong Northern sentiment in favor of Negro rights would eventually die out after the war, and the Negro would be left with no chance for social or political equality. ". . . I hoped the time should come when the foot prints of the white man should not be found on the soil of South Carolina," Lane declared; but since that eventuality proved unlikely, the best interests of the Negroes demanded consideration. By consideration, Senator Lane, in effect, meant something similar to Pike's "negro pen."[55]

Needless to say, nothing ever came of Pike's scheme nor of any of the others. In fact, except for the act establishing a Freedmen's Bureau in 1865, little or nothing was ever decided, as long as the war lasted and Lincoln lived, about post-emancipation problems in the South. Pike's ideas, however, do suggest, among other things, the deep-rooted racial antipathy which he and some of his contemporaries felt toward the Negro.

In Pike's case the idea of setting aside certain Southern states as Negro 'reservations' was closely connected with his notion that the Federal government had no choice in 1863-64 but to accept a compromise or negotiated peace with the Confederacy. This was another of the themes that dominated his political and military thinking about the terrible events at home.

[55] Fleming, "Deportation and Colonization," pp. 27-28; *Congressional Globe, 1863-64*, pp. 672-75. The committee on territories reported favorably on Senator Lane's bill, but it became buried in the rush of wartime legislation. None of these plans are to be confused with Thaddeus Stevens' "forty-acres" distribution idea of 1866.

V. Battles and Leaders
as Seen from Europe

PIKE, like other Americans in Europe during the Civil War, felt keenly that he was absent from the scene of the contemporary world's most stirring and epochal events. Within a month of his arrival in Europe, he began to struggle with the idea that he was missing the great drama of his own generation and land. "I should be glad to be able to help the country at home if I could see any post there in which I could be especially useful," he explained. Not only did Pike consider himself at fifty too "old to begin a military career," but his deep-rooted aversion to war and bloodshed made him unfitted for a soldier's life.[1] There seemed no alternative but to serve as best he could in Holland, and at the same time to follow scrupulously both the course of events in America and the European reaction to them.

In the interval between the attack on Sumter in mid-April and the first battle of Bull Run in July, 1861, Pike's primary interest lay in the attitude of Great Britain and France. Sharing the deep resentment of the North that these two powers had issued proclamations of neutrality, Pike at first judged English opinion to be in favor of peaceable separation and therefore hostile to the United States. He informed Fessenden that Englishmen and Frenchmen were convinced that the United States had better patiently submit to "dismemberment & disgrace rather than stop trade or have a fight." After

[1] Pike to Fessenden, June 22-24, 1861, JSP Papers; Notebooks No. 6, pp. 5-6; No. 9, p. 15.

conversing with Richard Cobden in Paris, Pike reported that
even this great Liberal espoused separation in America. But
Pike promised that the "damned fools will get their eyes open
directly."[2]

As for the major portion of the British press in the summer
of 1861, he astutely analyzed the situation. The *Times*,
Victorian England's mighty 'Thunderer,' filled its columns with
pronouncements which infuriated good Yankees. On June 1,
1861, for example, the *Times* declared with majestic complacency that India had been reconquered, the Chinese Empire
was dissolving, the Continental Old World grew faint-hearted,
and, forsooth, the United States had come to "the end of their
brief history."[3]   In addition to many statements of this type,
Pike had personal reasons for resenting the policy of the
Times. He submitted "an incisive article" on American affairs
to that journal only to find that it refused to print anything
that got to the "marrow" of the controversy. Angry though
he might be, he realized that in the long run neither the *Times*
nor any other newspaper would exercise as decisive influence
on the war as would cotton, the South's 'King' product and
England's major import.[4]

Pike's analysis of the crucial cotton question proved generally sound, and perhaps the Secretary of State found Pike's
information useful in the complex, continuous task of policy
formation and implementation. But he submitted much of
his economic data in a manner that Seward, proud and sensitive
as he was, may have found galling. In an early despatch, for
example, Pike loftily advised the Secretary that the government "cannot bear too constantly in mind the fact that in whatever England or France have done, or may do, on this seces-

---

[2] Pike to Fessenden, June 7, 1861, JSP Papers.

[3] *Times*, June 1, 1861. For the background of this attitude see Adams, *Great Britain*,
I, 48 ff.

[4] Pike to Fessenden, June 7, 1861, JSP Papers; Pike to Seward, No. 10, July 30,
1861, DoS Papers. Pike's unpublished article unfortunately seems lost, but the "marrow"
probably refers to slavery. For statements in the *Times* by John L. Motley and Cassius
M. Clay, see the issues of May 23-24 and May 20, 1861.

sion question, they simply mean *cotton*." The solution to keeping England and France quiet appeared to lie in letting them know that the United States would not imperil "their own domestic safety" by completely cutting off their cotton supply. "But this is a topic," the minister conceded, "which must have received your attention."[5]

In July, 1861, Pike visited London partially to study the economic situation. He arranged a "free and full" conference with Thomas Milner-Gibson, then president of the Board of Trade, and emerged convinced that the British "want to avoid difficulty, but they want cotton." Milner-Gibson believed that England could obtain cotton from sources other than the South, but the process of encouraging new supply areas would take more than one or two years. In the meantime, some relaxation of the United States blockade of Southern ports would not be too detrimental to the Federal cause. Pike, however, felt certain that neither Milner-Gibson nor the pro-Southern "cotton M.P.'s" had any distinct plan in mind for relieving the crisis when and if it did come.[6]

The simple truth about the European cotton famine was that it did not develop in the winter of 1861-62 as the Confederates had expected. This was owing to a number of factors, a chief one being the abnormally large cotton crops in 1859 and 1860 which Europe had imported. But the Confederates, self-hypnotized by their incessant paeans to King Cotton, failed to realize the situation. Their diplomatic policies had been predicated upon Europe's need for cotton, a need which the Southerners vainly attempted to hasten by their own embargo in 1861-62. The delay in the cotton famine's appearance until late 1862 threw the Confederate diplomatic schedule badly askew.[7]

By September, 1861, Pike had grasped the salient aspects of this cotton question. On the basis of his observations and

[5] Pike to Seward, No. 5, June 18, 1861, DoS Papers.
[6] Pike to Seward, No. 10, July 30, 1861, *ibid.*
[7] Owsley, *King Cotton*, pp. 146-65.

inquiries, he informed Seward that the mills could tide themselves over for another full year.   Cotton smuggled out
through Havana and Mexico would add another three or four
months to the safe period, and by that time if the matter were
yet urgent Eastern sources would probably have entered the
picture.   In other words, Pike seriously questioned the necessity of intervention by the Federal government to alleviate
the European cotton famine.[8]

This proved to be a correct estimate of the situation.
Whether Secretary Seward accepted it and carefully weighed
it against the whole mass of his information on the subject is
not known.   Adams in London judged that the cotton famine
would make itself acutely felt as early as the winter of 1861;
coupled with Adams' opinion, which differed from Pike's in the
vital point of timing, was the steady pressure from the English and French governments for a relaxation of the blockade.
In the face of all this, Secretary Seward firmly yet calmly
resisted all pressure in favor of altering the existing blockade
arrangements.   Pike's information about the existing and potential cotton supplies may have helped the Secretary of State to
arrive at his confident stand.[9]

Regardless of the use to which Seward put the information,
Pike continued to study and report the economic effects of the
American war on Europe.   Throughout the first two years of
the war especially, he passed on data about cotton supplies,
the wheat importation from the United States, and the general
European industrial reaction to the curtailment of American
trade.[10]   Pike found the Dutch largely unaffected by the
cotton shortage, since their mills used mostly flax and wool.

[8] Pike to Seward, No. 16, Sept. 11, 1861, DoS Papers.

[9] Bancroft, *Seward*, II, 210-22.   But see also Adams, *Great Britain*, II, 91-95.

[10] Pike to Seward, No. 27, Nov. 20, 1861; No. 34, Jan. 15, 1862, DoS Papers; No.
111, Nov. 18, 1863, *Foreign Papers 1864*, Pt. 3, p. 304.   Also Notebooks No. 1,
pp. 8, 13; No. 5, p. 23; No. 3, p. 4; No. 9, p. 38.   G. J. Kloos, *De Handelspolitieke
Betrekkingen Tusschen Nederland en de Vereenigde Staten van Amerika, 1814-1914*
(Amsterdam, n.d.), pp. 66 ff., deals with the long-range results of the protectionist
policy of the United States after 1861 rather than with the immediate effects of the war.

The American war did pinch the Dutch, interestingly enough, in the gin distilleries of Schiedam, Holland. There, where there had been more than a hundred distilleries, Pike reported things pretty much broken up by the "loss of the American demand."[11]

As interesting as European economic developments were to Pike, perhaps military events transpiring in America compelled more immediate concern. The first battle of Bull Run struck him, like most other Northerners, a sharp blow; and also like many others he became wise after the event. He had never believed raw troops could storm entrenchments in the war's first engagement. Turning on his former paper, Greeley's *Tribune*, Pike declared that he had "never failed to condemn & to damn with all the energy I possessed the insensate trash of the Press who were crying 'On to Richmond.'" The Yankees could learn the "trade of war," but the danger arose from the fact that this learning might be prevented by the popular clamor for an end to the war.

Concerning Greeley personally, Pike scorned the editor's attacks on training camps and on military professionalism in general. "Poor Greeley, after all his humiliating confessions, still ends his penitential cry, by declaring still against 'camps of instruction' for our troops, as if anything else was wanted." Pike's notion, more modern than the view held by some generals and congressmen during the Civil War, was that men "need to be taught how to *save* their lives in war & not how to throw them away."[12]

Pike's transfer from journalism to diplomacy obviously influenced his thinking about the role of newspapers. Throughout the war he clung to the notion that the United States

[11] Pike to Seward, No. 17, Sept. 18, 1861, DoS Papers.

[12] Pike to Fessenden, Aug. 22, 1861, JSP Papers. For the role of the newspapers in bringing on Bull Run, and Greeley's paper had much company, see Robert S. Harper, *Lincoln and the Press* (New York, 1951), pp. 100-106. For Greeley's personal role, which was not as simple as Pike imagined, see William H. Hale, *Horace Greeley: Voice of the People* (New York, 1950), pp. 244 ff.

needed a more or less absolute censorship. More than mere humor was involved when Pike declared that he would "like to suppress every newspaper in the United States, and hang every correspondent of the European journals." War and newspapers could "never be made to go together; certainly not side by side." Ironically enough, Pike, whose political articles and editorials of the 1850's were considered extreme even in the North, now informed Seward that the American press had destroyed its prestige and might even "ruin the country, by its ignorant & captious criticisms & assaults upon the civil and military administration."[13] Wartime diplomacy and distance were furnishing Pike a new perspective on some issues.

The *Trent* affair, for example, found him extremely moderate and cautious. Like other envoys and agents of the United States in Europe, Pike immediately perceived that Captain Charles Wilkes's seizure of the Confederate diplomats from aboard a British steamer had placed the Federal government in a dangerous position of inviting war with Britain.[14] News of the capture of James Mason and John Slidell reached Europe late in November, 1861. Within a few days Pike reported to the State Department that the current of opinion everywhere went against the United States. "The event is regarded as untoward any way," he commented, "and ruinous if endorsed by our government." Pike concluded on an almost plaintive note with the statement that unless "we cannot avoid it, I suppose we shall keep out of all other wars till we finish the one we have on hand."[15]

Pike encountered many Europeans who predicted that the democratic United States would be unable or unwilling to

---

[13] Pike to Fessenden, Nov. 30, 1864, JSP Papers; Pike to Seward, No. 11, Aug. 7, 1861, DoS Papers. Also Notebooks No. 9, p. 8; No. 16, p. 9.

[14] For the reactions of Adams, Thurlow Weed, and others in Europe, see Bancroft, *Seward*, II, 230-31. The feeling in the United States, with a few exceptions, was enthusiastic approval of Wilkes's action.

[15] Pike to Seward, No. 29, Dec. 4, 1861, DoS Papers. A marginal note indicates that this despatch was received on December 25, the day on which Lincoln's cabinet finally decided to return the Confederate diplomats (Randall, *Lincoln*, II, 48-49).

avoid war with England in late 1861. He angrily observed that "the fools are apparently numerous who believe, or profess to believe, that our government is under the control of an unthinkable mob, instead of being in the hands of persons of moderation & wisdom." Queen Sophie of Holland, the first wife of King William III, enjoyed a reputation for intelligence and literary talent, but she provoked Minister Pike when she insisted on the inevitability of war between Britain and the United States. The American protested that the President and his Cabinet should not be the victims of an "injurious & shallow suspicion." Rather, they were entitled by virtue of their positions and their individual characters "to be regarded as wise, discreet, & independent men, fully conscious of their duties and responsibilities." He pointed out to the "accomplished and engaging" Queen that the government of the United States was no more under the control of vague and frightful influences, "rendered hideous to the European apprehension under the term 'mob,' " than were the governments of other civilized countries.[16]

Despite the scepticism of some Europeans, Pike could only hope that his government would weather the serious *Trent* crisis. When news of the peaceful settlement reached him on January 9, 1862, Pike breathed more easily; he believed that surrendering Mason and Slidell would "vastly elevate and improve the position of the United States government at every court in Europe." Continental ruling classes had avowed that a "headlong democracy" must crash to ruin in such a delicate situation; but the fact that the United States had acted upon "the counsels of discretion" compelled all "Europe's involuntary respect and admiration."[17]

[16] Pike to Seward, No. 61, Dec. 11, 1861, DoS Papers. Pike's letter to Fessenden, Dec. 28, 1861, elaborates the same theme and is published by B. C. Weber in the *New England Quarterly*, XXI (Dec., 1948), 531-36.

[17] Pike to Seward, No. 33, Jan. 9, 1862, *Foreign Papers 1862*, Pt. 2, p. 595. For the *Trent* settlement, see Randall, *Lincoln*, II, 37-53, including bibliographical references.

Pike's optimism, arising from the peaceful denouement of the *Trent* matter, survived only briefly. Within a few months he privately came to consider the Union cause hopeless enough to make a compromise or negotiated peace seem highly desirable. Pike had a plan, dating back to the 1850's, for converting some of the Gulf states into a "negro pen."[18] Now the government's wartime financial policy vastly alarmed him, and added another cause for his despair concerning the war. Depressing news from America in 1862 about Union defeats, such as Second Bull Run and the failure of McClellan's peninsular campaign, only served to strengthen his inclination toward a negotiated settlement with the South.[19]

Pike considered that the most suitable Federal policy would be to fight for a boundary. By this he meant that the United States should make sure of the trans-Mississippi country and of border states like Missouri and Kentucky. Then, having seized such a line and restricting itself to defensive measures, the United States could "let events shape themselves." Pike lamented to Fessenden that "we must be approaching the end in some way." Financial pressures, public impatience, and assaults from the Democratic party "must be too much for us to stand forever." The single task of keeping an army together and in a state of repair looked formidable enough; to give that army larger, additional tasks appeared futile. The President's emancipation policy wobbled insecurely, for the "paltering policy is no policy." Since the North apparently could never affiliate either politically or socially with the Negroes ("the mass of barbarism being so large"), their expulsion would be for their own benefit. In short, rather than trying to restore the Union by abolition in the Gulf states, the United States should first secure the border

---

[18] See above, pp. 94 ff.

[19] The politico-military story of McClellan's final ousting in November, 1862, may be found in T. Harry Williams, *Lincoln and the Radicals*, pp. 19 ff. Randall, *Lincoln*, II, 62-125, has a sympathetic approach to McClellan while Kenneth P. Williams, *Lincoln Finds a General* (New York, 1949), II, 472-79, takes the opposite view.

states to the cause of freedom. The rest of the South could, in so many words, find its own way out of the dilemma posed by the presence of the Negroes.[20]

Federal military setbacks later in 1862 and in 1863, such as those at Fredericksburg and at Chancellorsville, deepened Pike's gloomy conviction that a compromise peace was inevitable. His general dissatisfaction with the scope and nature of Lincoln's emancipation program also entered into the web of ideas that made him a defeatist. In the spring of 1863 Pike confessed to a fellow diplomat, George G. Fogg, in Switzerland, that events seemed to make it increasingly plain that the "old Union" had disappeared forever. This result he did not lament so much as many others did. "If the old Union goes another will take its place." And even if the Union crumbled, the American people and New England remained. Yet Pike did not desire an immediate laying down of arms.

There were two objects he envisioned as prerequisites to negotiations. "One is to destroy the race of slaveholders, who are the greatest of criminals, and the other is to dictate our own boundaries in case we find it best to let some of the slave States go." Pike foresaw great difficulties in accomplishing the destruction of "the race of slaveholders," which was for him the paramount object of the whole war. If the United States destroyed slavery purely by force, he explained, the opposition at home and abroad would be "near about universal." But if the Federal government could not "destroy the slaveholders as a class" it ought nevertheless to endeavor to ruin them. This could be done by overwhelming the slaveholders with debt. Southern pride, "which some times accompanies poverty that likes to make a figure in the world," would prevent repudiation. "If there were no other object then in pursuing the war I think this alone a very tangible one," he declared.[21]

Pike's vindictive war aims, so patently different from those

---

[20] Pike to Fessenden, Jan. 13, 1863, JSP Papers.
[21] Pike to George G. Fogg, March 5, 1863, Notebook No. 5, pp. 27-29.

officially advanced by the administration at Washington, were shot through with defeatism. This mood occasionally cropped up in the North, in varying degrees and quarters, from First Bull Run until Atlanta's fall in September, 1864.[22] But Pike's case is interesting because of his European situation and in relation to his notions about other topics such as slavery and finance.

Moreover, other members of Lincoln's foreign corps shared many of the Maine diplomat's ideas. Minister Fogg in Switzerland, for example, agreed wholeheartedly with Pike that disunion appeared inevitable. Fogg wished to see the Union restored to its ancient, correct form if the rebellion could be crushed. But with "the rebellion *not* crushed," Fogg explained, "I am for *any* new *free* nationality not *smaller* than New England."[23] After Pike indicated general agreement with this position, Fogg again wrote that he did not regard "a division of our Union as, by any means, the greatest of evils." He had long regarded that "as a not very improbable result of the war."[24] George P. Marsh in Italy, while not apparently as reconciled to the dismemberment of the Union as were Pike and Fogg, wrote gloomily that the Federal cause looked hopeless unless a "revolution shall place the control of affairs in a different set of hands from those which now direct the destinies of our country."[25] Young Henry Adams in London, ruefully analyzing British opinion on the long-drawn American conflict, wrote in May, 1864, that the "current is dead against us, and the atmosphere so uncongenial that the idea of the possibility of our success is not admitted."[26]

In Pike's case one factor which helps explain the extent of his pessimism is that accurate, reliable information on Ameri-

[22] For example see Hale, *Greeley*, pp. 249-50, 265-71; James G. Randall, *The Civil War and Reconstruction* (Boston, 1937), pp. 614-17.

[23] Fogg to Pike, Jan. 15, 1863, Pike MSS.

[24] Fogg to Pike, March 12, 1863, *ibid*.

[25] Marsh to Mrs. Pike, Aug. 20, 1862, Pike MSS.

[26] Henry to Brooks Adams, May 13, 1864, in Worthington C. Ford, ed., *A Cycle of Adams Letters* (Boston, 1920), II, 126.

can affairs was hard to come by. Secretary Seward in many of his despatches inclined to overconfident, sweeping assertions and glowing prophecy, which, regardless of the possible effects on domestic public opinion, were not calculated to inform and forearm diplomats abroad.[27] In addition to this, Pike more than once found that telegraphic accounts in European papers were permeated with "lying intelligence or adverse speculation" about American events.[28]

If Pike's official and public sources failed to furnish much reason for hopefulness with regard to the war, the same thing may be said of his private information. As early as September, 1861, for example, his brother Charles, who published a newspaper in Wisconsin, wrote that the majority of Northern people seemed to share the dark conviction which he had gained during a spring visit to Washington. Charles Pike declared that "the President and Cabinet—*as a whole,—are not equal to the occasion.* The *impression,* which I then got, has haunted me like a night-mare ever since, despite my resolute endeavors to shake it off."[29] Dana late in 1861 reported increasing dissatisfaction with the administration. "Horace [Greeley] is pretty well," Dana added, "but regards every thing as lost & nothing but disaster in store for the country or its people."[30]

Another brother, Congressman Frederick Pike, furnished depressing insight into Congressional as well as public opinion. Associated with the Radicals in the House of Representatives, Fred Pike assailed the "Washington stupidity" which ignored the changed public feeling toward the war. "Thus far it has been reckoned treason to say a word against the President,"

[27] Bancroft, *Seward,* II, 502-6. Bancroft states that Seward's despatches often "represented hope rather than belief or sober judgment" (*ibid.*).

[28] Pike to Seward, No. 56, Aug. 6, 1862, *Foreign Papers 1862,* Pt. 2, p. 615; Notebook No. 7, p. 21. Confederate propaganda agents in London and Paris had made strategic arrangements with certain continental news agencies, which probably explains a part of Pike's trouble. See Owsley, *King Cotton,* p. 184; the author's M. A. thesis at Emory University, "*The Index:* Confederate Newspaper in London, 1862-1865," deals with Henry Hotze, one of the most energetic of the Confederate agents.

[29] Charles E. Pike to Pike, Oshkosh, Wisconsin, Sept. 15, 1861, Pike MSS.

[30] Dana to Pike, Nov. 8, 1861, Pike MSS.

Fred commented in August, 1862, "but unless he follows along after public sentiment more rapidly than he seems disposed to do there will be howling before the snow flies." There was altogether too much deference to Kentucky opinion; in fact the congressman thought that the Federal cause would have been better off if Kentucky had gone with the Confederates.[31]

Even the preliminary emancipation proclamation did not cool brother Fred's hot dissent. A month later he issued another private blast against the administration and the army. "If the President would leave off story telling long enough to look after the war & drive the drunken generals out of the army & cashier those who wish for the success of the rebels [,] which would include a large share of the regular army," Fred Pike breathlessly declared, "we might hope for a successful prosecution of the campaign." He characterized General McClellan as "a mere boy & timid at that" who was expected to lead off in the conquest of seven hundred thousand square miles. "It is clear the war can[']t continue much longer," Fred moaned. The administration and West Point had entire control of things military and "nothing but the extremest disaster can wrest it from them." Nothing less than a revolution would suffice to place control of the war in the proper hands.[32]

Presumably Fred Pike referred to the well-known Congressional attempt to wrest military supremacy from the executive and give it to the Committee on the Conduct of the War.[33] But it is interesting to note that George P. Marsh in Italy apparently not only speculated about revolution in Washington but seriously "feared that we shall be driven to choose between bowing the neck to Southern Rebellion and bending the knee

---

[31] Fred Pike to Pike, Aug. 3, 1862, Pike MSS. An interesting contrast to this view may be found in Professor Randall's essay on "Lincoln and the Southern Border," in *Lincoln and the South* (Baton Rouge, 1946), pp. 49-80; or Potter, *Secession Crisis*, pp. 280 ff.

[32] Fred Pike to Pike, Oct. 22, 1862, Pike MSS.

[33] See Williams, *Radicals*, pp. 62 ff.

to some foreign adventurer, who shall prove himself to possess qualities which we have vainly hoped for in soldiers of native birth." The North shall end by succumbing to the South, Marsh predicted to Pike, "unless we are rescued from that shame by the strong hand of a military dictator."[34]

This was the general context of Pike's own defeatist attitude. Running through all of the above comments is the obvious derogation of President Lincoln and especially of his early administration. The notebooks in which Pike scribbled all sorts of ideas and opinions, as well as copied many of the letters which he wrote, contain nothing specifically relating to his own estimate of Lincoln until late in 1863. His silence itself adds force to the theory that at least until well into 1863 he considered the White House occupant to be inadequate, perhaps dangerously so. In the opening phase of the war he requested Fessenden to remember him to Benjamin Wade, Ohio's fiery Radical senator who led in assaults upon the administration. Pike explained that he implicitly relied on Wade "in this great emergency."[35] As late as July, 1863, he noted that the "great lack" of the United States seemed to be in sound men in "the councils of the country." Perhaps wishing to remain discreet, Pike observed merely that our "executive men too do not seem to be of the first order." They had on the harness of war but they ran in the ruts of peace.[36]

Other diplomats apparently were as cautious as Pike in expressing their private sentiments. From Switzerland, Fogg grumbled that while the brains and heart of the rebellion were obviously in Richmond he wished he knew as well "where the brains of the Union are."[37] Marsh too refrained from naming names, but he remarked that the great national crisis had failed to produce "a single *man*, but had, on the contrary, dwarfed every puppet whom we had hitherto thought a man."

[34] Marsh to Pike, Aug. 20, 1862, Pike MSS.
[35] Pike to Fessenden, June 22-24, 1861, JSP Papers.
[36] Pike to Fessenden, July 3, 1863, *ibid.*
[37] Fogg to Pike, March 2, 1863, Pike MSS.

Marsh felt especially discouraged that the American people manifested "no indignation at the unparalleled imbecility of our rulers and military leaders, but are content to be led by fools and traitors to die in ditches. . . ."[38]

Pike corresponded regularly with one person who came to Lincoln's defense. This was Charles A. Dana. Fired from the *Tribune* in 1862 after more than a decade's prominent association with the paper and with Greeley, Dana found employment with the War Department in 1863 and soon became an Assistant Secretary of War.[39] It was probably his close association with the administration which allowed Dana to see the President in a different light from Pike and the others mentioned above. Dana discounted the swelling complaints and noisy impatience of 1862; he thought that on the whole the North should "thank God & take courage." One fact that Pike might not realize in Europe was that "Abe Lincoln is the most popular man & the most confided in since Washington. Since the death of his boy led Mrs. Abe into retirement, there has been nothing to diminish the public trust and attachment. Certainly, if not the wisest, he is the luckiest of men."[40]

Pike himself late in 1863 approached a slightly increased appreciation of Lincoln, despite the distance at which it was gained. Scribbling leisurely in his notebook about the physical and mental organization which war demanded of men, the Downeaster observed that if Lincoln had been of a "highly nervous organization" or gifted with too much brainpower, he would have died soon after the war began. "He went through because he had a hard, snug, limited mental force, a small brain of excellent quality on a wiry physique, and above all

[38] Marsh to Pike, Aug. 20, 1862, Pike MSS.

[39] For Dana's account of his dismissal, see Dana to Pike, April 9, 1862, Pike MSS; also Dana, *Recollections*; Hale, *Greeley*, pp. 250-52.

[40] Dana to Pike, May 26, 1862, Pike MSS. Dana also expressed disagreement with Pike's idea that the Federals were fighting for boundaries. "The people will keep the whole, & govern it for fifty years if necessary by military power. No division of the nation, no matter what it cost to prevent it, is their policy or I am much mistaken" (*ibid.*).

was endowed with a[n] irrepressible vein of native humor whose springs never died." This calm praise, which is left-handed as far as Lincoln's mental power went, suggests that Pike would have enjoyed studying the President's "head bumps." The minister to Holland could never shake off a strong suspicion that phrenology could teach men a great deal.[41]

"Snug, limited mental force" aside, Pike's estimate of Lincoln mounted steadily and sharply. By March, 1865, with the war almost won and about a month before Booth martyred the President, he considered Lincoln "one of the most unalloyed bits of human nature to be found in history." Of all American statesmen, he picked Lincoln as the wisest and the least selfish. He speculated about the President's being chosen for a third term, "notwithstanding certain superficial imperfections, which are discernable in his nature, & his writings." The *Tribune's* famous correspondent considered Lincoln's Second Inaugural "a most curious production" which proved how the President insisted upon printing his speeches without washing and dressing them "according to the rules of good writing society."[42] But despite these reservations, which are typical of the usual hypnosis produced by 'good taste,' Pike had the perception and understanding to anticipate a part of history's verdict of Abraham Lincoln.

Other wartime leaders of the United States did not rate so well as Lincoln in the caustic judgment of Minister Pike. His opinion of Seward, for example, may be briefly summarized here. In view of the long-standing political enmity between them, it is not surprising that the former *Tribune* man had an outspokenly low opinion of the Secretary of State. He made a valiant, even if futile, attempt to silence himself on the sore subject of the New York statesman. After conveying his

[41] Notebook No. 10, pp. 11-12.
[42] Notebook No. 17, pp. 26-28; for other comments, see Sandburg, *Lincoln*, IV, 95-96.

general disagreement with Seward on a diplomatic matter in
a letter to Fessenden, Pike added that he had "sworn a vow"
never again to oppose Seward. "If he swears the Moon is the
Sun I will not deny it. Fire shall not burn nor ice freeze any
thing out of me to his prejudice.—On this point my determination is iron clad with forty inch plating."[43]

Despite his heroic effort at discreet silence, Pike's true
opinion of Seward would not stay repressed. In the interval
between the end of the war and his resignation in 1866, he
tallied his final score on the Secretary of State and concluded
that Seward had no rule of political action except to aquiesce
whenever any pressure made yielding convenient. Pike then
proceeded to review the chief diplomatic events of the war,
hitting Seward on each one for pusillanimity and timidity. The
Secretary of State's conservative stand on the slavery question
came in for special condemnation, for it was this as much as
anything which helped blind Pike to a more just appreciation
of Seward's qualities and performance.[44] "If the United States
are today treated with respect or reserve by other powers,"
Pike summarized, "it is not because of the tone in which our
foreign affairs are conducted, but solely because of the spirit
of the people, as shown in the war, and as manifested in
Congress."[45]

Strangely enough, however, it was neither Lincoln nor
Seward about whom Pike most constantly concerned himself.
Salmon P. Chase, old friend of the Pikes and long the white
hope of the Radicals, became the target for Pike's most consistent attack. Before the war ended, the Chase-Pike friendship

[43] Pike to Fessenden, March 26 [1864], Notebook No. 12, p. 3.
[44] Notebook No. 20, pp. 16-18.
[45] *Ibid.* In connection with this point it does seem that Bancroft, *Seward,* II,
502-9, is a bit naïve in assuming that Seward's being a "very daring character" in the
conduct of his policy, especially toward Britain, somehow served to scare Britain into
neutrality or away from intervention. Perhaps Britain's relations with other continental
powers, such as Russia, Prussia, and France, deserve more attention in the matter of
Anglo-American relations than Bancroft gives. Bancroft's biography, by its masterfulness
in many respects, has prevented another full-length study since 1900, and is still the
chief basis for Seward's reputation.

had become badly strained. This happened because of Pike's thoroughgoing, vociferous condemnation of the Federal government's wartime financial policy. Chase, as Secretary of the Treasury until 1864, became the focus of Pike's financial despair. In order to make this clear, it is necessary to look briefly at the general outlines of the government's hurried measures for financing the war.

In his famous essay on "The Second American Revolution" Charles A. Beard has succinctly pictured the desperate efforts of the Federal government to meet the enormous, unforeseen cost of the Civil War. To a generation inured to stratosphere-finance, Civil War expenditures seem petty enough; but at the time the Federal army-navy expenditure of over three billion dollars during the war appeared dazzlingly large. To pay such costs the government resorted primarily to loans, with generous interest rates, rather than to unpopular taxation. Even after heavier taxes were imposed in the later phase of the war, loans produced much the larger share of governmental revenue. Beard refers to the "profitable principle," which lay behind this policy, that "the generation which directed the war should not bear the main burden of paying for it."[46]

In addition to the expensive loans and the delayed taxes, however, the Federal government in February, 1862, embarked on the controversial policy of issuing paper money, that is, making treasury notes into legal tender which could be applied to all debts save duties on imports and interest on government bonds. Necessity was the main argument advanced for this widely feared step. A severe financial crisis in December, 1861, threw the whole banking system off balance and resulted in the suspension of specie (gold and silver) payments. While Secretary Chase consulted leading bankers and vainly worked out a "counter plan" which partly anticipated his later national banking system, Congress apologetically opened the gates to paper

[46] Charles and Mary Beard, *The Rise of American Civilization* (New York, 1934), pp. 70-71, 107.

money. Chase himself came out belatedly in support of the measure, and in a matter of months he requested authorization from Congress to issue another $150,000,000 of the 'greenbacks.' By the close of the war the government had issued over $430,000,000 worth.[47]

The legal tender catapulted Pike into a fit of displeasure and genuine anxiety which continued throughout the war. In fact, one of his primary postwar concerns continued to be the vexing financial question. But in 1861, aside from his ideas on the country's fiscal policies, he had connections which gave the subject an immediate, personal interest: his friend Fessenden headed the Senate Finance Committee.

In the frenzied month of June, 1861, Fessenden gave the diplomat an initial private peep into official Washington's financial thinking. Fessenden, summoned to Washington for consultation several weeks before the convening of Congress, moved in to live with Secretary Chase during the critical period of preliminary planning. Fessenden estimated that the government would have to borrow $200,000,000 for the first year, but the big question was how and where to get this sum. A national loan, a foreign loan for the residue, and the limited issuance of treasury notes were to be the principal means. "Of course we shall tax the free list [of imports] all it will bear," Fessenden explained, "and may have to resort to a direct tax of some sort, by way of giving confidence—tho' that may be deferred to the next session." Fessenden admitted regretfully that the government "must come to" direct taxation if the war should last. And three weeks before First Bull Run he believed that

[47] For a more thorough discussion of the background and results of the legal tender act, see Davis R. Dewey, *Financial History of the United States* (New York, 1928), pp. 284 ff.; Randall, *Civil War*, pp. 450-52. Albert B. Hart, *Salmon Portland Chase* (New York, 1899), pp. 246-52, defends the role of Chase, while Don C. Barrett, *The Greenbacks and the Resumption of Specie Payments, 1862-1879* (Cambridge, Mass., 1931), pp. 25-57, denies that there existed any "necessity" for the greenbacks. Wesley C. Mitchell, *A History of the Greenbacks* (Chicago, 1903), pp. 403-20, discusses the augmented cost of the Federal debt because of the greenbacks; see also the newer study by Robert T. Patterson, *Federal Debt-Management Policies, 1865-1879* (Durham, N. C., 1954), especially pp. 19-43.

the war would last—"unless negro insurrections come to our aid as there is some prospect they may."[48]

Fessenden's private opinions contained nothing that would alleviate Pike's concern about financing the war, unless it be the reference to the possibility of slave insurrections as a short-cut to triumph. Without such insurrections, Fessenden obviously expected a long war even before Bull Run ended the picnic atmosphere of Washington. Yet the notion that the war would be of short duration is widely offered as one explanation for inadequacies in Federal financial policy.[49] Pike perceived the dangers in a policy which assumed a short war and minimized taxation, for he began studying the assets of the North. He calculated that the country could provide the first $250,000,000 of expenditures, but beyond that he already doubted that the North could furnish annually more than $100-000,000, which was a gross underestimation. Weeks before the event he nervously anticipated the suspension of specie payments with the consequent inflation and speculation.[50]

Pike's worst fears about specie suspension quickly materialized, and early in 1862 he began contemplating the baleful prospect of legal tender. The first definite forewarning of legal tender came in Representative Elbridge G. Spaulding's report for the Ways and Means Committee, of which Thaddeus Stevens was chairman. Pike reported to Secretary Seward that Dutch financiers were aroused lest the United States pursue an unwise, dangerous policy which would "evince a flagrant disregard of the rights of creditors and the interests of capital." Pike considered as unjustifiable any move on the part of the government which would lessen the "gradually widening confidence" felt in American investments by wealthy Dutchmen. While American words carried no great weight, government

[48] Fessenden to Pike, June 30, 1861, Pike MSS.

[49] See Hart, *Chase*, pp. 233, 237; Dewey, *Financial History*, pp. 276, 300. Chase's misconception about a short war seems to have survived Bull Run, judging from the tendency of his policy throughout 1861 (Dewey, *ibid.*, pp. 300 ff.).

[50] Notebook No. 1, pp. 6-7. Entry for Nov., 1861.

acts formed the basis of Europe's estimate of Federal power, wisdom, and integrity.[51]

The legal tender measure became law on February 25, 1862.[52] Fessenden at first opposed the measure in the Senate, but when that proved futile he suggested important amendments. One of these provided that the legal tender treasury notes could not be used to pay interest on government bonds; the other called for the issuance of $500,000,000 in bonds paying 6 per cent interest which could be purchased with either coin or treasury notes. In other words, holders of government bonds would receive only specie, yet the legal tender notes could be exchanged for the bonds. To his friend in Holland, Fessenden explained that he considered legal tender "odious" and "unnecessary." But the specie for interest "saved" the measure, he thought, and "*that* was mine." Fessenden confessed that he and the Secretary of the Treasury did not "entirely agree," and just how the government's finances were to come out in the end he could not foresee. "As yet we have done far better than I anticipated."[53]

Fessenden's mixture of complacency and anxiety proved justified. While the government did secure the vital revenue, some consequences of legal tender were in many ways unfortunate. Briefly put, one of the more serious results of the legal-tender policy was an increase in commodity prices which vastly added to the cost of the war. Another result was the disparity between the price of gold and the value of the greenbacks; this disparity provided ample opportunity for the speculation which flourished throughout the war, thereby increasing the difficulty of the Treasury's tasks.[54] Pike's brother, Con-

[51] Pike to Seward, No. 36, Feb. 5, 1862; No. 37, Feb. 11, 1862, DoS Papers.

[52] For Representative Elbridge G. Spaulding and a defense of the whole policy, see his *History of the Legal Tender Paper Money* (Buffalo, 1869); also the sketch by Frederic L. Paxson in the *Dictionary of American Biography*, XVII, 436-37.

[53] Fessenden to Pike, Aug. 2, 1862, Pike MSS. Fessenden, *Fessenden*, I, 195, 295-303 (despite its filiopietism the only biography). The clause allowing Treasury notes to be converted into bonds was dropped in 1863-64.

[54] Dewey, *Financial History*, pp. 292-97; Mitchell, *Greenbacks*, p. 419.

gressman Frederick A. Pike, admitted that the rise in the price
of gold, which was another way of saying the depreciation of
the Treasury notes, had endangered the prestige of Chase, who
"was supposed to be quite a financier when everything went
smoothly. . . ." Fred Pike expressed the idea which undoubtedly underlay much Congressional as well as popular opinion
when he confessed to his irate brother that "we hope for victories by & by that will answer every purpose of statesmanship
& finances."[55]

Diplomat Pike anathematized the idea that generals and
armies could rectify or compensate for the government's
mistakes. In his eyes a "Higher Law" of finance had been
dangerously violated. The government had "rashly and unnecessarily" interfered with debtor-creditor relations, and had
inflicted a "vital wound upon the rights and interests of capital."[56] These views were reinforced in Pike's estimation by
Dutch financial conservatism. The Dutch taxation system included no tax on property or income since, as Pike explained,
the Dutch considered that such levies would "stand in the way
of industrial & commercial development" and would "operate
to expel capital."[57] In the midst of such staunch economic
orthodoxy, no wonder wealthy Dutchmen looked askance at
Federal legal tender experiments. Pike, while not completely
sharing the Dutch aversion to property taxation, did not have to
look far to find abundant support for his own denunciation of
the legal tender.

As Pike repeatedly insisted in private letters and in des-

[55] Fred Pike to Pike, July 13, 1862, Pike MSS.

[56] Pike to Seward, No. 38, Feb. 19, 1862; No. 40, March 5, 1862, DoS Papers.

[57] Pike to Seward, No. 41, March 12, 1862, DoS Papers. At the request of the
House of Representatives, President Lincoln transmitted Pike's analysis of the Dutch
revenue system to the House. Up to that time Pike's despatch was the only one on the
subject received by the State Department. Seward apparently arranged for the House
to request the information in the first place. Seward to Pike, No. 48, April 2, 1862,
DoS Papers; Lincoln to the House of Representatives, April 5, 1862, in John G.
Nicolay and John Hay, *Complete Works of Abraham Lincoln* (New York, 1905),
VII, 140.

patches, the foreign market for bonds of the United States appears to have been adversely affected by the successive issues of legal tender notes, among other factors.[58] Chase belatedly sent Robert J. Walker, Southern Unionist and former Secretary of the Treasury under Polk, as his secret agent to Europe in 1863. Walker, whom Pike privately described as a "sublime ass," had small success in his twofold task of propagandizing against Confederate bonds, which long sold well in western Europe, and encouraging Europeans to purchase Federal issues. Only toward the end of the war did European financiers evince much interest in Federal securities, and then largely in the Frankfort market. Jay Cooke, the "financier of the Civil War," showed no interest in the European market and even actively opposed selling to Europe. The Philadelphia banker believed that his domestic appeal to patriotism would be weakened by European sales and considered that the United States only stood to suffer by being in debt to foreigners. Pike's hopes for greater utilization of the European market were more than offset at home by Cooke and the attitude he exemplified.[59]

Pike never relinquished his hope that the government would see the error of its financial ways. Late in 1862 he mistakenly believed he saw a spark of hope in Chase's annual report which outlined a plan for national banks and a national bank currency. Pike wrote directly to the Secretary of Treasury in a vain attempt to encourage resolute action against the legal tender. "You may not care to hear this from me," Pike

[58] Barrett, *Greenbacks*, pp. 41-48, discusses the failure early in the war to utilize European credit and the general causes of this policy. Ellis P. Oberholtzer, *Jay Cooke: Financier of the Civil War* (Philadelphia, 1907), I, 513 ff., treats the flurry of European investment in Federal securities which began toward the close of the war.

[59] Pike's description of Walker in Notebook No. 5, p. 19, is partially scratched out but legible. Amos E. Taylor, "Walker's Financial Mission to London on Behalf of the North, 1863-1864," *Journal of Economic and Business History*, III (Feb., 1931), 296-320, must be used carefully; Oberholtzer, *Jay Cooke*, I, 285-89, is more complete on this subject than the newer Henrietta M. Larson, *Jay Cooke: Private Banker* (Cambridge, Mass., 1936), p. 126. Two of Walker's propaganda pamphlets on "American Finances and Resources" (London, 1863) are available in the Princeton University Library.

admitted, "but I take the profoundest interest in our finances believing it to be the pivotal point of our disorders & knowing the imminent danger we are in of being pressed into a policy which can only end in general ruin." The legal tender measure was the "one rotten spot" which promised to spread and ruin everything.[60]

Pike's direct appeal apparently elicited no response from Chase, who was much more occupied with his national bank plan than with legal tender. Congress had earlier rejected the banking scheme, but now, in 1863, it was presented by Chase and others as absolutely essential for the sale of government bonds. The enormous and powerful facilities of Jay Cooke, who had at first opposed the plan, were now at the disposal of Chase. Newspapers carrying advertisements of government bonds were requested by the Cookes to editorialize in favor of the national bank measure, and Jay Cooke or his brother, Henry, wrote many articles stressing the urgent need for such banks. Having hometown clippings placed on the desk of each senator and representative has been described as the master stroke of the Cookes in this campaign for the national banks.[61]

Late in February, 1863, Secretary Chase and the Cooke interests won their goal. The new national banking system, as it finally emerged in 1864, provided for the establishment of local banking associations authorized by the Federal government. On the basis of government bonds, which the new banks purchased and for which they received interest, these new national banks could issue banknotes up to 90 per cent of the par value of the bonds. These banknotes in turn could be lent to borrowers at the current discount. Aside from furnishing a stable currency, Chase's national banking system proved highly advantageous to those fortunate enough to share

[60] Pike to Chase, Dec. 31, 1862, copy in Pike MSS.

[61] Larson, *Cooke*, pp. 137-39; brief explanations of the system itself, on which the next paragraph is based, may be found in Dewey, *Financial History*, pp. 320-28; Randall, *Civil War*, pp. 455-58; Oberholtzer, *Jay Cooke*, I, 326 ff.

in the establishment of the new banks. But it was not this
feature nor the possibility of banking concentration in the
Northeast to which Pike objected. His principal basis for
attacking Chase's scheme lay in the timing and the continued
reliance on the odious legal tender notes.

Pike declared to his congressman brother that Chase's
strangling of the state banks was "a d—— outrage." The
National Banking Act, however, did complement the vile legal
tender measures and thus completed Chase's "paper machinery." Pike prophesied that the measure would be a failure
and finances "go from bad to worse until the legal tender bill
is repealed & all the banks put on a specie basis." He could
not understand how such a "financial revolution" as Chase
seemed to desire could be peaceably carried out. Pike "hated
to feel this way about an old friend," but "the honest truth"
was that Chase's "desire of being President has been the guid-
ing impulse of a series of financial actions which are threatening the country with infinite disaster."[62]

Pike not only lashed out at Chase in private letters to his
brother, to Fessenden, and to Dana, but his despatches to
Seward, especially after 1862, dwelt increasingly on the poor
financial situation of the United States government and the
consequent alarm of himself and European financiers.[63] Pike
begged the Secretary of State to believe that he reported these
criticisms with the "deepest pain" especially since they "are
accompanied with the expression of disappointed expectations
and the profoundest fears of the result of Mr. Chase's apparent
policy."[64] But it would have taken more than such sugar-
coated statements as this, which appeared in the published
diplomatic correspondence, to assuage the injured feelings of
Salmon P. Chase.

[62] Pike to Fred Pike, May 8, 1864, Notebook No. 13, p. 20.

[63] Some samples: Pike to Seward, No. 75, Feb. 11, 1863, *Foreign Papers 1863*, Pt.
2, pp. 808-9; No. 121, Jan. 27, 1864, *Foreign Papers 1864*, Pt. 3, 308; No. 130,
April 27, 1864, *ibid.*, pp. 313-14.

[64] Pike to Seward, No. 137, June 8, 1864, *ibid.*, p. 317.

Seward forwarded many of Pike's despatches concerning finances directly to the Secretary of the Treasury. To some of Pike's criticism Seward himself responded with vague, airy assertions. For example, when the diplomat complained of the European effect of the currency's depreciation, Seward reminded him that "citizens and foreigners, all alike, may bear their losses and be thankful that the government maintains itself, and so preserves all private personal interests from ruin." On another occasion in early 1862 Seward indulged in his characteristic optimism by calling Pike's attention to the fact that all classes of the people already accepted the prospect of an early end to the war, and the United States would "perhaps be ceasing to borrow while those who have little faith in republican institutions are considering whether it is safe to lend." Seward was no nearer the truth when he asserted that the country was "likely to become quite independent of foreign credit, while its industry will be invigorated to an extent unknown in our former history."[65]

Even if Seward viewed the finances in this rosy light, he probably felt no pangs when passing Pike's criticism along to Chase. So the hurt Secretary of the Treasury thought. Several months after he had become Chief Justice, Chase wrote Mrs. Pike a curious letter which furnishes an interesting glimpse of himself. After remarking that "both you & Mr. Pike have maintained a profound silence ever since the seas parted us," Chase recalled one occasion on which Pike showed a "quasi-recognition" of his (Chase's) existence. "*That* came at a time & under circumstances which do not allow it to be forgotten."

Then Chase explained that Pike's "quasi-recognition" came just about when he resigned from the Treasury post. "All the sensitiveness there is in my nature," Chase wrote, "—and whatever others may think, you, I believe, will agree that it

[65] Seward to Pike, No. 79, Nov. 21, 1862, *Foreign Papers 1862*, Pt. 2, pp. 624-25; No. 44, Feb. 27, 1862, *ibid.*, p. 597; No. 46, March 10, 1862, *ibid.*, p. 598.

is not devoid of that quality—had been put on the rack by the
assaults made on me by the open enemies of the Administration
& those who claimed to be the most capital friends of the President. . . . Moreover I was overwhelmed with anxiety concerning the finances. . . . And, just at this time, when thus assailed
& thus struggling, the President, as if my perplexities and difficulties were too small, yielded to the importunities of politicians & required me to yield also where I firmly believed that
yielding was equivalent to a surrender of control on appointments. . . . It was during those days, that Mr. Seward, whose
Alter Ego Weed was among the most bitter of my assailants,
sent me an extract from a despatch of Mr. Pike in which he
expressed the astonishment of the Dutch Financiers & his own
that 'Mr. Chase persisted in swelling the volume of paper.'
Mr. Chase, whose utmost efforts had been directed to its
restraint, & who had just withdrawn over seventy millions of
Legal Tender interest notes for the purpose of such reduction,
after vainly endeavoring to induce congress to put the reduction [of currency] where it ought to have been put, on the
Circulation of State Banks: a pure loan from the people to
the Banks at a time when the People needed all they could
get for their own urgent wants. It was one of my bitter
moments when I tried it. 'How can I hope to be understood'
was my sorrowful thought."

Chase continued by noting that he could have endured all
this if Lincoln had not "yielded to politicians the substantial
control of important appointments in my department." That
could not be endured. Self-respect required resignation. " 'If I
have misconceived him [Lincoln]' I thought, 'he will seek an
explanation. And he will too if I have not & he is willing to
put matters on an acceptable basis.' He accepted it & that
proved I was right in offering it."

Then Chase explained that he had not lost interest in
"our cause" despite the wrongs done him but had campaigned
for Lincoln's re-election. "I made no claim for so doing; but

the people, who, after my resignation, gave me unexpected & most gratifying proof of their attachment & confidence, demanded, with unprecedented unanimity, my appointment as Chief Justice; and he nominated me to the Senate. I must do him [Lincoln] the justice of saying that I believe his own inclination was with the wishes of the People. I accepted the post not without some reluctance & misgiving, but with the determination with God's blessing to do my duty. And I am trying to do it."[66]

Aside from revealing wide historical and human interest, this document also clearly reveals that Pike had offended an influential friend. His answering explanation to the Chief Justice was perhaps even stranger than Chase's letter, for the minister to Holland squirmed and sweated without ever actually getting around the fact that he had held and expressed low opinions of Chase's policy. Pike first wrote a long paragraph about friendship saying, among other things, that "it would be unnatural for me to unnecessarily wound any fibre of the delicate relations of a friendship I am proud to acknowledge." Then, bravely plunging ahead to the finances, he noted that it was "the fate of public men, often, to be misapprehended, as well as to be judged in a spirit of severe criticism sometimes . . . even by their friends." Any "unintentional injustice" would just have to be charged to "human imperfection." Rather feebly, Pike concluded that after "these general observations, I do not find I have much to add." But he did console Chase by pointing to the fact that as Secretary of the Treasury he had made a European reputation.[67]

The Chief Justice might well have pondered just what sort of reputation Pike referred to, but apparently Chase felt forgiving and forgetful. He not only accepted Pike's explana-

[66] Chase to Mrs. Pike, March 17, 1865, Pike MSS. For a more comprehensive account of Chase's departure from the cabinet, which came as a shock to him after Lincoln's earlier refusals to accept his frequently offered resignation, see Hart, *Chase*, pp. 309-18.

[67] Pike to Chase, April 19, 1865, Notebook No. 17, pp. 49-51.

tion but now thought his own letter to Mrs. Pike had not been "fortunate in the choice of expression." Chase referred again to "a certain pleasure" Seward seemed to feel in conveying Pike's criticism—"certainly I remember no praise or cheer from any quarter that ever reached me through him [Seward]." (So Seward obviously was more culpable for persecuting Chase than was Pike.) Anyhow it was all over now, Chase continued, and he looked back on his financial achievements with great satisfaction, particularly the national currency. Had he remained at the treasury and "been supported properly" he should "long since" have resumed specie payments.[68]

The way had now been cleared for an eventual resumption of friendly relations, and such Reconstruction issues as Negro suffrage drew Pike and Chase again into contact. But long before that, Pike had had finances on the brain. Following Chase's resignation Fessenden had reluctantly allowed himself to be drafted for the difficult job.

Fessenden had several good reasons for not desiring to be Secretary of the Treasury, among them being his preference for the Senate, where he headed the powerful Finance Committee and earned wide respect for independence and courage. On the slavery issue Fessenden voted with the Radicals, which in many cases led him to oppose the administration. But Lincoln considered the Maine senator as being without "the petulant and vicious fretfulness" that characterized many of the Radicals. Fessenden's principal reason for wishing to avoid the job, however, arose from his chronically poor health.[69]

Pike, upon hearing of Fessenden's appointment, first thought of his friend's poor health. Perhaps, too, Pike regretfully realized that Fessenden had moved steadily toward

---

[68] Chase to Pike, July 8, 1865, Pike MSS.

[69] Fessenden, *Fessenden*, I, 315 ff.; Sandburg, *Lincoln*, pp. 113-25. Sandburg seems to have more material on Lincoln's relations with the treasury than any of the other recent studies; in his splendid three-volume study of *Lincoln: The President*, Professor Randall ignores the subject.

Chase's views on financial matters. Now, for example, Fessenden even championed the new national banks. Pike's concern led him to a brash move aimed at keeping Fessenden out of the treasury. Considering finances the most crucial aspect of the war, Pike had discussed the subject with every Northerner he encountered in Europe. He tended to form his judgment of other American diplomats and agents according to the degree of their agreement, or disagreement, with his own views on that subject. With Charles Francis Adams in London, Pike had on several occasions discussed American affairs. In June, 1863, for example, he called on the Adamses and afterwards recorded that "Mr. Adams is a very plucky & composed man & talks about the war with great good sense." Adams rated indeed well, for Pike described him as "one of the men with whom I hardly ever disagree."[70]

Pike took it unto himself to have Seward secure Fessenden's appointment to the London mission and Adams' transfer to the Treasury Department. In his letter to Seward, Pike explained that Fessenden's physical condition was dangerously poor; on the other hand, Adams' reliability in diplomacy was matched by his soundness in finance. Pike argued that by switching the two the country could save the services of both valuable men in "two of the most difficult posts we have to fill." Adams might refuse, Pike admitted, but his personal wishes were not paramount in such critical times. Moreover, Pike was "quite certain" that Adams had "no desire to remain in Europe."[71]

Whether or not Charles Francis Adams knew of Pike's suggestion, before it was made or later, is not known. Pike visited in England until late May, 1864, and might have sounded Adams out on his future plans and on the financial situation.

[70] Notebook No. 7, p. 2; entry for June 19, 1863. Indirect evidence supporting Pike's opinion of Adams' views may be found in *Moran Journal*, II, 1047; Charles F. Adams, *Charles F. Adams* (New York, 1900), p. 146; Ford, ed., *Cycle*, II, 224-25, 231-32.

[71] Pike to Seward, July 23, 1864, Notebook No. 14, p. 25.

Pike did advise Fessenden about the plan and urged that he "make Mr. Lincoln recall Mr. Adams & put him in your place." Fessenden could "get relief & health by crossing the ocean" and filling the London post, and Pike promised his widower-friend that Lizzie Pike should travel over and "make things go easy . . . & take care of you as only a woman can."[72]

None of Pike's arguments changed the decisions about the treasury post which had already been made. The whole scheme was a bit farfetched, and is interesting mainly as an indication of Pike's concern about the country's financial condition and Senator Fessenden. Seward had many reasons for being satisfied with Adams' performance in London; on the other hand, Fessenden had a record of conspicuous enmity to the Secretary of State and to his policies.[73] Seward apparently took no cognizance of Pike's suggestion nor is there any evidence that President Lincoln ever knew about it. Pike had no alternative but to hope, first, that Fessenden's health would survive the ordeal—and, secondly, that he had not been irretrievably converted to legal tender and the new national banks.

Actually, Fessenden still shared many of Pike's opinions. Denouncing Secretary Chase's policy of depending primarily on loans and legal tender, Pike had also clamored for more taxes and reduced expenditures. Pike insisted that "our only resource lies in two words *war taxes*." The war had to be put on a basis of "indefinite continuance," and the government and the people had to become reconciled to paying the costs.[74] As much as any of the economically conservative legislators of the Civil War era, Fessenden tended to agree with Pike about taxation. The Maine senator not only favored the income tax of 1861, which was of much greater social significance for the

[72] Notebook No. 13, pp. 13 ff.; Pike to Fessenden, July 23, 1864, Notebook No. 14, p. 25.

[73] Fessenden, *Fessenden*, I, 231 ff.; Gideon Welles, *Diary of Gideon Welles* (New York, 1911), II, 65, 173, gives a typical glimpse of Cabinet politics as seen through the eyes of the Secretary of the Navy.

[74] Pike to Fessenden, Feb. 2, 1863, Notebook No. 5, pp. 18-20.

future than of financial import during the war, but Fessenden in 1862 proposed and secured the first graduated income tax.[75]

But by 1864 Fessenden had, as Pike feared, partially changed his mind about the finances. While he strove successfully to avoid swelling the already large volume of currency and thereby worsening the inflation, Fessenden now accepted the national banks as a useful innovation. Furthermore, he found himself compelled to employ the services of Jay Cooke for selling government bonds. Altogether, Fessenden's brief record as Secretary of the Treasury (he resigned on March 3, 1865, to reoccupy his Senate seat) was brighter than that of his predecessor. Fessenden inherited a bad situation at a particularly critical juncture, for the summer of 1864 found Federal financial as well as military stock at a low point. Yet Fessenden worked no miracles in reshaping the machinery and policies he inherited from Chase. Fortunately Pike had the good sense not to expect more than the competence his friend revealed.[76]

Pike admitted that Fessenden had a well-nigh hopeless task; whereas Chase had been "flying his kite & playing out line," Fessenden now had the slow, irksome task of winding it in. Pike advised him that the prospects for a foreign loan

[75] The progression principle was not adopted for its own sake but merely to provide additional revenue made necessary by other tax changes. From the flat 3 per cent on all incomes over $600, as the House bill provided, the Senate, on Fessenden's suggestion, called for 3 per cent on incomes between $600 and $10,000; 5 per cent on those between $10,000 and $50,000; and 7.5 per cent on those over $50,000. The conference committee knocked out the 7.5 per cent bracket. This act of July 1, 1862, was actually the first income-tax measure put into operation, since Chase "seized every excuse to avoid use of the income tax." Fred Pike also was an outstanding advocate of the measure, giving the Radicals their rallying cry of "Tax, Fight, Emancipate." See Sidney Ratner, *American Taxation: Its History as a Social Force in Democracy* (New York, 1942), pp. 64-73; Williams, *Radicals*, p. 157. As an illustration of the relative unimportance of the wartime income tax, the $20,294,000 collected under it in 1864 should be compared with $719,476,032 from loans in 1863-64 or the $102,316,152 from customs in the same year (Dewey, *Financial History*, pp. 299, 305).

[76] For Fessenden's secretaryship, see Dewey, *Financial History*, pp. 314-16; Ratner, *Taxation*, pp. 92-99; Fessenden, *Fessenden*, I, 326 ff.

now looked inauspicious, since "all the money that Europe wants to invest in our securities" had already been tapped through existing channels, primarily in Amsterdam and Frank-fort. "I know full well that what you do will be watchfully done," Pike concluded, "and with a single eye to the public good, and I will not suffer myself to doubt that we shall sur-mount the difficulties of the situation, and come out into the sunshine at last with our feet on the solid rock." Pike reverted to the language of his Downeast days when he consoled Fessen-den with the reflection that the first thing to be done with a water-logged ship was to "get the water down & keep her afloat." After that Fessenden could start worrying about his destination.[77] Sherman's victories in the deep South and Lin-coln's re-election soon made the remainder of the voyage appear surer and safer.

Pike's general criticism of Federal financial policies and of Chase have been largely substantiated by a number of modern historians and economists.[78] There is wide agreement today that, as Pike insisted from 1862 on, the government might well have relied earlier and more heavily on taxation rather than on the issue of legal-tender notes and the excessive dependence on loans. Nevertheless, Pike allowed his belief in the importance of finances to blind him to certain political and military realities. As explained above, Pike's notion that the Federal financial policies were doomed reinforced both his desire for a negotiated peace and his inclination to accept a Southern "negro pen" about which the government need not concern itself. When Pike suggested increased taxation he also insisted on reduced expenditures; and reduced expenditures in the death-struggle that was the Civil War might well have meant a compromise peace or worse. In a word, Pike allowed

---

[77] Pike to Fessenden, July 20, 1864; July 23, 1864, Notebook No. 14, pp. 19-25.

[78] Ratner, *Taxation*, pp. 64 ff.; Barrett, *Greenbacks*, pp. 13 ff.; Randall, *Civil War*, p. 445. Even Dewey, *Financial History* (1902), p. 300, to a certain extent, is critical of Chase.

his own fears to become so exaggerated that they helped to make him a defeatist.

Pike's old friend Gurowski, who sooner or later attacked just about every public man north as well as south of the Mason-Dixon line, never criticized Pike by name. But Gurowski seems to have been chastising Pike when he declared that the published diplomatic correspondence "contains many commonplaces about the finances of the country." The Polish count believed that "even the best among our diplomats abroad lose the domestic scent, the perception, and the appreciation of domestic affairs." Foreign bankers and foreign nations inspired the "nonsense" about loans and credit, but the United States would "again play a trick upon European notions of political economy."[79]

Despite the strangely xenophobic aspect of the Polish count's comment, Pike does seem to have lost some of the "domestic scent." Chaotic finances failed to destroy the Confederacy. And regardless of the inefficiency, high cost, and serious postwar consequences of Federal financial policy, there is no reason for believing that Northern aims would have been better answered by reducing expenditures and "fighting for a boundary," in the manner that Pike advocated.

In addition to his overzealous but honest convictions, Pike's personal position might have encouraged him to view the financial picture in an excessively dim light. His income depended on moderate savings and small investments; yet it was just this type of personal security which wartime inflation undermined. Unlike many of his contemporaries, Pike had long before relinquished the desire and the opportunity of making a quick million. Would he, in his late fifties, return to America only to find his economic security destroyed and his old way of life shattered?[80]

Meanwhile from several sources Pike received abundant evidence that some Americans thrived under wartime economic

---

[79] Gurowski, *Diary*, III, 92-93.

[80] Writing to a Boston businessman about the advisibility of exchanging "N. York

conditions. As early as the fall of 1863, Fred Pike gleefully described "these flush times when everybody has abundant employment at full wages & businessmen everywhere are getting rich. . . ." Never had there been such "flourishing operations," and even little Calais, Maine, had its new crop of affluent capitalists. Fred admitted that prudent businessmen inevitably looked at their large gains and mentally struck off 25 or 33 per cent to bring them down to the gold standard. But there was even less of that than the absent diplomat might think. Common laborers received only the "1.25 they always got," but actually Fred thought money could be acquired with little difficulty.[81]

Fred Pike spoke for the Maine picture. Charles A. Dana told a comparable story for New York City. After a visit to the burgeoning metropolis, Dana declared that he had never seen the city "in such splendor, or so universally animated by the spirit of gambling." Everybody bought everything on speculation, and every woman dressed magnificently. Splendid "equipages" rolled constantly down Broadway. Dana assured Pike that all the city's former pomp was "entirely outdone by its present displays."[82]

As businessmen in Calais and New York and elsewhere in the North giddily prospered in the war economy, Pike spent quiet days at The Hague. And when the Dutch capital became tedious, the Pikes were happy to embark on far-ranging jaunts to places as different as the Riviera and Scotland.

Central 6 pr cts (1861) for some of the Convertible 1869, 8 pr cts of the Mich Central," Pike noted that persistent inflation took away all protection for the "mere *bond* holder" (Pike to James M. Forbes, Feb. 24, 1864, Notebook No. 11, pp. 15-16).

[81] Fred Pike to Pike, Oct. 11, 1863, Pike MSS.

[82] Dana to Pike, July 10, 1864, Pike MSS. For a scholarly description of the same general condition, see Harold U. Faulkner, *American Economic History* (New York, 1943), pp. 342 ff.

VI. *Seeing Europe*
and Europeans

THE HAGUE in the latter half of the nineteenth century ranked as "the most fashionalble, the handsomest, and the most modern-looking town in Holland." This was the judgment of a fastidious English traveler who found "gaiety" in The Hague's broad and handsome boulevards. The Englishman believed the atmosphere to be one that was invariably conferred by "the presence of a [royal] court."[1] A more ingratiating Italian traveler declared that he felt like "a very poor devil" in the elegant, half-French city where the population, being largely affluent and official, was of a "more refined order than that of the other Dutch cities."[2] Perhaps it was just as well that Minister Pike did not produce the travel book he seems to have contemplated, for, while admiring the broad streets and handsome buildings, he actually found a diplomat's life at the Hague quite dull.

Like the majority of his colleagues from America, Pike possessed few of the usual talents of the experienced diplomat. In the matter of language, for example, he apparently considered learning Dutch as out of the question. (The Italian traveler, incidentally, thought Dutch sounded like German "spoken by a man with a hair in his throat. . . .")[3] Dutch was not essential, at any rate, since French remained the

---

[1] Charles W. Wood, *Through Holland* (London, 1877), pp. 31-33.
[2] Edmondo de Amicis, *Holland and Its People;* trans. Caroline Tilton (New York, 1888), pp. 130-31.
[3] *Ibid.*, p. 141.

language of diplomacy, and his official duties were executed in that language. Pike's early notebooks indicate that he did struggle with French. There are scribbled vocabulary studies and laborious conjugations of the trying French verbs. But self-education proved inadequate in the intricacies of French, especially conversational French, and Minister Pike had to console himself with the thought that forcing "a free born American" to learn two or three foreign languages constituted virtual enslavement. He reasoned that a man's learning foreign languages after reaching the age of fifty resembled that same man's going to a gymnasium to acquire acrobatic tricks. "He can do it, but the old joints supple themselves slowly."[4] Pike managed to clear linguistic hurdles apparently without serious mishap. But there were other reasons besides 'foreign chattering' which caused his dislike of the diplomatic routine.

Zealous republican and egalitarian though he might be, Pike quickly discovered that European diplomats made an intricate, expensive art of their profession. The baffling problems of dress and entertainment soon arose, for, as Pike and most other Americans were apt to forget, diplomatic practice had been perfected at monarchical courts long before the American Republic made its appearance on the international scene. Secretary William L. Marcy's famous "Dress Circular" of 1853, which ordered American diplomats to don simple, citizen's clothing, created certain problems even if it did cater to American nationalism and republicanism. Henry C. Murphy, Pike's predecessor at The Hague, advised the Downeaster to get a uniform. Without gilt lace Pike would only be a "rara avis at this court." Murphy related how he had first adopted a blue coat with eagle buttons only to find that he was "continually mistaken for the waiters who deal out ices and champaigne [sic]. . . ." Such embarrassing situations convinced Murphy that "a modest uniform" made by a Parisian tailor would also

---

[4] Notebooks No. 15, p. 33; No. 17, p. 35.

best answer Pike's needs. "If all diplomats were Ben. Franklin and had a reputation which made them soar above the gilded crowd," Murphy reasoned, "it would be very well; but believe me I advise you to this course for your own convenience." Affecting singularity was of dubious value as an expression of democracy.[5]

Whether or not Pike accepted his predecessor's advice is not known. He probably did, at least in part, for he too became convinced that republican-black could be painfully embarrassing. Pike argued that simple attire served well enough as long as the government specifically prescribed the outfit, thus relieving the individual diplomat of any responsibility. He asserted that "nobody but a pachydermatory ass wishes or can endure the notoriety which comes of arbitrary singularity."[6]

Regardless of his appearance, Pike maintained cordial relations with the Dutch court. After the traditional ceremony of receiving credentials, King William III inquired about Pike's previous diplomatic experience. The former journalist coolly admitted that "our American diplomatists generally were not educated after the European method." But he also had the grace to add that they "labored under some disadvantages in consequence."[7] Pike found Queen Sophie, a former Württemburg princess who was estranged from her husband, an eager and pleasant conversationalist despite the fact that Her Majesty's sympathies were with the South in the American war.

A little colloquy between Pike, the Queen, and several diplomatic wives, which took place at one of the many social

[5] Murphy to Pike, May 15, 1861, Pike MSS. For background of the Dress Circular, see Thomas A. Bailey, *A Diplomatic History of the American People* (New York, 1940), pp. 282-84. In an era when monarchy is admired by many Americans it is interesting to note George Bancroft's reply when the British ambassador in Berlin asked him why he appeared in undertaker's black. The famous American historian-diplomat retorted that "we [Americans] could not be more appropriately dressed than we are—at European courts, where what we represent is the Burial of Monarchy" (*ibid.*, p. 284).

[6] Unsent letter to Charles Sumner, chairman of the Senate Foreign Relations Committee, on March 21, 1867, Notebook No. 24, pp. 20-21.

[7] Pike to Seward, No. 1, June 8, 1861, *Foreign Papers 1861*, pp. 333-34.

affairs, illustrates the general attitude of Europe's aristocratic classes toward the Civil War. The Queen opened verbal fire with the observation that the United States had no history, to which Pike answered that the defect was just now being rapidly repaired. When the Yankee suggested that the Queen draw upon her imagination for America's future history, she replied, "O Yes, no doubt, *you will be masters then*. That is just the history I do not want to read."

This first skirmish going in the vivacious Queen's favor, Minister Pike rallied by alluding to the unfortunate secessionist sympathies of Lady Buchanan, the British ambassador's wife who sat near by. The Queen admitted her own initial approval of secession but insisted that she had changed her mind. Lady Buchanan not only confessed her secessionism but reminded the American that England had allowed the colonies to leave the fold. Why should not the South now have the same privilege? Pike feebly parried this commonplace thrust by pointing to the seven years of war which the Americans had waged to escape Britain and suggested that the United States be given at least that many years to settle the current issue. Then he advanced to stronger ground by reminding the British lady that Ireland might find the secession doctrine useful. This Irish reminder eliminated Britannia from the fray. But the French ambassador's wife, who claimed Southern descent on the maternal side and whom Pike described as "young, buxom, & full of animal spirits with a plethoric purse," pointed to the deep sectional hatreds that divided America. Pike explained this by the institution of slaveholding, insisting that once the detested "race of slaveholders" had been extinguished amity would reign again. Supper and dancing soon scattered the group, but Pike had gained additional evidence for his belief that aristocratic Europe felt little good will toward the United States.[8]

Unfortunately not many of his official evenings furnished

[8] Notebook No. 2, pp. 6-8. Feb. [?], 1862.

Pike with such lively conversation. After aʙouτ τwo years at The Hague, he concluded that of all the diplomats he had known there, only two or three were more than third-rate men. A paucity of ideas made their conversation of little interest. (He excluded the fox-hunting British minister who had "some *running* ideas on that subject.") To Pike it appeared that the foreign corps concerned itself largely with "horses & carriages & servants" and left most business to secretaries and attachés. High society, the thrifty New Englander had discovered, was meant less for enjoyment than for rivalry, and the game could be exorbitantly expensive if taken too seriously.[9]

Harsh economic facts compelled him to moderate his expenditures. His ministerial salary of $7,500 annually looked even smaller when compared with the $18,000 paid to the British minister or $16,000 to the Russian. Pike's personal income, while more than adequate in normal times for comfortable living in America, could not safely be stretched to cover lavish expenditure abroad, especially when the Federal financial situation threatened to be indefinitely unstable. And he possessed his share of Yankee prudence and dollar-sense. The upshot was that Minister Pike and Mrs. Pike kept their feet on the ground. They gave occasional dinners, complete from "Consommé de Volaille printanière" to an impressive choice of wines, but Pike resolved that it was better to "show the cotton" a little than to try and put everything on a genuinely "silk" basis.[10]

The Pikes' frugality disturbed at least one pretentious American in Europe. Benjamin Moran, London legation official, described Lizzie Ellicott Pike as a "tall, coarse, ill-mannered woman whose vulgarity would make her conspicuous

---

[9] Notebooks No. 8, pp. 1 ff.; No. 11, pp. 35-37. Pike characterized many members of The Hague's diplomatic corps in an amusing yet not unkindly manner, but the material is hardly relevant here.

[10] Notebooks No. 1, p. 2; No. 13, p. 3; No. 15, p. 37. *Congressional Directory* . . . (Washington, 1861), p. 47, for American diplomatic salaries.

anywhere." Not only did she join her husband in frequen
absences from his post, but, alas, she did "her own household
work." Moran scored Pike himself as a "most unfit man for
an U. S. Minister," but then so were "all the men connected
with the newspaper press whom Mr. Lincoln has appointed
to diplomatic posts."[11] Acidulous as Moran was by nature, his
patently unfair attack on the Pikes probably resulted from
foggy London weather, poor digestion, or perhaps a combination of both. Moran himself had earlier described Pike as a
"man of more than ordinary intellect and intelligence" whose
high forehead and strong features would allow him to be
called "fine looking anywhere." Despite a "lack of refinement
not proper to a Minister," Moran not only liked Pike at this
first meeting but expected him to "make a tolerable representative." But as for Lizzie Pike's household work, the haughty
London diarist was right. Lizzie even had the effrontery to
preserve strawberries in the 'legation' dining room.[12]

Actually Mrs. Pike seems to have been an intelligent,
generous, and modest woman. Pike's notebooks do not contain
a great deal about her, but the few glimpses that do come
through are the more revealing because they are indirect and
unself-conscious. Pike himself apparently eschewed conven-
tional religious practice, but Elizabeth Ellicott had been raised
in a devout Quaker family. Her religion seems to have
retained the quiet intensity which sometimes characterizes the
Friends. Owen Lovejoy, brother of the martyred Illinois abolitionist and himself a fervent Radical congressman, once wrote
to Friend Lizzie Pike: "I hope thee will have grace to keep
humble with the many honors that cluster around thee."[13]

The strawberry preserves indicate that Lovejoy need not
have concerned himself about Lizzie's humility. As for her
intellect, Mrs. Pike possessed abundant common sense. The

---

[11] *Moran Journal*, II, 1299. Entry for May 21, 1864.

[12] *Ibid.*, II, 847. Entry for July 18, 1861. Notebook No. 7, p. 24. It should be
remembered that there was no American legation; the Pikes merely had rooms.

[13] Lovejoy to Mrs. Pike, Feb. 15, 1864, Pike MSS.

vivacious Queen of Holland enjoyed her conversation, and after one of their talks about religion and other topics Queen Sophie complimented Lizzie by saying "with great sincerity" that she was a "very remarkable woman." Even Minister Pike, typical Victorian spouse though he might be in some respects, secretly confessed to his notebook that he had the great, good fortune to be married to a woman of "native dignity and repose of character."[14]

But marital bliss did not reign undisturbed. Lizzie suffered from "rheumatic complaints," which were aggravated by the damp climate of The Hague. This served as an added incentive to travel, which Mr. Pike apparently relished anyhow. On one occasion, however, when both Lizzie and he acquired "prodigious" head-colds while shifting from drafty railway cars to stuffy hotel rooms, Pike growled that, on the whole, "travelling with Lizzie is like carrying a piano on your travels for the sake of its music."[15]

Another reason for the Pikes' extensive travels was that from 1862 on he found his diplomatic duties consuming less time and energy. After the first year's negotiations over Dutch neutrality and maritime regulations, Pike could find very little in the diplomatic line which required constant, serious attention. Seward had suggested that Pike encourage Dutch immigration to the United States. This was a touchy subject, especially in wartime, and Seward stated that while Pike could not hold out inducements of rewards or bounties for soldiers, he could let it be known "that any foreigners arriving in this country will probably find no difficulty in finding military employment." Seward also ordered Pike, and other envoys, to advertise the glowing facts about American economic prosperity and homesteading opportunities.[16]

[14]Notebooks No. 14, p. 3; No. 9, p. 22.
[15] Notebook No. 19, p. 50.
[16] Seward to Pike, No. 21, Sept. 5, 1861, *Foreign Papers 1861*, p. 346; Seward circular to Pike, etc., No. 19, Aug. 8, 1862, DOS Papers. In 1856 the Federal government expelled the British minister and three British consuls for their activity in

Despite Seward's interest in this immigration matter, which sprang from obvious economic and military reasons, Pike found that the Dutch were simply not "an emigrating people." He explained this by the fact that the Dutch, while enjoying prosperity and contentment at home, were not to be enticed towards "a great, unfinished, active, bounding country like ours." The figures prove the correctness of Pike's analysis, for while the Irish especially poured into the North, and into the Union army, partially as a result of encouragement offered by Federal agents, the Dutch remained unenthusiastic.[17]

Concerning immigration to the United States, it might be noted parenthetically that Seward's circulars ordering his envoys to advertise the military and economic opportunities in America infuriated the Confederate agents in Europe. Ambrose Dudley Mann, the Confederate agent in Belgium, somehow acquired a copy of one of Seward's circulars about immigration. Mann saw that the Continental and London papers received copies of the Seward circular, and he also took active steps to counteract the influence of Seward's propaganda in Germany and Switzerland as well as in Belgium. Mann later undertook the Confederacy's special mission to the Vatican in an attempt to procure papal aid in discouraging Catholic immigration to the United States.

The papal mission being temporary, however, the ambitious Confederate agent repeatedly begged Secretary of State Judah P. Benjamin to allow him to enlarge his sphere so as to include Holland. Mann argued that "at some future period" the

---

enlisting American for Crimean War service (Samuel F. Bemis, *A Diplomatic History of the United States*, New York, 1936, pp. 334-35).

[17] Pike to Seward, No. 81, April 1, 1863, DoS Papers. From 1861 to 1870 there were only about 9,000 immigrants from the Netherlands as compared with about 436,000 from Ireland alone or 787,000 from Germany (Samuel E. Morrison and Henry S. Commager, *The Growth of the American Republic*, New York, 1942, II, 787). Seward's immigration policy needs further investigation, but see William D'Arcy, *The Fenian Movement in the United States:1858-1886* (Washington, 1947), pp. 61 ff.; Owsley, *King Cotton*, pp. 517-26; and *Foreign Papers 1864*, Pt. 3, pp. 173 ff. The last suggests some of the foreign complications that arose over the encouragement given to immigration.

proud kingdom of Holland might "enquire why it was that she was not regarded as of as much consequence by the Confederate States as Belgium." The Amsterdam bourse also offered an opportunity for discreetly disparaging the state of Federal finances. Despite all his pleas, Mann received no authorization to extend his mission. Pike was thus spared one annoyance which might have complicated his own tasks at The Hague, for elsewhere in Europe Confederate agents developed resourceful techniques for furthering their cause.[18]

Since Pike had no Confederate machinations to combat and could do little in the way of promoting Dutch immigration, he devoted a large part of his time to observing and studying various phases of European life. Agricultural methods and conditions greatly interested him, and he acquired much information about the dairy industry in which the Dutch excelled. He made excursions to study the newest type dairy barns and investigated Dutch techniques for inoculating cattle against certain diseases. In the latter case he even communicated with the Boston Board of Trade concerning his findings. In being thus concerned with the practical and utilitarian aspects of European life, Pike placed himself in the tradition of American travelers that extended at least as far back as Thomas Jefferson.[19]

Pike found Dutch politics less compelling than their animal husbandry. The language barrier undoubtedly limited his appreciation of Dutch political life, but there were other factors. Dutch parliamentary life suffered from the usual European malady of splinter parties, and the resulting fluidity in ministries and the cabinet-shuffling gave the whole picture an unreal

[18] Mann to Judah P. Benjamin, June 30, 1862; Sept. 1, 1862; Nov. 17, 1864; Dec. 16, 1864, in *Official Records of the Union and Confederate Navies in the War of the Rebellion* (Washington, 1922), Series II, Vol. III, pp. 451, 521, 1240, 1251. Owsley, *King Cotton*, pp. 517 ff.

[19] Notebooks No. 1, pp. 11 ff.; No. 12, p. 21. In France, Pike enjoyed inspecting the Emperor's farm and in England he attended stock shows and agricultural fairs (Notebooks No. 3, pp. 6 ff.; No. 15, pp. 8 ff.). Several separate notebooks in the Pike MSS devoted to English and continental agriculture suggest that Pike gathered the material with some sort of book in mind.

aspect for Pike.[20] Moreover, contemporary issues in Dutch politics must necessarily have seemed uninspiring to one who had been so intimately associated with American national politics during the turbulent 1850's. Politico-religious divisions in the Netherlands between orthodox Protestants, Catholics, and secular Liberals underlay most questions of the day, particularly that of primary education and whether the state or the churches should control the schools. This struggle, which characterized a large portion of Continental parliamentary life in the last half of the nineteenth century, quickly became arid and futile; yet it proved a fountainhead of political strife in Holland for a half-century. When the Liberal party led by John Rudolf Thorbecke, Holland's "first constitutional prime-minister" under the constitution of 1848, split over a colonial question in 1863-64, political issues only became more hopelessly entangled as party lines became more blurred. Pike perhaps should be excused for not devoting greater attention to Dutch domestic politics.[21]

Yet Pike found a great deal to admire in the Dutch people. Indeed, he found them happily resembling his fellow New Englanders in their thrift and industriousness, cleanliness and independence. The essentially bourgeois-republican spirit which animated the nation gratified Pike, who like most of his countrymen retained a vigorous hatred for monarchy in the abstract. As much as he esteemed the Dutch character and appreciated the national achievements, he confessed that "as a country to live in, I think Holland detestable, and not to be endured." Consequently he escaped to more lively, agreeable locations whenever possible. As Pike later advised his successor at The Hague, he considered that London and Paris were

---

[20] Notebook No. 1, p. 14.

[21] George Edmundson, *History of Holland* (Cambridge, 1922), pp. 411-16. C. J. Hayes, *A Generation of Materialism* (New York, 1941), p. 56, points out that Dutch suffrage extensions made in 1887 and 1896 increased the electorate only from 2 to 14 per cent.

"built mainly to succor Hague Diplomatists."[22]

London, more than anything else in Europe, satisfied and interested Minister Pike. Yet he went abroad with an acute, albeit typical, case of Anglophobia that he never fully overcame. Outspoken dislike for Britain continued throughout most of the nineteenth century in America, and the Civil War only intensified the old issue. Secretary of State Seward himself had earned ill-will in England for indiscreet statements in the 1850's, and British statesmen never overcame their suspicions of his motives. At the outset of the war, when Britain's neutrality policy outraged sentiment in the United States, two of President Lincoln's newly appointed foreign envoys, Cassius Clay and Anson Burlingame, made public addresses in Paris in which they attacked England in challenging tones that the English press and public widely resented. Much of this, of course, was the sheer bumptiousness of a nation on the make, to borrow Professor Thomas A. Bailey's phrase. But in many cases, concrete political and economic reasons underlay the superficial prejudice.[23]

In Pike's case, desire for the annexation of Canada gave substance to the Anglophobia. American lust for Canada in the 1860's survived in many instances as a vestige of the rambunctious expansionism of the 1850's, particularly as the New England expression of Manifest Destiny. Pike and others kept a clear grasp on the realities of the situation throughout the Civil War. Concerning the expiring Canadian reciprocity treaty of 1854, for example, Pike urged Senator Fessenden to consider the political reasons for abrogating the treaty, which Congress soon did. Pike insisted that United States policy ought first to be to sever the provinces from England, and this could be accomplished by high tariff duties on Canadian goods. In

[22] Notebooks No. 2, p. 13; No. 4, pp. 2-3; No. 6, p. 30; No. 9, p. 13. The last item is from Pike to Hugh Ewing, March 12, 1867, No. 24, pp. 19-20.

[23] Thomas A. Bailey, *The Man in the Street: The Impact of American Public Opinion on Foreign Policy* (New York, 1948), pp. 103-6; 212 ff. For Clay and Burlingame, *The* [London] *Times*, June 3, 1861. Bancroft, *Seward*, II, 203, 224-26.

other words, the United States could employ the tariff as a politico-economic weapon to compel Canadian withdrawal from the Empire. Also when the Anglo-American war came, which Pike expected or claimed to expect, New England and especially Maine would be the theater of war if the Canadian provinces still belonged to England.[24] As this letter shows, Pike's enmity towards Britain was no mere social reaction to British class distinctions; rather, he and some of his countrymen kept a clear focus on Canada while they twisted the lion's tail. Nevertheless, Parliament, the Crystal Palace, Carlyle and Dickens, and other facets of British life were immensely gratifying to Pike.

As an experienced Washington political correspondent, Pike took great interest in attending sessions of Parliament. Just as he had scrutinized and characterized Clay, Webster, and other American leaders during the 1840's and 1850's, he now studied Gladstone, Disraeli, John Stuart Mill, John Bright, and their contemporaries in the spring of 1866. Aside from his subtlety and weightiness in debate, Pike noted that Gladstone, who was then Prime Minister, lolled "on his seat like any American." Disraeli as leader of the Conservative opposition maintained an impassive, even icy demeanor when listening but on his feet became "the most lithe & animated of speakers," with lightening-like responses to queries and pungent, witty retorts that brought forth much cheering.[25]

Greatly impressed by the intelligence and experience found in the House of Commons, Pike also discovered that private interests could triumph over impartiality even in that august body. In a debate on the new naval ironclads, for example, Pike, with the aid of an astute young stranger who knew the

---

[24] Pike to Fessenden, June 30, 1864, JSP Papers, and this is but one example of many such statements. Congressman Fred Pike shared these views and championed them in the House. For Canadian-American relations during the Civil War and immediately afterwards, see L. B. Shippee, *Canadian-American Relations, 1849-1874* (New Haven, 1939), chaps. vi, vii; D'Arcy, *Fenian Movement.* Bancroft, *Seward*, II, 470-74, is ambiguous on the matter, as was Seward himself.

[25] Notebook No. 20, pp. 26 ff.

backgrounds of the members, observed that a certain "great railroad contractor" pleaded eloquently for ship construction by private contractors. Another contractor and shipbuilder argued for the adoption of a certain type of turret, but Pike discovered that the member's own firm had filled Admiralty contracts with unsatisfactory ships of that type. Conceding an element of humanitarianism and moderation, he nevertheless concluded that British society and politics reflected the "knock down and drag out school of philosophy."[26]

Lord Palmerston and John Bright were two luminaries of the day who impressed him in a very different manner. Palmerston, stooping slightly at the age of seventy-nine but still Prime Minister when Pike met him in 1863, seemed a bit on the facetious side. Pike observed that despite thin white hair and a heavy gait 'Pam' appeared to be a "jolly old man with a stereotyped laugh, or a laugh by rote." When Pike diplomatically expressed his own desire to see the continuance of Anglo-American peace, Palmerston replied, "Then you are not like *all* your countrymen, Ho, Ho!" John Bright, on the other hand, by personal mildness and simplicity as well as by political sympathy with the North, won his warm admiration. During the war and afterwards, when the struggle between Congress and the President had begun, Bright continued to discuss American affairs with Pike.[27]

Altogether, the British government, as Pike saw it in action in Commons and in the House of Lords as well as through some personal contacts, seemed more impressive than the Congress he had known. Parliamentary decorum and order made the Washington brawling and dueling look all the worse. More important, close observation suggested to Pike that Parliament was composed of talented and experienced individuals

[26] *Ibid.*, pp. 46-51. Pike apparently never saw American politics in such a harsh but clear light.

[27] Notebooks No. 7, pp. 12-14; No. 21, pp. 10-12. On the final occasion in 1866 when Pike visited Bright in the Reform Club, the second reform bill, giving the suffrage to industrial workers, loomed as the chief issue in English politics; but the conversation apparently dealt largely with American affairs.

whose services would have been lost in America by sweeping political rotation which cast aside public officials and turned them "out to grass." Even the French Chambers, he judged, excelled the American Congress in the quality of its members. Leaving "everything to the fortuitous results of populous elections" without any attempt to salvage talent and experience seemed a fundamental American mistake.[28]

Pike thought highly of English Parliamentary life, but he made one friend in London who denied approval not only to Parliament but to almost everything else in the contemporary scene. That was Thomas Carlyle. Pike first saw the great Scottish writer in circumstances which he described in the following manner: "To-night I saw the greatest thing in London. It was Dickens reading Pickwick's Trial to Thomas Carlyle. I thought Carlyle would split, and Dickens was not much better. Carlyle sat on the front bench and he haw-hawed right out over & over again till he fairly exhausted himself. Dickens would read & then he would stop in order to give Carlyle a chance to stop. Of course the whole crowded audience were in the same mood and the uproar was tremendous. I laughed till my jaws ached, and I caught myself involuntarily stamping."[29]

Despite the laughter, and its ghostly contagious quality, the Carlyle of this era suffered from near-exhaustion caused by his labors on *Frederick the Great*. In addition, a deep personal gloom and philosophical bitterness had settled around him. But when Pike boldly requested that he be allowed to call, since at Dickens' reading he had observed "that you are human," Carlyle's wife replied with an invitation to tea in

[28] Notebooks No. 17, pp. 36-39; No. 20, pp. 37-38.
[29] Notebook No. 6, pp. 11-13; April 28, 1863. After an earlier visit to hear the novelist read from his works, Pike wrote a brief but vivid description of Dickens' appearance and dramatic technique. The passages of Pike's notebooks in which he describes his encounters with Dickens, Carlyle, and Tennyson have been published by Professor Harold Davis in the *Atlantic Monthly*, CLXIV (Dec., 1939), 810-19.

virtue of her husband's "humanness." Thus began a relationship which Pike found enriching and enjoyable.[30]

Among the many topics on which Carlyle expounded in Pike's company, ranging from 'modern' architectural monstrosities to the righteousness of Germany's claim to Schleswig-Holstein, the Scot's references to American affairs probably most interested Pike. Carlyle's views on the Civil War and on the related slavery question were indeed such as to compel attention. As early as 1849, in an article on "The Negro Question," with particular reference to the emancipated British West Indian Negroes, Carlyle had lashed out at his "philanthropic friends" whose solicitude for the Negro only pointed up the contrast of their callousness toward the Irish and their utter disregard for the overworked, starved British wage-slave. Just as the Southern proslavery apologists, Carlyle scorned the "benevolent twaddle" about "Black Quashee" and reiterated his belief in "fixed relations" for all classes, black and white.[31]

Granted these views, no one could have expected Carlyle to see the Northern cause in the favorable light of a humanitarian crusade deserving sympathy from the enlightened spirits of the world. Carlyle explained to Pike that the American slavery question seemed to be a dispute as to whether it was "better to employ servants for life or for short periods. . . ." He thought the short-period type of employment was "a miserable system and one going to perdition" since it allowed no satisfactory relations between employer and employed. More

---

[30] Notebook No. 6, pp. 13, 15. Emery Neff, *Carlyle* (New York, 1932), pp. 246 ff. Another American who visited Carlyle at the same time as Pike was Moncure D. Conway, who bore a letter of introduction from Carlyle's close friend, Ralph Waldo Emerson. Conway later published *Thomas Carlyle* (New York, 1881), which was partially based on conversations and observations from this period.

[31] Thomas Carlyle, "Occasional Discourse on the Negro Question," *Fraser's Magazine*, XL (Dec., 1849), 670-79. Neff, *Carlyle*, pp. 225-29, sympathetically interprets this as deliberate exaggeration on Carlyle's part in order to shock contemporaries out of their "fatally mistaken liberalism." While this may be true, the original article also reveals Carlyle's contempt for the Negro race as well as his approval of the institution of slavery, to a certain degree.

succinctly even, Carlyle stated conversationally to another friend that the "South says to the Naygur, God bless you, and be a slave! The North says, God damn you, and be free!"[32]

Pike's notebooks suggest that he did not say a great deal in these conversations with Carlyle. The reason was simple: he had no opportunity. Pike nevertheless made allowances for the great man's "nervous irritability" which seemed to supply most of the driving force to his mental power. There is a touch of humor in his admission that to question Carlyle's argument was "to pull his nose, . . . to dispute his facts is to knock him down." One wonders if Pike's knowledge of Carlyle as disputant had the reinforcement gained from painful experience. Regardless, he wisely perceived that Carlyle, in all his fierce paradoxes, remained a "sort of combination of John Knox and David Hume," at once a "tremendous believer and a tremendous skeptic." Humanity being too great a problem for him, Carlyle's "fullness overflows and inundates rather than gently irrigating the natural fruits of his intellect." And on the third and last visit Pike had with Carlyle, then seventy-one and bereaved by the death of his wife, the old man tenaciously clung to many of his views but he "was not so confident on the general subject of everything going to everlasting smash as he has seemed to be on previous occasions."[33]

That Carlyle made a deep impression on Pike is obvious. Despite the fact that he recognized certain limitations and exaggerations in the explosive Victorian's thought, he continued both to read and to admire much of Carlyle's writings. Nor were Carlyle's racial assumptions incompatible with Pike's own. The American would never have expressed his ideas so coldly and bluntly as did Carlyle; but Pike's own attitude toward the American Negroes bore many traces of Carlyle's description of the Northern war aims with regard to the slaves —"God damn you, and be free!" Years later, after Pike had

---

[32] Notebook No. 15, pp. 18 ff.; Neff, *Carlyle*, p. 249. See also Carlyle's brief "Ilias (Americana) in Nuce," *Macmillan's Magazine*, VIII (Aug., 1863), 301.

[33] Notebooks No. 6, p. 24; No. 23, pp. 2-8, entry for June 3, 1866.

gone to South Carolina and observed the Negro's role in the Reconstruction government there, he sent Carlyle a copy of *The Prostrate State*. Pike though this "unique but melancholy" account might afford Carlyle a half hour's entertainment, for here in *The Prostrate State* " 'Quashee' " could be seen in "his virgin attempt at self government." And appropriately enough, Pike's interpretation of "Sambo," as he personified the Negro legislator and voter, must have gratified Carlyle. Unjust as he was, Pike offered in 1874 what seemed to be confirmation of the Scot's dire prophecies about emancipation and universal suffrage.[34]

In contrast with his fortunate bid for Carlyle's acquaintance, Pike more or less came a cropper when he made an overture to Queen Victoria's Poet Laureate, Alfred, Lord Tennyson. Having embarked on a leisurely tour of southern England in the summer of 1863, Pike happened to hear that Tennyson lived close by and, with characteristic spontaneity, the American "suddenly formed the determination to call on him." He sent his card in by the hack driver, and soon the Pikes, trying to "soften the abrupt features" of their visit, were talking with Mrs. Tennyson. Pike's description of the approaching poet merits quotation: "Mr. Tennyson soon came in, in a coarse short coat & trousers loose & over long, with a look comical from its disconsolateness. He neither looked up nor down nor round about but with a trudging gait marched in silently & walked across the large parlor with the air of a large school boy about to be flogged."

Nobody spoke. Nobody sat. Probably swallowing bravely, Pike spoke first and elicited a solemn, constrained reply from the noble bard. Then the resourceful diplomat hit a lucky note by referring to "the beauty of the situation," that is, the scenery. Tennyson himself now rallied a bit, began to point out views, and launched the Pikes on a tour of the garden and farm yards. The visit soon ended with pleasantries, Tennyson

[34] Pike to Carlyle, April 16, 1874, Notebook No. 31, p. 35.

following his visitors out to their carriage and inquiring about Longfellow. But the brash Americans were not to escape so lightly: Tennyson begged them not to spread the news that they had been admitted without a proper letter of introduction, since it was his standing rule to require one because of the public's intrusiveness. Poor Pike, subdued if not flattened, confessed that the Englishman's manner clearly said, "Now do go, and don't for God's sake send anybody else." Pike regretted the visit, but still he felt that the long-haired and bearded Tennyson, who wore an "inexpressibly sad & anxious expression," had betrayed a streak of that damnable "chronic exclusiveness" which marked the English character. The whole affair ended, as far as the bruised American was concerned, with the proud observation that "few men of distinction are so large as not to show that their reputation is a weight which it troubles them to support."[35]

The only remark with any political bearing which Lord Tennyson had volunteered was an expression of his astonishment at the North's violent expressions against England. Pike apparently had felt too humiliated to argue the point. In contrast to Tennyson's view, however, he heard another opinion during the same trip that pleased him. This was at Osborne, where Queen Victoria hid herself in deep mourning for Prince Albert. The Osborne gatekeeper warmed to the friendly Yankee's overtures about the near-by potato vines and cabbages. The old fellow had been in America about a half century earlier, and in the meantime had served George IV and William IV as well as carried young Victoria in his arms. Having long ago refused an opportunity to become an overseer in the South, the veteran gatekeeper now followed the American war with interest. He thought it unfortunate that the English newspapers were so much opposed to the North, but his private suspicion was that some of the "big folks [in England] had property in the South."[36]

[35] Notebook No. 6, pp. 33-35; entry for May 31, 1863.
[36] Notebook No. 6, p. 39; entry for June 7, 1863.

Regardless of the validity of the gatekeeper's economic interpretation, it is interesting and suggestive to compare his attitude with that which Palmerston, Carlyle, and Tennyson had revealed. Pike kept his balance even in the face of opinions which subtly indicated coolness and hostility towards the United States. He reasoned that he and his countrymen could afford to be "sublimely indifferent" to opinions of contemporary writers and politicians. History would do the United States full justice, while contemporaries in Europe who misjudged the situation or saw only half the picture would merely impair their own future reputations. And in the cases of many of the English *literati* and members of the ruling class this has proved to be a sound prophecy.[37]

In addition to political and literary diversions, Minister Pike thoroughly enjoyed himself in England in a strictly non-diplomatic, tourist sense. There is no need here to follow him as he toured the Crystal Palace, where Victorians marveled at man's splendid new machines and gadgets, or as he wandered through the labyrinthine passages of the Bank of England. English churches offered magnificent variety in architecture and tradition, and Pike visited proud Anglican cathedrals as well as the vast Metropolitan Tabernacle where the Reverend Charles H. Spurgeon roared Baptist fundamentalism to an aroused flock and prayed for Abraham Lincoln. Perhaps Pike's most human indulgence is exemplified by the three or four trips he made to see a certain London magician whose lady assistant disappeared from a large wicker basket. Baffled and annoyed at being deceived, the diplomat returned repeatedly to the spectacle, moving closer to the front each time, only to admit in the end that the wily magician had triumphed over careful scrutiny.[38]

Thus the wandering minister spent his time in London. He had also recommended Paris as the other important refuge

[37] Notebook No. 9, p. 8.
[38] Notebooks Nos. 6, 7, 18-21 contain descriptions of many aspects of English life.

for "Hague Diplomatists." Yet he never fully savored Parisian or French life, except in a superficial sense. There were several reasons for this, including no doubt the language, but one strong factor was that Pike bore a deep aversion to Emperor Napoleon III, an aversion which the Mexican venture only intensified. Republican animus against Bonaparte's imperial trappings inspired him to describe Napoleon's early Mexican moves as part of the side show which the "royal Barnum" felt compelled to present to his public in general and especially to his Catholic subjects.[39]

As the Emperor's Mexican plans began to materialize in 1863, Pike felt an increasing dislike for the whole French Imperial regime, and he peppered his despatches to Seward with protests and advice concerning the Mexican affair. Pike judged that the Emperor had no real intention of recognizing the Confederacy, especially so long as he found it expedient to act in accord with Britain. His flirtations with the South, Pike believed, looked toward averting or qualifying "a contingent Southern hostility" to the French future in Mexico rather than to any serious purpose to act precipitately. Still, Seward might possibly find it advantageous somehow to add to Spain's troubles in Santo Domingo, where native revolts caused the Spanish endless headaches in their attempt to regain the island. European rulers needed constant reminding, according to Pike, that they could not meddle in New World affairs with impunity.[40]

Pike allowed his own wrath at the Emperor's and the Archduke Maximilian's ambitions to provoke him into immod-

---

[39] Pike to Seward, No. 42, March 19, 1862, DoS Papers. Although this pungent description of the Emperor was tactfully omitted from the published *Foreign Papers*, other candid but perceptive observations from Pike slipped into print (*Foreign Papers, 1862*, Pt. 2, p. 609). Seward's critics seized on this as another example of the State Department's careless indiscretion. See [William B. Reed], *The Diplomatic Year: Being a Review of Mr. Seward's Foreign Correspondence of 1862* (Philadelphia, 1863), pp. 22-23.

[40] Pike to Seward, No. 96, Aug. 5, 1863; No. 105, Oct. 14, 1863, DoS Papers. For the Santo Domingo and Mexican moves of Spain and France, see Dexter Perkins, *The Monroe Doctrine, 1826-1867* (Baltimore, 1933), pp. 280-317; 357 ff.

eration, which Seward fortunately never did until after the war when he could afford to talk strongly. Pike personally thought that Napoleon, "the biggest of asses who . . . ever wielded supreme power," meant to challenge republicanism in America. This suggested to Pike that the United States should turn the tables and propagandize in Europe, particularly in Venetia and Hungary, where Austrian power still reigned despite the protests of native Italian and Magyar nationalists. He advised Senator Fessenden that the position of the United States with regard to the Mexican matter appeared pusillanimous from Europe, where even many Continental journals displayed more "manliness" than did the press of the North. He urged the influential senator to see that Congress took some prompt action, "though of course with prudence."[41] Unfortunately, Pike never gave Seward adequate credit for the patient fashion in which he handled the French intrusion into Mexico. Resisting the dangerous temptation of catering to public and Congressional opinion until after the war, Seward made his Mexican diplomacy one of the more creditable aspects of his career.[42]

In addition to France's uncongenial type of government and provocative foreign policy, Catholicism made the Downeaster distinctly uncomfortable. Not that Pike had run with the Know Nothings in the 1850's or that he entertained strong prejudices with regard to religion. He seems, in fact, to have tended toward mild skepticism or, at most, an undefined deism. But intellectually and psychologically he found it impossible to sympathize with the Roman church. His strong rationalistic tendencies made him suspicious of all Catholic miracles, which he considered as mere superstitions. He explained the flourishing state of Catholicism on the ground that the world loves "humbug." Despite his own relative cosmopolitanism,

---

[41] Notebooks No. 8, pp. 12, 22, 30; No. 9, pp. 23-24. Pike to Fessenden, Sept. 3, 1863, JSP Papers.
[42] Perkins, *Monroe Doctrine*, p. 531. Bancroft, *Seward*, pp. 419 ff., but with caution.

Pike thought it extremely odd to see European Catholics enjoying Sunday in typical holiday fashion, with sidewalk cafés serving the same gay crowds that came out from the cathedrals. Such frivolities could only inspire the American, whose Puritan ancestors were not after all very far removed, to remark piously: "We in New England use Sundays as the stepping stones to Heaven."[43]

The Pikes spent less time in Germany than in either France or England, but in the Rhineland they felt satisfaction that the newspapers favored the United States more than did the French or English press. Pike found the city of Frankfort alive with heated discussion of the German nationality question. He thought the presence of both Austrian and Prussian soldiers somewhat belied Frankfort's position as a Free City, but regardless, the atmosphere of excited rallies and patriotic debates seemed to indicate a healthy freedom. Pike also sensed the more fundamental stresses of Germany and Europe on the eve of Bismarck's wars. He described Europe in a despatch to Seward as a "pent volcano, with only here and there a standing ground not torn with threatening fissures." Pike insisted that the insecurity and dangers in European politics were preeminently present in the 1860's. Subsequent events proved that he correctly summarized the situation.[44]

Even with the tense atmosphere and varied scene, however, Europe's charms began to wear thin for the Downeaster. Travel allowed temporary escape from dull routine and stuffy officialdom at The Hague, but even touring could produce its own type of ennui. Pike's earliest declarations of homesickness, in letters to Fessenden and to Dana, may perhaps be discounted as sentimental indulgence; but by 1864 and 1865 he quite clearly had the return trip on his mind. The diplomat, who found his tasks too limited and infrequent and his appetite for new sights and experiences becoming surfeited,

[43] Notebooks No. 8, pp. 19, 35; No. 14, p. 22; No. 15, p. 48.

[44] Notebook No. 4, pp. 28-29. Pike to Seward, No. 43, March 16, 1862, *Foreign Papers 1862*, Pt. 2, p. 600.

now reflected: "I guess the most useful & most agreeable thing I ever did was to catch smelts off the wharf on a pleasant spring flood tide." Maine's charms became increasingly attractive to one who felt himself practically an expatriate.[45]

Too, Minister Pike was not exactly a free agent, and Secretary Seward found it necessary to remind not only him but the entire diplomatic corps of this fact. State Department regulations required that diplomatic and consular officials take no extended leaves of absence unless satisfactory reasons of a public nature were offered. Seward circularized a warning about these instructions in the fall of 1863; but in February, 1864, he found it necessary to emphasize the regulation by advising offenders that they "must expect to incur the serious displeasure of the President."[46]

Pike at first adopted a rather cavalier attitude toward the regulation concerning leaves of absence. George P. Marsh in Turin wrote that he detested the leave rule. Marsh thought American ministers in the [Democratic] past were admittedly "too peripatetic," but now under the new dispensation they should at least be allowed more freedom within their respective countries. Pike agreed with Marsh that "vagabonds would abuse" the opportunity of leaving their posts, and the existing regulations were well suited to the "precious administration" of President Pierce. For his part, Pike explained to Marsh that he went as much as he liked, although without getting too far from the capital. "I do not make it a point to stand here idle when I want to do something elsewhere,"

---

[45] Notebooks No. 14, p. 4; No. 16, p. 57; No. 18, p. 45. Pike wrote during these years many recollections of early Maine and Calais in particular which convey much flavor and color and have proved of value to local and regional historians. Davis, *International Community*, is the best example.

[46] Seward Circular, No. 46, Feb. 6, 1864, DoS Papers. Another circular, No. 25, Oct. 1, 1862, prohibited diplomatic and consular officers from making public addresses except on those "festal occasions" where innocuous remarks might be offered; even then Seward urged the utmost caution with regard to political matters. Pike was not guilty of any breach related to this, although Seward was having some trouble with other overzealous democrats who tended to forget the delicacy of their positions. Theodore Canisius, the German printer and friend of Lincoln, for example, stirred up trouble in the Vienna consulate (Monaghan, *Diplomat*, p. 256).

Pike confessed. He endeavored first to attend to "the weightier matters of the law" and recommended that Marsh do the same thing and then "go when you like and where you like."[47]

After Seward's warning circulars, however, Pike became more careful about his absences from The Hague. Mrs. Pike's poor health necessitated trips to various places, like the Riviera or Scotland, where a noted specialist treated her. But the diplomat now cautiously requested leave from Seward before embarking. Although in each case the Secretary of State granted the private requests,[48] there is evidence that Seward felt annoyed with the minister to the Netherlands, perhaps because of his proclivity for travel. In mid-1864 Seward had a small mission for Pike to fulfil, and the Secretary of State advised him that the "time seems to have come at last for you to go upon active service." Then when the assignment, which dealt with supposed Confederate ships at Amsterdam, proved unnecessary, Seward congratulated him on escaping "from the responsibility" in the matter.[49] Whether Pike smarted under the veiled insinuation is not known, but he had no reason to expect much more from his old political enemy in the Department of State. Looming larger and larger in Pike's own mind was the question as to how much longer he should remain abroad.

After Lincoln's death in April, 1865, a shudder of insecurity ran through the diplomatic corps. Would President Johnson prefer to fill some of the choice posts, traditionally regarded as among the ripest patronage plums, with men of his own naming? From Lisbon, James E. Harvey reported hearing that Washington expected a "general change," especially

[47] Marsh to Pike, April 30, 1862, Pike MSS. Pike to Marsh, June 9, 1862, Marsh collection, University of Vermont; courtesy of Mr. David Lowenthal.

[48] Pike to Seward, Aug. 10, 1864, Aug. 23, 1865, and replies, in DoS Papers.

[49] Seward to Pike, No. 163, June 27, 1864; No. 168, July 26, 1864, *Foreign Papers 1864*, Pt. 3, p. 321. Later in the same year Pike performed other duties in connection with Federal naval forces in European waters; see *ibid.*, pp. 321-23; also Seward to Pike, No. 188, Oct. 17, 1864; Pike to Seward, No. 12, Aug. 14, 1861, DoS Papers. Early in the war Pike communicated with Senator I. W. Grimes of Iowa, who was a member of the Naval Affairs Committee, concerning British ironclads (Pike MSS).

as the time for the convening of Congress drew nearer and the clamor for political spoils became intensified. "I have made up my mind to pack my carpet bag," Harvey admitted, "and be ready when the bell rings for the train to be off, so as not to be caught napping, and I advise all other probable travelers to be in a similar state of readiness."[50]

Harvey's estimate of the situation proved sound. Somebody in Washington was shaking the political tree. Norman B. Judd and George G. Fogg, ministers to Prussia and Switzerland respectively, were apparently the first to fall. Seward intimated that Fogg could "confer a favor" on President Johnson by resigning. And Judd in Berlin also had received a similar invitation. Fogg assured his friend Mrs. Pike that the prospect of going home held its own attractions. But still, he did think it odd that he and Judd had been singled out for recalling. To Fogg it looked as though "*somebody* was avenging the wrongs which *somebody* suffered at the hands of the Chicago Convention," especially since he and Judd were "supposed to have 'brewed the malt' that worked out the nomination of Abraham Lincoln." At any rate, there were now two down and dozens to go.[51]

Nor had Pike been forgotten in the reshuffle. His little private note from Seward soon arrived, and the Secretary of State informed him that friends of "other parties" were making urgent requests to President Johnson to appoint a successor to Pike at The Hague. Seward assured Pike that thus far the petitioners had received no consideration, because "as perhaps you are aware, you were appointed to that mission upon my recommendation of you to the late President Lincoln." Never-

---

[50] Harvey to Pike, July 17, 1865, Pike MSS.

[51] Fogg to Mrs. Pike, June 22, 1865, Pike MSS. For the roles Fogg and Judd played in the nomination of Lincoln, see Reinhard H. Luthin, *The First Lincoln Campaign* (Cambridge, Mass., 1944), pp. 139, 171; for both men's parts in the unending cabinet-juggling that went on in the winter of 1860-61, see William E. Baringer, *A House Dividing: Lincoln as President Elect* (Springfield, Illinois, 1945), *passim*. Both tended to be anti-Seward in that furious intraparty battle, but whether that fact actually influenced their recall is not known.

theless, rumors had reached the State Department that Congressman Fred Pike had spoken of his brother's desire to leave Holland. The Department should merely like to be correctly informed.[52]

Seward's note, while kindly put, could also be interpreted as a clear indication that if Pike wanted out, nobody desired to stop him. And it is true that Pike had repeatedly stated to his brother, as well as to Fessenden and others, that his diplomatic life had become stale. Harvey in Lisbon had thought it wonderful "how quick they hear the first whisper of a returning intention, but not more perhaps than how prompt they are to suggest such a possibility. . . ." Harvey believed these "gentle admonitions" would not find everybody "as well prepared and disposed as the Minister at the Hague."[53]

Harvey overestimated Pike's equanimity. He had no intention of being rushed when Seward informed him that "other parties" were clamoring for The Hague post. In fact, Pike promptly advised the Secretary of State that, while he had often expressed his weariness in being abroad, he had never specifically mentioned resigning. Only now, in mid-1865, could he settle upon a definite time for resigning which would not involve a personal loss, and that time would be the summer of the following year.[54]

Presumably he referred to financial reasons for remaining another year, and Seward left the situation at that. Finally in the spring of 1866 Pike submitted his formal resignation to take effect on June 1. Some slight confusion arose in the matter of Pike's successor at The Hague, since General Daniel E. Sickles, then military governor of the Department of South Carolina, declined the ministry when it was offered to him. Pike merely obtained leave of absence from the State Department so that he could sail in early June as planned.[55]

[52] Seward to Pike, June 15, 1865, DoS Papers.
[53] Harvey to Pike, Aug. 10, 1865, Pike MSS.
[54] Pike to Seward, July 5, 1865, DoS Papers. The fact that Mrs. Pike was receiving European medical treatment may have partially influenced this decision.
[55] Pike to Seward, March 10, April 11, 18, 27, May 29, 1866, DoS Papers. The

Pike began to assess the value of his years abroad by summarizing his views on the key American diplomats of the Civil War era. Henry S. Sanford in Belgium earned top place on Pike's list of transplanted Americans who aped European aristocracy and forgot their republican origin. Sanford also had the great misfortune, in Pike's eyes, of being one of Seward's "clerks" and would have been "a good McClellan man if that notability . . . had been elected President [in 1864]." Nothing worse could be said of Sanford.

William L. Dayton, minister to France until his death late in 1864, fared better with Pike than did Sanford. Pike believed that Dayton's cautious judgment and considerate actions well suited the necessities of the situation under Napoleon III's sometimes erratic control. John Bigelow, on the other hand, who had succeeded Dayton, spoke "broken French" and aside from that had few qualifications other than a groveling subserviency to the Secretary of State.

Harvey at Lisbon had acquitted himself with great credit, showing promptitude and resoluteness when the need arose, while Charles Francis Adams had "never failed to be equal to his position." Adams, "made by nature for a statesman & improved by education," possessed firmness and moderation at the same time, and his views were both comprehensive and sound. Both John Motley in Vienna and George P. Marsh in Turin allowed their scholarly predilections to blind them to realities. Marsh had "a whole pocket full of languages at command but they would all fail to give him sound judgment in a difficult crisis." Thus Pike rated his colleagues, some generously and others perhaps unfairly, after five years of relatively close observation.[56]

United States consul at Amsterdam, Albert Rhodes, served as chargé at The Hague until December, 1866, when Major General Hugh E. Ewing arrived to fill the post.

[56] All set forth in a long, "private & confidential" letter of Sept. 20, 1865, to Dana, now editor of the Chicago *Republican*; Notebook No. 18, pp. 58-62. Pike's intense dislike of Sanford, who in the 1850's helped stir up much of the silly furor over the Dress Circular, is a tiresome story that may be traced through many of the notebooks and letters. Unfortunately, Pike's personal feelings seemed to have influenced his oppo-

Looking back on his own experience, Pike concluded that having had America and then Europe, in "alternate doses," had been both pleasant and rewarding. The "long reach of history backward" of many particular parts of the Continent had unfolded an existence, a way of life, which Americans generally overlooked in surveying the Old World from a distance. The New Englander claimed that he returned to America "with my accumulations gathered here, strapped to my back rather than incorporated into my life." But he oversimplified. Without Europe, how would he have concluded that Americans were not only "newspaper educated" but were also the example *par excellence* of a "nation of blowers." Only foreign residence could have given him comprehension of the "magnificence of this national failing." But whether his new insight and understanding could withstand the fierce partisanship of Reconstruction is another story.[57]

Taking his farewell of Queen Sophie, Pike found the sprightly monarch alarmed at the prospect of having the notorious General Sickles and his scandal-spattered wife as the next representatives from America. In vain, she plied for information concerning the pair. The Queen's "shameful & inexcusable" gossip left Pike uncomfortable, but the King sent him off with nobler memories. King William III, on the morning Pike bade him good-bye, had Bismarck and the threatening Austro-Prussian war largely on his mind. When Pike stated that he had not had the pleasure of meeting the famed Prussian statesman, the King "congratulated" him on having missed the dubious honor. But as for America, the King spoke warmly of the genuine amity between the Netherlands and the United States and said other kind things which cheered the departing diplomat. He left thinking, in a veritable glow of interna-

---

sition to a treaty with Belgium concerning the Scheldt River dues which Sanford negotiated. See Miller, *Treaties*, VIII, 939-47; and for Sanford the sketch by M. B. Griffen in the *Dictionary of American Biography*, XVI, 348-49.

[57] Notebooks No. 15, pp. 43-44; No. 19, p. 56; No. 12, p. 20.

tional good will, "in five years more the King & I would be excellent friends."[58]

Official duties now ended, the Pikes left for Liverpool via Paris and London. After last-minute shopping and the purchase of a feather bed for Lizzie's comfort on the voyage, they boarded a steamer in the drizzling rain on June 9, 1866. The voyage was tedious and uncomfortable, with fog sticking "closer than a brother," but finally on June 21 Boston came in sight. In a matter of hours, Pike was surveying the sprawling bustle of postwar New York and finding democracy a bit difficult to take. The muddy streets annoyed him, and his nostrils were "saluted by a stink." Even the "free & enlightened" population of New York appalled him, for he noted that those "who are not German are Irish, those who are not Irish are Chinese, & those who are not Chinese are nigger."[59] This was home again.

[58] Notebook No. 22, pp. 21-23; entry for May 18, 1866. For an account of Sickles, who became minister to Spain as well as one of Queen Isabella's numerous lovers, see Edgcumb Pinchon, *Dan Sickles: Hero of Gettysburg and "Yankee King of Spain"* (New York, 1945).

[59] Notebook No. 23, pp. 11 ff.

VII. *Reconstruction:*

From Radical to Liberal Republican

P IKE RETURNED to the American political arena at a time
when fateful divisions were destroying the Union party
coalition which had won the war. After Lincoln's assassination,
Dana had written him in May, 1865, that Andrew Johnson's
accession to the Presidency removed the probability of "any
serious division" in the Republican ranks. Dana even believed
that Johnson's administration would be an improvement in
that the new President was surrounded by fewer persons "who
wish to get rich out of contracts or privileges of various kinds
conferred by the government." To complete this optimistic
analysis, he added that the "thoroughness of the subjugation"
in the defeated South was "wonderful." After a trip into
Virginia, the newspaperman, who was soon to become famous as
the editor of the New York *Sun,* declared that "no people were
ever so entirely conquered, and what is true of Virginia is true
of the whole South."[1]

Dana's belief in the fundamental unity of the Republican
party and its harmony with the chief executive soon proved
totally erroneous. When Congress convened in December,
1865, the Radicals, led mainly by Thaddeus Stevens, Charles
Sumner, and Benjamin Wade, challenged the Lincoln-Johnson
approach to reconstruction, that is, the prompt readmission of
the reorganized Southern states in accordance with the Constitutional theory of an indestructible Union. The Radicals
blocked the seating of the new congressmen from the South,

[1] Dana to Pike, May 10, 1865, Pike MSS.

and launched a violent struggle with the President that culminated in the impeachment proceedings of 1868. President
Johnson escaped the complete humiliation prepared for him by
the Radicals, but he lost the even larger fight over Reconstruction.[2]

Pike's preferences in this struggle were largely with the
Radicals. The actual reasons for his support of "Radical Reconstruction" seem at variance with the reasons which he
advanced at the time. The former diplomat's position on the
crucial question of universal suffrage for the freedmen, that
is Negro voting, makes this clear and throws much light on
his initial attitude toward Reconstruction. Indeed, he might
be taken as typical of those Republicans, certainly not all, who
were willing to fight for a program of Negro voting in the
South both for the political gains which might thereby accrue to
the Republican party and for the preservation of the economic
gains of the business class which that party had come to represent. In the long run this program, which the Republicans
virtually renounced in the compromise of 1876-77, may have
delayed the Negro's opportunity for a more meaningful role
in American democratic life. It also played a vital part in the
continuation of bitter sectionalism and the concomitant political
bankruptcy of the nation which lasted for years after Appo-
mattox.

Long before Negro suffrage had become an open issue in
Washington, Pike had come to believe that the freed slaves
must be given the vote. As early as April, 1865, the diplomat,
exultant over the final Federal triumphs, wrote Dana that the
North would have to "resort to that very rough implement,
negro suffrage." He remembered that Georgia's Robert
Toombs had commented that revolutions went to the bottom
of things. "When one of his niggers is elected Governor of

---

[2] The most comprehensive account of Johnson's Presidency is George F. Milton,
The Age of Hate: Andrew Johnson and the Radicals (New York, 1930), but Howard
K. Beale, *The Critical Year: A Study of Andrew Johnson and Reconstruction* (New
York, 1930), is particularly good for the politico-economic story.

Georgia, chosen by his fellow slaves," Pike prophesied, "I suppose he will be impressed still more deeply with the appositeness of the reflection."[3]   A portion of the bitter wit in this passage must be credited to understandable elation over the hard-won Northern victory.   But the references to Negro suffrage were not intended for irony, as Pike's correspondence with Chief Justice Chase proves.

Their long-standing friendship had been strained by disagreement over financial policy, but the two veteran antislavery champions now enjoyed a *rapprochement* which centered on the suffrage issue.   The Chief Justice stepped out in favor of unrestricted Negro suffrage in the various Southern states even before the Radical leaders in Congress. Only a few days before the President's assassination, Chase wrote to Lincoln stressing his belief that the "easiest and safest way" to effect reconstruction lay in enrolling "the loyal citizens without regard to complexion," and encouraging them in reorganizing state governments under constitutions securing universal male suffrage.   Lincoln failed to endorse this program in his last speech of April 11.   The Chief Justice immediately called attention to the omission and explained that once he should have been at least partially satisfied with "suffrage for the intelligent [Negroes] and for those who have been soldiers; now I am convinced that universal suffrage is demanded by sound policy and impartial justice."[4]

After Lincoln's death the Chief Justice continued to urge the adoption of his voting scheme.   In May and June, 1865, he visited principal Southern cities to observe conditions among both Negroes and whites.   He informed Pike that the conspic-

---

[3] Pike to Dana, April 19, 1865, Notebook No. 17, p. 53.

[4] Chase to Lincoln, April 11 and April 12, 1865, privately printed copy in Pike MSS; also in J. W. Shuckers, *The Life and Public Services of Salmon Portland Chase* (New York, 1874), pp. 515-17. Lincoln's preference, but not insistence, that the vote be "conferred on the very intelligent [Negroes], and on those who serve our cause as soldiers," was included in his last speech of April 11, when he addressed a celebrating crowd on the White House lawn (Sandburg, *Lincoln*, IV, 219 ff.). This was three days prior to the assassination.

uous features among the freedmen were their "eagerness for education, especially of the children; anxiety to own land; and desire for support" in their new status as freedmen. In New Orleans the Chief Justice had advised a committee of colored men that native freedmen were citizens of the United States and "consequently entitled to the rights of citizens. . . ."[5] The Chief Justice realized that the legal basis for this claim needed Constitutional shoring, but that was precisely one of the functions of the Fourteenth Amendment, which Chase approved.[6]

An early biographer of Chief Justice Chase, J. W. Shuckers, candidly explains that universal suffrage for the freedmen "was a necessity which the Republican party could not escape." If the Negroes should not vote and support the Republicans, that party "must die." Albert B. Hart, writing a life of the Chief Justice twenty-five years later, points to the continuous interest in the Negro's welfare which Chase had felt during the war. And, at the same time that he admits Chase's ever-present Presidential ambition, which revived toward 1868, Hart interprets his advocacy of Negro suffrage in the South, at a time when the doctrine was unpopular in the North, as a logical extension of his earlier liberalism and humanitarianism concerning the Negroes.[7] Regardless of Chase's motivation in this crucial question about which Reconstruction politics revolved, there is evidence which suggests that his friend Pike's conversion to the Radical program lacked sincerity and honesty as well as vision.

The starting point for Pike's ideas on postwar problems was his belief, widely held throughout the triumphant North,

[5] Chase to Pike, July 8, 1865, with enclosure of letter from Chase to committee of colored men, New Orleans, June 6, 1865, Pike MSS.

[6] Aside from the citizenship aspect in which Chase was primarily concerned, Congress added sections which included its own Civil Rights Act of 1866, which had been repassed over President Johnson's veto (Hart, *Chase*, pp. 340-41); W. E. B. DuBois, *Black Reconstruction* (New York, 1935), pp. 286 ff., explains the complicated situation concerning the amendment.

[7] Shuckers, *Chase*, p. 546; Hart, *Chase*, pp. 335 ff.

that "the great labor of our day and generation has been gloriously accomplished." For him, the victory meant that "the broad untainted territories" had been saved from slavery. The great "unwieldly carcase of slavery" might still remain and be offensive in its "process of putrefaction," but in due time the remains should be gotten underground. In other words, the major battle had been won and the remainder of the task could be wished away with a few vague references to carcasses and burying, while everybody relaxed after the ordeal. This notion actually meant that the wartime sense of urgency and dedication might be dispensed with in the task of reuniting the disrupted nation.[8]

Despite this shortsighted reaction to victory, Pike forced himself to consider the merits and potentialities of Negro suffrage. He began his reasoning with the premise that the freedman "is ignorant, debased, & totally unfit to exercise the duties of citizenship, as any man can be—as any Irishman fresh from Donnybrook." But the Negro had been given his freedom in communities which regarded him as fit only for bondage, and without protection the freedman would be oppressed and wronged at every step. There were two ways of protecting him in this situation: by Federal bayonets or by giving him the vote. The military approach not only would cost excessively but would be embarrassing and provocative of violence and increasing complaints. That left the other alternative of Negro suffrage. The program should be experimental, however, in order to ascertain if the two Southern races could live together in a state of political equality. Nothing would test this question so thoroughly as universal suffrage, for "if they cannot or will not vote together, they will vote apart." In other words, white and black would live and vote together in peace or quiet; or else they would live and vote apart still in harmonious circumstances. It was that simple. The vote

[8] Notebook No. 18, p. 18; Pike to Chase, Aug. 8, 1865, Notebook No. 18, pp. 36-37.

would act as the magic catalytic agent in the complex Southern social mixture.[9]

This question worried Pike, who was yet abroad at the time. A few pages beyond the above section in his notebook he returned to the problem, and once again somewhat tortuously reasoned around the matter. In a manner that was to be characteristic of his postwar writing and thinking, he denied the validity of the freedman's "actual or supposed right" to the suffrage. That was an abstraction, and (in contrast to the 1850's) the abstract should be scrupulously avoided. Of course the government had no right to deny "first principles." But when it came to applying them to the ex-slaves "enlightened expediency" must be the standard. Whatever the Federal government did must be experimental only, and since Negro suffrage was "more radical than anything else, and goes deeper & wider into the whole ground of discussion on the subject," it deserved to be tested. After all, the freedmen had "the virtue of loyalty" and their votes would protect them and defeat "the efforts of treason both now & hereafter." They might not at first understand the use of the new weapon; but that could be learned.[10]

The holes in his logic need scant exposition, for the premise about Negro ignorance and debasement undermined a good portion of the whole structure. Although he recognized the need for education in the future, how were the contemporary Negro citizens to "protect" themselves with a vote if they were to be regarded as lacking intelligence and character? Or for that matter, how could Pike, who had earlier talked about "sloughing off the mass of barbarism" and cramming all the blacks into a "negro pen," now honestly concern himself about the freedman's well being? Had Federal victory produced

[9] *Ibid.* pp. 46-50. This argument, which is much longer in the original, apparently was included in Pike's letter of Aug. 8, 1865, to Chase.

[10] Notebook No. 18, 52-54. Distressed by the widespread English sympathy for President Johnson, Pike defended the Congressional plan in an article in the London *Daily News*. See Pike to Fessenden, March 15, 1866. JSP Papers.

in him a new concern for the Southern Negro's safety and political fulfilment? The harmonious voting together or voting apart which he envisaged appears to be little more than the most superficial of wishful thinking. Perhaps the key, after all, lies in the meaning attached to the words "loyalty" and "treason." Like many of his Republican contemporaries, the Downeaster recognized only one trustworthy, "loyal" political organization.

Congressman Fred Pike put the whole matter in a clearer, more candid fashion when he confessed in the fall of 1865 that the "rebels" had to be kept out of the Federal government. The congressman explained that the Southerners had to be held off until "we can get our debts saddled off on the General Government." His hope, which proved futile, was for the United States government to pay the loyal states so much per man mustered into military service ("say 150$"). That would mean that Maine could receive about nine million dollars, "enough to discharge the State debt & the most of the town debts." While the Federal taxation could be borne "pretty well," the local taxes, which were largely on property and which had been increased during the war, were nothing but a "nuisance."[11]

Fred Pike's interest in keeping the Southerners out of Congress might be compared with Senator Charles Sumner's concern on that score. Secretary of Treasury Hugh McCulloch appealed to Sumner not to make a political issue of the national debt by threatening that the returning Southerners would or could repudiate the war obligations of the United States government. Although Northern Democrats hastily supported a resolution affirming "the sacredness and inviolability" of the public debt as soon as Congress convened, Sumner had already used the threat of repudiation in his political speeches and arguments against President Johnson. Sumner

[11] Fred Pike to Pike, Nov. 12, 1865, Pike MSS. For Northern state and local taxation during the war and after, see William J. Shultz, *Financial Development of the United States* (New York, 1937), pp. 310, 341-43.

also expressed deep concern over the welfare and treatment of the freedmen.[12]

Concerning the Negro issue itself, Congressman Fred Pike was less aroused than the Massachusetts senator. In the fall of 1865 he confessed that it was difficult to keep the Negro out of politics or to determine "what sort of a hoist he will give parties this time." The Connecticut elections, where Negro suffrage had been rejected by a considerable majority, damaged "us radicals." If the North itself would not tolerate Negro suffrage "it will be hard to make it a shibboleth of admission of the Southern States." But the case was not hopeless, the congressman insisted, since the Southerners "as a whole are behaving badly & that helps us." Aside from "rebels," the congressman also thought poorly of the Irish, who repeatedly voted Democratic. The Radicals would have to fight both of these low elements if the Southerners were readmitted, so "now that we have the rebels at a disadvantage I am inclined to hold them as long as possible."[13]

Enough has been said to indicate the general political orientation of Minister Pike when he returned from Europe in the summer of 1866. Like his brother, he followed along with the Radicals in denouncing Andrew Johnson and the Southern state governments which vainly sought readmission into the Union in 1865-66. This was also the general editorial policy of the *Tribune* in this period, and Pike gradually returned to his former position as a Washington correspondent for Greeley's paper. One of his first concerns in the summer of 1866 and the following winter, during the Congresssional session, was to re-establish old contacts and to feel out the political

---

[12] James F. Rhodes, *History of the United States from the Compromise of 1850* . . . (New York, 1904) V, 549-50; Moorfield Storey, *Charles Sumner* (Boston, 1900), pp. 302 ff. One section of the Fourteenth Amendment also dealt with this inviolable debt, declaring null and void all Confederate debts.

[13] Fred Pike to Mrs. Pike, Oct. 15, 1865, Pike MSS. Politics aside, Fred Pike rejoiced in the "jubilee of wealth." Not only were handsome "turn outs" and pretentious residences becoming plentiful, but even "the monuments in the grave yards are larger & more numerous."

situation. He visited Seward, whom the Radicals still attacked as during the war, and argued with the Secretary of State about the propriety of readmitting the reconstructed Southern states. Seward held that Negro suffrage might "be very proper 100 years hence," but he was opposed to it as a practical measure for the present. Pike, on the other hand, dodged this view by insisting that any truly "practical" approach necessitated the reduction of "rebel" political power. And he included, as part of his justification of Radical methods, his current interpretation of the Constitution as an instrument which should be changed in accordance with the "growth & development" that had occurred in the country during the war.[14]

Seward and Pike continued to differ on fundamental issues just as they had in 1860-61 and throughout the war, the Secretary of State standing loyally beside the Lincoln-Johnson policy while Pike chose the path marked out by the Radical leaders in Congress. Actually, politics interested the former diplomat less than did certain economic issues, such as the finances. But he occasionally sent political letters to the *Tribune*. During the impeachment crisis of 1868, for example, he joined in the clamor for Johnson's removal, admitting initially that the nomination of the Tennessean as Vice-President in 1864 had been "one of those unhappy freaks of a popular assembly sometimes committed under an impulse at once groundless and evanescent." The notion that the President could not be impeached except for an "indictable offense" appeared to be "wholly untenable." The President could and should be removed from office simply because he was "justly amenable to charges of high misdemeanor throughout the whole course of his career. . . ."[15] In other words, the impeachment should candidly be placed on political grounds and the President elimi-

---

[14] Notebook No. 23, pp. 14 ff.; entry for July 1, 1866. On another occasion, early in 1867, Pike and several Republican veterans enjoyed "whiskey punches & cards" at Seward's home; unfortunately the penciled account is illegible (Notebook No. 24, pp. 8 ff.). For Seward, see Bancroft, *Seward*, II, 443 ff.

[15] *Tribune*, March 2, 1868.

nated as an obstacle to the Radical Republican policies. This was nothing more than the *Tribune* proclaimed editorially throughout the first half of 1868, but Pike's statement was clear and forceful, perhaps embarrassingly clear. William M. Evarts, a chief member of the President's defense counsel, cited Pike's article in his impressive summation as an excellent statement of the political charges against the hated President, a statement which openly dismissed the technical, formal allegations of crime as paltry, untenable grounds. Unfortunately, from the Radicals' point of view, the whole impeachment structure had to rest on "technical and formal crimes."[16]

The failure of the Radicals to oust the President came as no bitter disappointment to Pike. Even before the trial ended he published in Greeley's journal a weak, ambiguous defense of those independent senators who refused to allow partisanship to control their every utterance. Senator Fessenden, who ultimately bolted the Radical camp to cast one of the seven decisive votes which saved Johnson, must have been in Pike's mind and probably helped him see the Stevens-Sumner-Wade technique in a less favorable light.[17] He had written the Maine senator during the trial that whoever could not "go for hanging Andy on suspicion will be held as hostages for his future good behavior & for future political successes." But when Radicals in Congress and in the press, including the *Tribune,* bitterly attacked Fessenden and the other party 'apostates,' Pike sided with his friend from Maine. In fact, he either changed his mind about the whole impeachment procedure or else had concealed his real views during the trial, for there is an undated memorandum in his personal papers which con-

[16] *Tribune,* Jan.-May, 1868; for Evart's speech, *Tribune,* April 30, 1868. Congressman Pike shared his brother's views and, because of them, received a stern scolding from Gideon Welles, who continued to serve as Navy Secretary under Johnson. See Welles, *Diary,* III, 360-61.

[17] *Tribune,* April 27, 1868; this initialed article is datelined April 6. Except for Wade, Pike had long had little personal respect for the Radical leaders themselves; Stevens had been instrumental in the legal-tender "folly," and Sumner he considered a learned, dogmatic "sluice."

demns the move. The reasons there given are simply that the action was politically inexpedient, would be a step toward "Mexicanizing our institutions," and was unnecessary since the Radicals had a two-thirds majority in Congress and could do pretty much as they pleased regardless of the "isolated, powerless" President.[18]

Pike's ultimate coolness toward the impeachment program of the Radicals also indicated his relative detachment from Republican party affairs, which in this era centered increasingly on personalities. In the years after his return from Europe, the American political scene, in his eyes, became increasingly empty of vital content. In 1868, for example, he felt only mildly hopeful about Grant as the Republican nominee. The Presidential election year had brought the usual revival of the Chase candidacy, which Greeley and the *Tribune* pushed until the Grant boom became embarrassingly widespread.[19] Pike also preferred the Chief Justice for the Republican candidate, but he took no great part in the maneuvering that went on throughout the first half of 1868. When Grant won the race against Horatio Seymour, the Democratic nominee, in a strange campaign in which neither the candidates nor the electorate knew what issues were involved, Pike seems to have been satisfied with the great Union general, who was a magnificently unknown quantity in political life. Chase had sought the Democratic nomination after Grant's availability became irresistible to the Republicans, but the Chief Justice confessed to Pike during the campaign that neither party suited him, that he was "a neutral quantity" in the political struggle. His altruistic stoicism had a strained note in it, but the frustrated

[18] Pike to Fessenden, [April, 1868?], JSP Papers. The memorandum is in Pike's handwriting but is undated, Pike MSS. When Fessenden died in September, 1869, Pike wrote a long eulogy defending the senator's vote against convicting the president and pointing out that the "great industrial and moneyed interest of the country had unbounded confidence in his judgment and discretion" (article in the Pike MSS, pasted in *Memorial Addresses on the Life and Character of William Pitt Fessenden*, Washington, 1870).

[19] William B. Hesseltine, *Ulysses S. Grant: Politician* (New York, 1935), p. 116; Hart, *Chase*, pp. 361-63.

Chief Justice explained that he just wanted "to plod on in a quiet way, doing what good I can to my country & my country-men, *without distinction* &c, and taking, with resignation, what-ever, in the way of administration, may happen to come."[20]

Pike, like his eminent friend in the Supreme Court, tried to be philosophical about the election of the Union general, but his attitude had an element of uncertainty. Like thousands of other Republicans, he consoled himself with the reflection that Grant had "good sense to build upon" and on all subjects relating to government he would surely "grow wise with years." Still, he believed the general to be "patently igno-rant" on important issues like the finances. But, never mind, "we pardon everything to the soundness of his general expres-sions."[21] If he was uneasy about Grant in 1868, it was prima-rily because Pike felt a keen interest in such economic matters as the currency, the public debt, and the tariff. Grant as President proved "sound" on these issues; that is, his position and Pike's were relatively close for a long time. So the Maine journalist had no substantive economic quarrel with the admin-istration during the ensuing four years. Eventually he parted ways with the Grant Republicans. But the "Grantism" at which Pike came to rage had nothing whatsoever to do with the tariff or the finances or with any other economic matter.

The financial question with which the Maine journalist so much concerned himself after the war was largely a contin-uation of a wartime problem. Pike's intense disapproval of Federal war finance has been discussed earlier.[22] The chief cause of his displeasure had been the issuance of the legal tender notes, the greenbacks. In 1865, and for several years

---

[20] Chase to Pike, Oct. 5, 1868, Pike MSS. For the 1868 election, in which the Republicans talked mostly about the "rebocracy" and "repudiation," Grant proclaimed enigmatically, "Let us have peace," and the Democrats hedged dismally on their chosen economic issue (taxation of bonds, more greenbacks, etc.) by nominating a conservative, hard-money candidate; see Charles H. Coleman, *The Election of 1868* (New York, 1933); Hesseltine, *Grant*, pp. 122 ff.

[21] Notebook No. 25, p. 27.

[22] See above, pp. 114 17.

after, the greenbacks continued to be the source of a great controversy in which many voluble people took part and about which more was said than done. The problems, in brief, were these: first, over $400,000,000 in greenbacks was in circulation at the close of the war and the question as to what was to be done about them became a hotly debated issue. Debtor groups generally demanded their continuance and even expansion; the creditor interests, on the other hand, clamored either for their immediate redemption in specie or for the inauguration of a program looking toward their ultimate redemption. This was the core of the "specie resumption" debate. The second and related problem arose in connection with the long-range handling of the national debt. In the fall of 1865 the Federal indebtedness reached about $2,760,000,000, less than one half of which was funded. A great many of the government bonds were bought during the war with the depreciated greenbacks, but the various loans were not uniform as to the mode of repayment; that is, some of the acts specified payment of interest and principal in specie while others remained silent on this point. When the matter of funding the debt arose, the "heretical" suggestion began to be made, particularly among Western farmers, that since many of the bonds had been purchased with "cheap money" (i.e., greenbacks) they should be repaid in the same unless the issuing act clearly called for specie payment. And the same groups that advanced this notion usually demanded that revenue from government bonds be subjected to taxation like any other property.[23] Clearly, these were issues which might cut across the sectional walls which divided the country.

Reconstruction political duels, however, were never fought on economic lines. In the first place, Radical Republicans chose Negro suffrage as their cardinal weapon, and because of the circumstances which prevailed in 1865-66 their choice was

---

[23] Dewey, *Financial History*, pp. 331 ff.; Barrett, *Greenbacks*, pp. 108 ff.; Coleman, *Election of 1868*, pp. 24-40.

the most powerful element in the situation. But it should also be noted that the Democrats themselves virtually rejected the economic issue which the financial debate soon afforded them. This is perhaps best epitomized by the nomination of Horatio Seymour in 1868. The Democratic platform included the "Ohio Idea" of paying bonds in greenbacks, but the candidate himself was a conservative, hard-money champion. In brief, as Professor Charles Beard points out, the Democratic party in 1868, crippled by the odium attached to "rebellion" and dominated by business interests, began the practice of hovering around the mercantile metropolis of New York when seeking its Presidential canditates. This was the financial and political background against which Pike waged his persistent campaign for the withdrawal of the greenbacks and for specie payments in full to bondholders.[24]

Pike's financial articles appeared in the *Tribune* at irregular intervals throughout 1867 and 1868. Although he and Greeley occasionally disagreed on minor points in the financial debate, their differences were of an intramural variety; no serious harm was done to the "honest money" camp by the occasional editorial exceptions which the *Tribune* took to Pike's arguments. Pike thought well enough of his financial articles to collect them into pamphlets, one of which appeared in 1867, another in 1868, and the last in 1875; then all three of these were combined into a small book entitled *The Finances: 1867-1878* which he issued privately in 1878. Even without following him into the myriad by-ways of the complex, verbose controversy, it is easy to fix his position. In monetary matters he never strayed away from that Gibralter of nineteenth-century economic thinking, "the mighty laws of supply and demand."[25]

---

[24] Beard, *Rise*, II, 299.

[25] The three pamphlets are: *The Financial Crisis: Its Evils and Their Remedy*; republished from the *Tribune* (New York, 1867), 38 pp.; *The Restoration of the Currency*; republished from the *Tribune* (New York, 1868), 52 pp.; *Contributions to the Financial Discussion, 1874-1875* (New York, 1875), 44 pp. The latter contains material

The core of Pike's financial thinking lay in his belief that the greenbacks were an insidious and unjustifiable component of the nation's currency. He argued, reasonably enough, that the North's war prosperity sprang originally not from the issue of legal tender but from the increased demands forced on the government and the country by war needs. After the war, he was consistent in his demand for the elimination of the greenbacks and the return to a specie standard. He frankly believed and admitted that the nation must inevitably pass through a period of "depression and prostration," that is, suffer the deserved distress of the deflationary process. Government had entered the sacred realm of self-regulating economic life and now it would only compound its sins by remaining in the picture.[26]

The most glaring danger of the greenbacks, however, arose from the fact that they tempted the "inflationists," whom he described as "public enemies," to destroy, to repudiate the national "honor" and credit by paying the bondholders in inflated paper currency. Pike paid no heed to the suggestion that a large portion of the government securities had been purchased with this same paper money or that many bondholders had already received interest payments in specie which were larger than the original cost (in gold) of the bonds. To those who advocated that the bonds be taxed he replied with a stout affirmation of the sanctity of contract, arguing that the government's provision that no state or municipality should tax the Federal issues implied a moral obligation on the part of the government to refrain from such a step. In short, nothing could shake Pike from his profound loyalty to the bond-holding class.[27]

---

from Dana's *Sun*, for which Pike wrote many editorials in the 1870's. The quote is from Pike, *Crisis*, p. 10.

[26] Pike, *Crisis*, *passim*.

[27] Pike, *Crisis*, pp. 35-38; *Tribune*, Feb. 23, 1867. Even Dewey, *Financial History*, p. 352, admits that exempting the bonds from taxation made an invidious distinction as well as contributed to the snarling of financial legislation.

This loyalty was largely an unconscious affair. Economic writing and thinking, such as Pike engaged in, was common enough. But economic thoughts translated boldly into political terms was something else again during the postwar era. A *Tribune* editorial early in 1868 furnishes an apt illustration of this state of affairs; appropriately enough it appeared in the column adjacent to one of Pike's financial letters. The editorial dealt with the "dangerous significance" betokened by the cries of "bondholders" and "moneyed aristocrats" which were increasingly heard. "Many of the leading Democratic organs, especially in the West," the New York paper declared, "are opening their columns to rash denunciation of men who have money or other property, stigmatizing them as privileged classes, exempt from taxation. . . ." This could only incite a spirit which was "at variance with right and justice, and dangerous to our Government," for such "incendiary" appeals might influence the thousands of people who seldom studied issues carefully. With a figure of speech that had often been cried from the South in prewar years, the *Tribune* concluded its plea for economic peace and quiet: "It is not the part of wisdom to flourish a lighted torch in a powder magazine."[28]

The torch was doused in 1868 by the Democratic nomination of a hard-money man. Most of the powder was safely scattered by the election of Grant. In his inaugural address the General announced that the debt would be paid in specie in order to "protect the national honor," and one of the first acts of the Congress in March, 1869, was the passing of an act reaffirming Grant's promise and pledging the nation to redeem the greenbacks at the earliest practicable time. To be sure, only the first step had been taken toward an "honorable" settlement of the financial question, but it was an important step. The long arguments which followed were essentially about method, and in 1875, after a great deal of backing and filling, Congress finally committed itself to a resumption of

[28] *Tribune,* Jan. 21, 1868.

specie payments four years thence, that is, in 1879.[29]   In the view of Pike and the other economic conservatives of both Democratic and Republican camps, the law of supply and demand had been satisfied.

When Pike, the economic pamphleteer, expounded his ideas on laissez faire principles, he specified that the government should merely establish fixed standards of weight, measure, and value; but he added, with candor at least, that it should also "enact general provisions of law for the generous development and adequate protection of its industry."[30]   In other words, like so many others of his era and later, he apparently saw no contradiction between his adherence to self-regulating economic "laws" and a tariff wall of unprecedented height behind which American industrialists, primarily in the northeastern states, enjoyed their expansion and prosperity. The tariff suffered the fate of other economic questions during Reconstruction: it was buried under the avalanche of controversy over Negro suffrage and other political aspects of the Southern question.[31]   When the tariff revisionists, or revenue reformers as they were called, did begin to organize and to agitate for some reductions or adjustments, Pike joined Greeley in ridiculing them as wild free traders and impractical visionaries.   Still a foremost champion of extreme protectionism, Greeley flew into Secretary of the Treasury Hugh McCulloch in 1866 when that official suggested that excessive protection encouraged the growth of monopolies.   The *Tribune* editor described this notion as a "sheer, bald, palpable fallacy," and Greeley followed a characteristic pattern in handling any threat to the tariff by suggesting, a bit illogically, that the Secretary

---

[29] Dewey, *Financial History*, pp. 352 ff.; Hesseltine, *Grant*, pp. 144, 157.

[30] Pike, *Restoration*, p. 1.

[31] For an able study of the Radical strategy in avoiding a test of their tariff policy at the polls, particularly in the crucial elections of 1866, see Howard K. Beale, "The Tariff and Reconstruction," *American Historical Review*, XXXV (Jan., 1930), 276-94. Also F. W. Taussig, *The Tariff History of the United States* (New York, 1923), pp. 171-78.

was against home monopolies while he favored foreign ones. To ardent protectionists like Greeley any mention of tariff reform equaled free trade, and that was "foreign," or worse still, "British."[32]

Pike demanded one important exception to protectionism, and this arose from his interest in American shipping. George W. Dalzell in *The Flight from the Flag* has described the startling decline of the United States' merchant marine during the Civil War, when fear of Confederate cruisers and the concomitant high insurance rates virtually destroyed the shipping industry. After the war many factors combined to prevent the recuperation of the traditionally prosperous shippers and builders, but one of these causes is generally acknowledged to have been the heavy protective duty on iron which greatly retarded American construction by increasing the cost of the domestic product.[33]

This sad state of American shipping distressed Pike, whose native state of Maine had formerly led the country in this field, and he wrote many *Sun* editorials deploring the situation. "However prosperous and powerful we may be internally, we are not masters of our national dignity and honor, nor the secure guardians of the national rights," he proclaimed, "unless we possess a commanding maritime position." To the suggestion that foreign vessels be purchased, he replied, bristling with loyalty, that the "lively and patriotic sense of nationality" of American seamen would be humiliated if they rode in foreign bottoms. The remedy he and others from the seaboard suggested was that the raw materials needed for shipbuilding be

[32] *Tribune,* Dec. 7, 1866; signed editorial; *ibid.,* Dec. 19, 1866. Despite their general agreement, Pike and Greeley engaged in another of their intramural disputes about 1870, when Pike was writing *Sun* editorials and toying with the notion that 40 per cent duty might furnish enough protection as well as revenue. Greeley called this "twaddling." See *Sun,* Dec., 1870. For Pike's loyalty to protectionism in general, see *Sun,* March 31, 1871. These and the following *Sun* citations are from scrapbooks in the Pike MSS in which he collected his own articles and editorials as well as some related material.

[33] Dalzell, *Flight,* pp. 237 ff., treats this more fully.

allowed to come in duty free. "Give us but cheap iron, copper, hemp, and other raw material," he argued, "and we will again build as cheaply as England or Scotland."[34]

The countersuggestion to this cry for duty-free raw materials was that the Federal government should subsidize the shipping industry. Any move to lower the tariff for whatever reason encountered strong opposition from the protectionists; one hole in the dike, particularly in the strategic iron tariff schedules, might lead to the disintegration of the whole structure. The railways had leaned heavily on government largess; might not the same "national interest" that dictated this generous, paternalistic policy justify government aid to the shipping industry? Though many shipbuilders and related interests thought so, Pike thought not. And in arguing against subsidies he went a long way toward demolishing his own protectionist principles, although that apparently did not occur to him. He insisted that the shipping interest, old and well established, was no "infant crying for sustenance." All it demanded was that it should not be "oppressed and borne down by the burdens of an overwhelming taxation." Just as the shipping industry ought not be crushed by taxation in the form of a protective tariff on its raw materials, it should not be artificially built up by subsidies.[35]

He offered as his reason for opposing the shipping subsidies that economic cliché of the century about competition's being the life of trade. Pike insisted that as "a general proposition, no one can question that all donations, gifts, bonuses, bounties, or subsidies given by legislation to individuals or companies to support a tottering industry constitute a miserable and ruinous policy, even from the protectionist point of view."[36] But laissez faire dogma could hardly extract the Downeaster

---

[34] *Sun*, Dec. 26, 1870. See also *Sun*, Jan. 20, 1872.

[35] *Sun*, Jan. 5, 1871. For background on the shipping crisis and the subsidy schemes, see Grosvenor M. Jones, *Government Aid to Merchant Shipping* (Washington, 1925), pp. 38-41; David B. Tyler, *Steam Conquers the Atlantic* (New York, 1939), pp. 352-66.

[36] *Sun*, Jan. 5, 1871.

from his dilemma, for if he rejected subsidies and viewed duties on the shipping industry's raw materials as "an overwhelming taxation" of that industry, might not other consumers of iron products also object to the taxation? Suppose the purchasers of farm machinery raised the same cry? This was precisely the danger that Greeley, for example, envisioned, and the editor warned that lowering the tariff would "give the lower order of demagogues an excellent lever for upsetting our entire Tariff, by crying, 'Farmers! why shouldn't *you* have your Iron, &c., free of duty as well [as] those millionaire ship-owners?' " The *Tribune* editor seriously doubted that the United States could compete with Western Europe in the development of steamships "*without* the aid of Government subsidies."[37]

The truth of the matter was that Pike and others interested in the New England shipping industry were hoisted by their own protectionist petard. Throughout the decades preceding the Civil War, shipbuilding and shipping had centered on the northeastern seaboard. Maine had for a time led all the other states in supplying the ships of the merchant marine. Shipping and lumber, closely related industries in the days of sail, had made Calais a thriving, prosperous port during Pike's youth and early manhood, and much of his own savings had been accumulated from investments in those activities. The Civil War and iron ships brought revolutionary changes to American shipping, changes which gradually ruined the well established builders on the northeast coast.[38] By the late 1860's and early 1870's, the decline had become acute, and relief, such as cheaper iron from Britain, would have to come if any of these older shipbuilders were to survive the transition from sail to steam and from wood to iron. Subsidies in the postwar era meant aid to the steamship builders along the middle Atlantic

[37] *Tribune,* Feb. 6, 1871; see also Feb. 8, March 24, 1871. Greeley published his rebuttal to the argument for lowering the iron duties for shipbuilders at the same time he printed one of Pike's letters advocating such a reduction.

[38] For example, see Davis, *International Community,* pp. 221 ff., for the Calais and St. Croix valley decline.

and Pacific seaboards, and could hardly help the older industries of New England where wood and sail had been the rule. Pike, like so many others, spoke and pleaded in "national" terms. But he eventually showed his hand by declaring that "if there is any part of the Union more damaged than another by the hateful system of subsidies it is New England, and Maine above every other State."[39]

Pike told only half the story when he offered laissez faire scruples against subsidies. His brother had pitifully pictured the plight of the shipbuilders and demanded lower tariffs for them in an 1868 speech before the House. Greeley mischievously replied to the argument, in an editorial entitled "Pike's Pique," by suggesting that local Maine interests prompted the congressman. He was probably right, for Fred Pike, upholding protectionism in general, spoke also in terms of "national" interest and asked only for the same important exception to protection that his journalist brother demanded.[40] The upshot of all the bickering within the protectionist family was that Congress in 1872, after prolonged hearings and investigations by a special House committee on the decline of the merchant marine, voted an insignificant 10 per cent reduction on certain key materials, including iron, needed in ship construction. This election year reduction, which was eventually restored, also forestalled the growing demand for tariff reform. But also in 1872 Congress voted a generous subsidy, in the form of a mail contract, to the Pacific Mail Steamship company. Flagrant corruption surrounding the act led to its abrogation a few years later.

Needless to say, these inadequate measures failed to halt the decline of the American merchant marine, for the shipbuilding industries of the northeast coast were already too far gone to be saved by any such faltering step.[41] The significance

[39] *Sun*, Dec. 8, 1874; Jones, *Government Aid*, pp. 40-41.
[40] *Tribune*, May 11, 1868.
[41] Dalzell, *Flight*, pp. 258-59; Tyler, *Steam*, pp. 352 ff.; Taussig, *Tariff*, pp. 180-88.

of the whole matter, in connection with Pike, is to illustrate some of the insurmountable difficulties involved in being both a "liberal" economic individualist and a protectionist at the same time, in speaking and writing of "national" interests while economic realities were often still regional.

Such intra-Republican squabbles as this one between Pike and Greeley typified the problems facing a party which had inadequate opposition and which found it increasingly difficult to coalesce around any frank, positive program. Other Republican warriors were also quarreling among themselves. Some, like Sumner and Schurz, were leaving the camp, for reasons ranging from dissatisfaction with Grant's disposal of the patronage to honest indignation at the corruption which characterized the era and the administration.[42] As the party began to splinter under the strain of accumulated personal grievances, Pike bemoaned what he called the Washington "doldrums." In his *Sun* editorials of 1870 and 1871 he deplored the fact that it was "not an interesting period in the political life of Washington." While the "heat and glow of a great contest of ideas" had disappeared, nothing new had been regenerated except a civil administration of a "low type."[43]

Pike's criticisms of the Grant administration in 1870-71 illustrate the ambiguities and contradictions which beset many of the dissidents within the Republican party. Grant's message in December, 1870, emphasized his interest in acquiring Santo Domingo, but the Maine journalist declared this was not "what the intellect of the Republican party would have suggested." (Pike, like Senator Sumner, who became bitterly estranged from Grant about Santo Domingo, would have preferred Canada to any Caribbean acquisition.) Continuing a bit vaguely, the *Sun* editorialist stated that the "leading minds" of the party wanted to see the administration "lift itself out upon some distinct, intelligent . . . and commanding position, showing

[42] For the patronage fights, see Hesseltine, *Grant*, pp. 145-56.

[43] *Sun*, Dec. 12, 14, 1870. Pike also criticized Grant's grammar and style in the State of the Union message.

a worthy conception of the high and multifarious duties of a great government" after a civil conflict. Perhaps the "commanding position" could relate to the end of military rule in several Southern states? But concerning the Southern problem, Pike waved his own version of the bloody shirt. He insisted that the administration, while forgiving generously, should let the world know whether or not it proposed "to remember, or to forget and reward, the unspeakable crimes of the rebellion; and herein it might have spoken in a manner to blast pusillanimity and electrify a nation."

The Santo Domingo scheme was brazen and blundering, Pike argued. But the Republicans, speaking through Grant, might have declared "the principles and policy which should govern the nation in its future and inevitable absorption of the countries contiguous to our own, which may now or hereafter desire incorporation into our system." In other words, it was not the imperialistic principle behind the Santo Domingo scheme which bothered the Republican critics of the President's diplomacy, but merely the unskilful, hasty manner in which the President pursued his object. Altogether, the editorialist's complaints against the administration were flimsy. Yet he himself charged Grant with failing "to afford any mental sustenance to a great party which has performed an immense service for the country and to humanity, and now, in the full fruition of its hopes, contemplates suicide for want of brains in its chosen leaders."[44]

Despite his unconvincing indictment of Republican leadership, Pike had a deeper grasp of the problem facing his party, and early in 1871 he offered a perceptive editorial in the *Sun* entitled "Advice to the Republicans." He began by deploring the decline and threatening disintegration of "a great organization, so conspicuous in the past for its many noble deeds and

---

[44] *Sun*, Dec. 19, 1870. For the Santo Domingo imbroglio, see Hesseltine, *Grant*, pp. 196-203, 247-49; Allan Nevins, *Hamilton Fish: The Inner History of the Grant Administration* (New York, 1936), pp. 309-34. And for the journalist's own continuing interest in Canada, see the *Tribune*, Feb. 14, 1871; *Sun*, Feb. 24, 1871.

sacrifices, so vital in its ideas, so aggressive in its valiant assaults upon the great crime and scandal of our age—African slavery. . . ." The basic trouble seemed to be that party leaders failed to understand that "this is no time for a party of doctrinaires, such as the Republican party was at the period of its formation, and necessarily continued to be until its great objects were attained." The prewar and wartime Republicans had a great work to do in "revolutionizing a social and political condition which was the out-growth and fruit" of past centuries. "This work had to be performed inside the coffer dam of doctrines as rigid as cast iron." But with the completion of the "new structure" the task of the "doctrinaires" had come to an end.

Now, in 1871, many Republicans and all the Democrats seemed to think that the party still had to remain inside the "coffer dam" of ideas. From various Republicans came proposals of "a grand universal system of popular education" or of extreme, brazenly high tariffs—all proposals designed to furnish the party with a rallying cry. The flagrant error of these suggestions, Pike argued, lay in the belief that because the party had once been led by doctrinaires it must still be led by them, that because "it has triumphed by bearing aloft the flag of a cause whose strength consisted in the radical nature of its ideas, therefore nothing short of the same positive tone and equally positive dogmas on other issues can insure success to the party in the future."

This was Pike's diagnosis of the party's past history and its present dilemma. He also had some positive suggestions for the future. He considered it as natural and inevitable that the Republicans should now recognize that they had passed into what he called the "administrative stage." This phase became inescapable for all political groups and was but a part of their natural history of "rise, progress, and decay." Rather than "striking schemes" or "sharp-edged radical policies," the situation now called for "wise, cautious, conservative

measures" because the country had wearied of its "high excite-
ments" which had culminated in "a bloody and intoxicating
war." Republicans had to eliminate their "foolish leaders"
and various "rank schemes" and come out openly upon "the
broad platform of moderate and judicious measures." Leaving
unimportant and secondary foreign projects behind, the party
should adopt "a financial policy looking to an abatement of
the present excessive taxation, and tending directly toward the
resumption of specie payments." The country's maritime
interests and "naval capacities" cried for restoration. And as
for the tariff, the application of a "little vigorous common
sense" would prune off some of the excrescences and leave
protective duties which, if not "perfect," would "at least not
be so absurd, so oppressive, or so parital as to excite derision
and animosity."[45]

Clearly, one hitherto staunch Republican now had a sur-
feit of moral certainties and "radical" dogmas. What he
demanded was that the party should openly acknowledge and
urge its economic policies of protectionism (with the indefensi-
ble "excrescences" removed), low taxation, and the resumption
of specie payments. Having proclaimed these economic principles, the frankly "administrative" party could escape all the
noise and fury of petty, personal wrangling and devote itself
to the vital, internal concerns of the country. The striking
thing is that in the election year of 1872 the administration did
secure tariff reductions, albeit fairly trivial and temporary;
taxes had been coming down since the end of the war but the
widely attacked and shrunken income tax was finally dropped

[45] *Sun,* Jan. 19, 1871. The *Sun's* editor, Dana, added a phrase to this about the
"absurd pretensions of Grant to a renomination." Pike noted these additions to his
editorials in his scrapbooks, Pike MSS. For Dana, who had been disappointed in not
receiving Grant's appointment as New York collector of customs and who early began
attacking the administration, see James H. Wilson, *Life of Charles A. Dana* (New York,
1907), pp. 404 ff. For a later return to the idea that Republicans could no longer
be "doctrinaires" and that all "great questions of trade and industry" had been once and
for all settled, see *Sun,* Jan. 3, 1873. In this later editorial Pike argued that the
only concern of the day was to stop the corruption and robbery in government.

in the spring of 1872; and the Republicans were still firmly pledged to return to specie and the "honest" dollar.[46] Despite these economic moves in the direction the Maine journalist had urged, the election of 1872 was not to be concerned with tariffs or taxes or currency. Had he not forgotten that the "Southern problem" still occupied the attention of the wearied country?

Pike paid the South little attention during the first half of Grant's administration. Conditions there were still chaotic and abnormal, with frequent Ku Klux Klan outrages and with Federal troops supporting several Radical Republican state governments.[47] Like so many others, however, he was beginning to tire of all the furor and continual agitation. He had assented a few years earlier to the dogma of Negro suffrage primarily for political reasons, that is, to maintain the Republicans in power.[48] He had felt misgivings about the new doctrine then, but by 1870-71 he was more skeptical of the validity of such a policy, even as a party device. He explained his confusion on the point as early as 1867 when he wrote to an old friends and fellow Republican from the 1850's, Fitz-Henry Warren. "My aim in politics hitherto," he stated, "has been to keep the colored gentlemen out of the territories & to destroy the race of slaveholders[.]" These aims had been triumphantly accomplished, but the "precise thing to do next has never been exactly clear to my understanding [,] doubtless because of my want of penetration. But this is not my fault. It is said the brain secretes conclusions as the liver secretes bile. I am waiting for the operation. It may be an ossification has commenced which interferes with the natural processes. I have had a few mental glimpses however of what ought *not* to be done and this is encouraging."[49]

[46] Ratner, *American Taxation*, pp. 133-34; Hesseltine, *Grant*, p. 267.
[47] Randall, *Civil War*, pp. 854-58; DuBois, *Black Reconstruction*, pp. 381 ff.
[48] See above, pp. 161 ff.
[49] Pike to Fitz-Henry Warren, Nov. 10, 1867, Notebook No. 24, pp. 26-27. See also his questioning of "human rights" in Notebook No. 25, p. 3.

Dissenting so early from the program of Chase, Sumner, Greeley, and other Radical leaders, Pike's tacit skepticism about "universal suffrage" increased with the years. He now believed that "the nigger is a porcupine" who "fills with quills everybody who undertakes to hug him."[50] To those who spoke of abstract human rights and dogmatic first principles, he replied, on the private pages of his notebook, that in the abstract "there is nothing more absurd than that we in America should allow the ignorant tribes of Irishmen" to vote. And besides, the former antislavery crusader now thought that no man should feel confidence "in the expression of abstract opinions on public affairs till he has gone through one tremendous civil convulsion."[51]

The corollary of his disenchantment on the Negro suffrage question was the view that the Grant administration's Radical reconstruction program had dismally failed. In the spring of 1871 he asserted that the "whole process of genuine reconstruction has yet to be accomplished." And anticipating one theme of his book about Reconstruction in South Carolina, *The Prostrate State*, he explained that the "immediate cause of the outrages in the Carolinas and elsewhere in the South is to be found in the unparalleled robbery and corruption practised by the carpet-bag Governments with the help of the negro Legislatures." The recurring use of Federal troops to settle Southern controversies merely gave a temporary triumph to the Negro-carpetbagger alliance and settled nothing. The sword's justification had ended with Appomatox, and in every state which now enjoyed membership in the union "we shall be obliged to go back to the sway of public opinion." That "sway" might occasionally be "violent," but he hoped that no state could afford to be unjust to the Negroes "when it has lost the power to enslave them or control their movements."[52]

[50] Notebook No. 25, p. 14. And speculations about wisdom of complete political democracy, *ibid.*, pp. 17-18, with affirmative case winning only a slight victory.

[51] Notebook No. 25, p. 30; latter quote from a loose memorandum in the Pike MSS.

[52] *Sun*, March 28, 1871; Dana added another sentence directed against Grant's

An even more significant indication of Pike's changed views toward the "rebels" and "slaveholders" came in March, 1872. He published a lengthy article in Greeley's *Tribune* concerning South Carolina, "A State in Ruins." Strangely enough, practically every major point he made in his later book is mentioned in this piece which was written one year before he visited the South. He contrasted South Carolina in the days of her power, when the "dogmatic" but "high-toned aristocracy" ruled, and the present days of her tribulation when she suffered in proportion to her former glory. The majority of the Negro legislators he depicted as a "great mass of ignorance and barbarism" who were led by carpetbaggers and "a few intelligent colored people." These very leaders, he charged, were the miscreants and thieves who fattened on the flagrant corruption that was rampant. The former antislavery spokesman wailed that "300,000 white people, more or less, composing the intelligence and property-holders of the State, are put under the heel of 400,000 pauper blacks, fresh from a state of slavery and ignorance the most dense."

This *Tribune* article concluded with an apology for "the wild crimes of Ku-Klux youth" of South Carolina. Did not the acts of these Klansmen "foreshadow a possible future for that wretched people" and demand the attention of Northern statesmen? And the New Englander, indeed far from the old home base of "moral truth," declared: "One thing seems plain to the most ordinary apprehension. The condition of things now existing in South Carolina would not be borne a month in any Northern State without a taxpayers' league being organized to resist the payment of all taxes imposed for fradulent purposes and without the swift establishment of a court of lynch law. So much treason as that exists in the blood of every American citizen worthy of his birthright."[53]

upholding military governments in the South "for the mere purposes" of procuring Grant delegates for the next party convention.

[53] *Tribune*, March 5, 1872; datelined Feb. 22, 1872, Washington. For approving reaction to this article in South Carolina, see undated clippings in scrapbook, Pike MSS.

The sources for most of the information in this article may be indicated, for in February, 1872, Pike had several conversations with persons having direct interests in South Carolina. One of these talks was with William Sprague, a millionaire United States senator from Rhode Island and the husband of the Chief Justice's daughter, Kate Chase. Sprague had invested heavily in South Carolina ventures, and through his agent there he gained an unsavory picture of the political corruption among the Radicals. Sprague testified to Pike that for $75,000 he could have had his agent named senator from South Carolina; but the transaction was too disgraceful for the wealthy Rhode Island politician. Consequently he distrusted the whole batch of carpetbagger senators. Thus the journalist gained one opinion which influenced his article in the *Tribune*.[54]

An even more significant conversation which enlightened the Downeaster about Carolina conditions was with General Wade Hampton, whom Pike encountered at an agricultural convention in Washington. Hampton, who later played a leading role among the white "redeemers" of 1876-77, informed Pike about "oppressive taxation" levied by the Negro-carpetbagger legislature and the thefts perpetrated by the "adventurers" who unscrupulously used the colored voters. The Confederate general described the laborer's disinclination to work for wages, and the consequent loss through "his idleness and mismanagement" when he share-cropped. In short, Hampton gave the *Tribune*'s correspondent an insight into the distant situation; needless to say, the insight reflected a conservative, white point of view.[55]

---

[54] Notebook No. 28, pp. 1-2; entry for Feb. 15, 1872. See above p. 45 n.

[55] Notebook No. 28, p. 2; entry for Feb. 16-23 [?], 1872. About the same time Pike talked with a "Mr. Aiken of S. C. (near Abbeville)." This was probably D. Wyatt Aiken, a prominent agricultural leader and editor of the *Rural Carolinian*. Aiken advised the journalist about the voting situation; although "he was on the best of terms with the hands on his plantation . . . he had not the slightest influence over their votes." The Negroes still confided in their former masters in every respect except voting; there it was "only necessary for a man to represent himself as one of the men who freed the blacks to enable him to get all their votes to a man" (Notebook No. 28, pp. 2-3). For Hampton and Aiken, see Francis B. Simkins and Robert H.

The *Tribune's* rivals in New York joyfully seized upon Pike's article as proof of what they considered the purely expedient alteration of that paper's former Radical orientation. Was not the lurid article merely another manifestation of the anti-Grant drive? A *Tribune* editorial hotly answered that the assumption that "we set forth such facts as those which elucidate the swindling misgovernment of South Carolina for some political purpose" is "utterly groundless." The editorial pointed out that the author of the Carolina piece, James S. Pike, could not be considered an anti-Grant man, yet "there is nothing in his letter on South Carolina which differs by a shade from our oft-expressed convictions." Pike's strictures against the whole Carolina regime were simply "our sentiments, better expressed."[56]

Yet Greeley still clung to his belief in the righteousness of universal suffrage in the South, and in the "wickedness" of the carpetbaggers who had ruined the Radical experiment. But a new tone occasionally crept into the *Tribune*, aside from that shown in Pike's article. In April, 1872, for example, an editorial stated that in view of the Negro's ignorance and degradation under slavery the freedmen had done fairly well. But "they might and should have done much better." Their freedom would "not be assured and perfect" until they had become landholders. And why had they not already come into possession of lands? "Had they saved the money they have since 1865 spent in drink, tobacco, balls, gaming, and other dissipation, they might have bought therewith at least Ten Million acres of the soil of their respective States which would have given each family an average of ten acres of mother earth; and the free and clear owner of ten acres need never stand idle or accept half wages." Sloth and wild living were, therefore, the explanations for the freedmen's economic plight.[57]

Woody, *South Carolina During Reconstruction* (Chapel Hill, 1932), *passim*; Hampton M. Jarrell, *Wade Hampton and the Negro* (Columbia, S. C., 1949).

[56] *Tribune*, March 7, 1872.

[57] *Tribune*, April 12, 1872; see also March 23, 1872.

Thus Pike and his friends looked South, albeit through white eyes. The failure of Grant's Southern program had to be emphasized in 1872, for with no economic issues at stake how else could the administration be driven from office? The two powerful New York editors for whom Pike wrote, Dana and Greeley, had joined the dissident camp of the party long before Pike could bring himself to follow their example.[58] But his South Carolina article suggested that he might yet find the political nerve necessary for an open anti-administration move.

One development which aided the anti-Grant movement was the incredible amount of graft which characterized the times. Successive scandals titillated, more than alarmed, the public. These ranged from the Black Friday plot of Jay Gould and Jim Fisk in 1869, which involved some members of Grant's family, to the wretched Credit Mobilier affair which broke during the campaign of 1872.[59] The reaction to these developments was particularly marked among certain newspaper and political circles. Carl Schurz, for example, went to Washington as a senator from Missouri in 1869, and his greatest efforts were soon devoted to advancing the cause of civil service reform, and, along with his friend Sumner, to opposing the Grant administration. Schurz, who is described by his biographer as being untrammeled by political pledges and enjoying lofty ideals as well as ambitions, now repented his earlier enthusiastic endorsement of Radical methods in the South.[60] Thanks to the abundant fuel furnished by the Grant administration, he and other reformers, like E. L. Godkin of the *Nation*, soon had a first-class political blaze about unfit ap-

[58] Hesseltine, *Grant*, pp. 255-68; Hale, *Greeley*, pp. 324-27; Wilson, *Dana*, pp. 404 ff.

[59] For accounts of this aspect, Hesseltine, *Grant*, pp. 169-79, 308-12, is more judicious than the spirited Matthew Josephson, *The Politicos, 1865-1896* (New York, 1938), pp. 100-140. Carlton J. H. Hayes, *A Generation of Materialism*, pp. 79-81, gives an interesting perspective on corruption and the "Fruition of Liberalism" on the continent of Europe.

[60] Claude M. Fuess, *Carl Schurz: Reformer* (New York, 1932), pp. 154 ff.; Earle D. Ross, *The Liberal Republican Movement* (New York, 1919), pp. 28 ff.

pointments and "wicked corruption." Just as it had superficial-
ly appeased the tariff reformers, however, the Grant administration also rolled with the blows of the civil service champions.
In 1871 the harassed President approved Senator Schurz's
Civil Service Act and named a commission to devise examinations. He thus proceeded to identify the administration with
the popular cause, despite the alarm and indignation of his
staunchest friends in Congress.[61]

Grant stalwarts in Congress were not the only ones made
uncomfortable by all the idealistic, moral talk about competitive examinations and nonpolitical appointments to office.
Veteran political journalists like Pike and Greeley squirmed
when the civil service zealots began making reform noises.
Pike, for example, in an 1871 *Sun* editorial ridiculed one of
Senator Schurz's civil service speeches as being "too thoroughly
German in its character to be acceptable or even useful." He
conceded that the reformers were striving toward a noble goal
and, of course, he sympathized with them; but it did seem
that a thoroughgoing moral reform of all society would have
to take place before statutory regulations could help the government. There was nothing wrong with the present system so
much as with the men. "If the community will choose able
and good men for public station, beginning with the President,"
the Maine journalist wrote, "they can have the best and the
purest of governments with our present machinery." In other
words, remove Grant and all would be rosy.[62]

When the President's Civil Service Commission presented
Congress and the country with a definite program for examinations and merit appointments early in 1872, Pike continued to
regard the whole business with considerable disdain. He
reverted to an idea which had a Jacksonian ring when he
insisted that "want of capacity is not a general American weakness that needs to be especially guarded against." The com-

[61] Hesseltine, *Grant*, pp. 252-53, 263-65; Fuess, *Schurz*, pp. 162-63; Josephson,
Politicos, pp. 154-58.
[62] *Sun*, Jan. 27, 1871.

mission members who originated the reforms he characterized as "irresponsible" dilettantes whose powers were "unknown to the Constitution." The reformers talked about ending rotation in office. Why, Pike answered, the one thing "which most vitalizes our elections and inspires the public interest . . . is change in the *personnel* of the officeholders." The redistribution of the appointive offices was no more improper or illegitimate than redistribution of elective offices. In short, the *Sun* editorialist drew on his thirty years of experience in state and national politics and candidly announced that the civil service reformers were impractical and foolish.[63]

Thus the veteran Maine political writer wavered ambiguously in the confused first half of 1872. Should he stand loyally by the politically entrenched President or join Greeley, Schurz, Sumner, and the other dissidents in an anti-Grant drive? That was one question. Another matter which undoubtedly bothered him was the ground on which the variegated opposition to Grant might unite. Pike himself illustrates the dilemma of the dissidents. Being pro-tariff and anti-civil service reform, he was thus cut off from two important groups with some grass-root strength. Although not so closely identified with the original Radical program for the South as Schurz, Sumner, or Greeley had been, he had upheld the Radical demand for Negro suffrage and for keeping "rebels and repudiation" in quarantine, by troops if necessary.

Boldly recognizing the incongruities and contradictions of the situation, Pike in late February called on the anti-Grant Republicans to get back into line. In a strongly worded *Tribune* article, he discounted the noisy family squabbling that

[63] *Sun*, Jan.-Feb. [?], 1872; Pike's scrapbook, "Original Articles 1871-1872-1873," Pike MSS. There is no positive evidence on this point but Pike's candor about the limitations of civil service reform may have been too much for Dana, whose *Sun* was energetically attacking "official corruption." See Wilson, *Dana*, pp. 428-29. Pike's editorials in the *Sun* stopped rather abruptly in late January or early February, 1872, and his articles in the *Tribune* began in early March with the South Carolina piece mentioned above. If there was any disagreement with Dana, it was not serious or permanent, for after 1872 the freelancer again published editorials in the *Sun*.

currently characterized the Republicans. He called the Congressional vituperation and feuding among the Republicans "the scum and rubbish of public life." But what was most alarming to his anti-Grant friends, he demanded more "party organization" as the most "efficient corrector" of all the laxness and disintegration. More party discipline was just what the independents did not want, and here was a *Tribune* correspondent undermining their whole cause. Pike continued his call to the Republican faithful by suggesting that the great body of Republicans would look to the party convention at Philadelphia in June as the "authoritative exponent" of their views. In other words, even Grant, whose renomination was virtually certain, would have to be swallowed if the "authoritative exponent" spoke as was expected. Any encouragement of a third party movement, he concluded, would only help the Democrats; they, the traditional enemy, would then nominate a conservative candidate and write a moderate platform and "invite the disaffected from every cave of Adullam in the land."[64]

The basic error in Pike's calculations, and his trumpet call for Republican loyalty, was an overestimation of the Democratic control in the situation. At the time he wrote, Judge David Davis, a conservative Republican and long-time friend of Abraham Lincoln, had the favor of many Democratic congressmen; in addition, Davis had just been named Presidential nominee of a small labor group.[65] The Downeaster underestimated the powerful position of the rapidly forming anti-Grant coalition, and misjudged the desperate plight of the Democrats, who were in no position to do much more than accept as their candidate whomever the Republican bolters might name.

Pike mistook the drift of events. Greeley did not. On the day following Pike's untimely loyalty call, Greeley edito-

[64] *Tribune*, Feb. 27, 1872.
[65] Ross, *Liberal Republican*, pp. 77-81.

rially chastised his correspondent for demanding "party organization" when that was the very thing which characterized the political life of South Carolina. As for all the Republicans' looking to the Republican convention in Philadelphia, the editor reminded him that the "independents" and "reformers" had been called to a convention in Cincinnati on May 1. Meantime, other New York papers like the pro-Grant *Times* and the Democratic *World* picked up Pike's letter along with Greeley's answer and proceeded to make political capital out of the confusion within the anti-Grant ranks.[66]

The Maine journalist quickly tried to cover himself, but the attempt was feeble. With magnificent ambiguity he soon explained in the *Tribune:* "What I have written on a former occasion has been rather the expression of a philosophic résumé of the situation from an impersonal point of view than that very different language which an ardent personality lying behind it would utter if it sought to accomplish reform, and saw any way open by which it could be effected." Still, he stubbornly refused to recant wholeheartedly, for he dismissed the admitted corruption of the Republican party with a remark about the ancient "depravity of mankind." And he insisted that despite the corruption, President Grant deserved "unqualified praise" in his treatment of "our great national questions" like "Protection to American Industry." Grant also had treated the Indians humanely, had upheld the national credit and made repudiation an impossibility, and had maintained peace at home and abroad. On the other hand, it was certainly the business of the independent press to "pursue corruption and malfeasance in office, wherever and whenever it shows itself." He concluded by congratulating the *Tribune* on its strong and just stand toward corruption.[67]

After all his straddling, Pike became a Liberal Republican and a violent anti-Grant spokesman. In the final analysis,

[66] *Tribune,* Feb. 28, 1872; undated clippings, Pike MSS.
[67] *Tribune,* March 4, 1872.

pressure from Greeley must be considered as one factor. The editor begged the recalcitrant journalist to "Be reasonable." "We cannot reelect Grant, with his 15 to 18 relatives appointed by himself to office . . . ," Greeley argued, "and every thief in the Southern governments yelling [for] Grant with all his might." Pike must see the light and "help get Grant off the track."[68] A few days later the editor reminded his old associate of the tax frauds and other shameful practices which characterized the administration. "Pike, you know how I hate to fight my friends," Greeley declared, "but I now think I shall not support Grant in any event." Even Judge David Davis might be preferable, if nothing better could be had.[69]

The *Tribune* editor's speculations about a candidate with which to oppose Grant were appropriate and timely, for when the Liberal Republicans convened in Cincinnati in early May, none other than Horace Greeley was named to head their ticket. Not only that, but the Baltimore convention of the Democratic party in late June endorsed the editor of the *Tribune* as their nominee. The Democrats rubberstamped the Liberal Republican platform, which emphasized the withdrawal of Federal troops from the South and equivocated on the tariff issue.[70] Pike seems to have had no direct part in the maneuvering and nominating that filled the spring and early summer of 1872. Outside of embarrassing his friend Greeley by pointing to Grant's fundamental soundness on the "great national ques-

[68] Greeley to Pike, March 2, 1872, Pike MSS.

[69] Greeley to Pike, March 6, 1872, Pike MSS. Greeley apparently still had faint hopes of keeping Grant from the regular Republican nomination; he begged Pike not to say that "you can't go" Schuyler Colfax, the Vice-President under Grant. "I know all his failings," wrote Greeley, "—say that they amount to murder and treason—but he hasn't fifteen brothers-in-law and cousins sucking the life blood of the country" (*ibid.*). Pike could not bring himself to approve Colfax (Pike to Greeley, March 9, 1872, Notebook No. 28, p. 8), but the hope of side-tracking Grant at Philadelphia was futile anyhow.

[70] A full account of these political wonders, which were actually not so wonderful in the chaotic situation that existed, may be found in Ross, *Liberal Republican*; Josephson, *Politicos*, pp. 158-64, has a balanced brief account. John W. Kern, "The Presidential Election of 1872, and Its Effect upon the Democratic Party," unpublished Princeton senior thesis, treats a neglected aspect in a fresh light.

tions" like the tariff and finances, the only contribution which Pike had made to the fight against the administration was his picture of the South Carolina situation.

Greeley's nomination undoubtedly carried great weight with the Downeaster. Aside from the important personal aspect, the editor's nomination and subsequent endorsement by the Democrats made it quite certain that none of the economic issues were at stake. Greeley was just as sound economically in Pike's eyes as was Grant, so on that score it was Tweedledum and Tweedledee. On civil service reform Greeley was no more likely than Grant to swallow unrealistic programs about competitive examinations and such. That left the Southern question, that is, the matter of reconciliation, amnesty, and restoration of civil rule. This Southern issue became Greeley's primary concern, along with the corruption of "Grantism," and here his Maine friend also could go along.

Still, bolting the party that had saved the Union was no laughing matter in postwar Maine. As Pike painfully learned, the lot of a bolter there could be as bitter a dose as any white Southerner might have to swallow in later years if he dared step outside the Democratic fold. It must have been a difficult decision for him to make, but the local political situation also worked toward making him a Liberal Republican. Eugene Hale, who later served as senator from Maine for thirty years, had in 1869 succeeded Frederick A. Pike as congressman from Maine's fifth district. Hale was Senator Zachariah Chandler's son-in-law and a close political friend of James G. Blaine, but he ran into difficulty in the district Republican convention in the summer of 1872. Delegates from one county, Waldo, protested that Hale had promised to withdraw in 1872 in favor of a candidate from their county, which was one of the three big counties comprising the fifth district. Chagrined at Hale's flouting of the geographical rotation idea, a large number of delegates were ready for a bolt. Pike himself admitted that this was an "influential consideration" in the formation of a bolting convention, the local Liberal Republican convention which nominated Fred Pike as a candidate for his old seat in Congress. "I have been trying to secure a bolt these two weeks," the journalist wrote Greeley, "and we succeeded last week at the Convention which nominated Hale."[71]

Thus Pike became a Liberal Republican, for the simple reasons that Greeley was the nominee of that party, his brother hoped to win a Congressional seat, and a fortuitous quarrel among local Republicans in Maine's fifth district made a bolt possible. Regardless of his own interest in reconciliation and harmony with the South, an interest which was probably not great before 1872, Pike could hardly advise his brother to campaign in northern Maine on that issue. Maine voters were liable to be about as interested in the "Southern question," now devoid of its past moral aspects, as Mississippians would be in the hallowed question of the Newfoundland fisheries. Logically, then, the Pikes and their Liberal Republican allies had to fall back on corruption. The Pike brothers, both veteran politicians and former officeholders, launched a bitter fight against the current crowd of officeholders.

The journalist's campaign notes indicate that he excoriated Hale, corruption, patronage seekers, stipendiaries, and most appointed officials.[72] Still unreconciled to any fancy system of competitive examinations, he suggested that the true method of civil service reform was "to adopt the principle of election in all federal appointments."[73] Obviously the Pikes did not have much of an issue, and perhaps this in itself helps explain why the rancorous campaign so embittered Pike and many of his townsmen. Unable to attack the still popular general in the White House, Pike could only lukewarmly push Greeley.

[71] *Tribune* article by Pike datelined Aug. 25, 1872. Pike to Greeley, Aug. [?], 1872, Notebook No. 28, p. 13.

[72] Pike himself had tried to get Greeley appointed as minister to England in 1869, four days after Grant's inauguration (Pike to Elihu B. Washburne, then Secretary of State, March 8, 1869, Elihu B. Washburne, Jr., Papers, Library of Congress).

[73] Speech at Belfast, Maine, Aug., 1872, Pike MSS; the *Sun* endorsed Pike's idea; Pike also printed a campaign newspaper for his brother, the *Calais Tribune*.

His line was that Grant had made a poor President thus far and that Greeley might make a better one, though he considered neither of them an "ideal candidate." The Liberal prospects, under the circumstances, were none too bright.

Just as on the national level, the Liberal Republicans in Maine's fifth district were badly beaten. The Maine elections were in September, and the Grant victory there, though expected, came as a blow to the national hopes of the new party. Taking the defeat with ill grace, Pike wrote an article for the *Tribune* charging that Hale's sizeable majority resulted from nothing but bribery. He described his "respectable" home town of Calais as being covered with vote-buyers and corrupt officeholders. There was vote-buying in 1872, all over the country apparently, but Pike's excessive charges and rancor only earned him the illwill of his homefolk.[74]

The campaign of 1872 left Pike politically homeless for the remainder of his life. Throughout the canvass he stressed the fact that he and the other Liberal Republicans were "better" Republicans than the Grant crowd, but the charge made against him of party treason haunted him then and later. The Democratic endorsement of Greeley was a political kiss of death in orthodox Republican communities where past attacks on "copperheadism," "repudiation," and "doughfaces" had done their work only too well. In reply to the journalist's nationally aired charges of bought voters and Calais corruption, the local paper in Calais published a defense which concluded with the observation that the coalitionists had failed first, "because they had no principles," and secondly, "because the voters were republicans and could not be bought." But the former diplomat and famous *Tribune* correspondent coolly

---

[74] Pike's *Tribune* letter, datelined Sept. 11, 1872; the *Sun* picked up the story editorially on Nov. 13, 1872. For the national results, see Ross, *Liberal Republican*, pp. 178-91. For state politics in Maine, where the Democrats accepted the coalition with the Liberal Republicans and were defeated, see Louis C. Hatch, ed., *Maine: A History* (New York, 1919), II, 570-72. Greeley visited Maine but, worried and already exhausted, was unable to reach Calais. See Greeley to Pike, Aug. 7, 1872, Pike MSS.

announced that regardless of the temporary setback, he felt assured of the ultimate success of "civil service reform" and the escape of the "white men of the South" from under the "heel of the carpet-bagger." Therefore, he could afford to "gaze amiably" upon the terrible rage of "village journals."[75]

The death of Horace Greeley three weeks after his energetic campaign ended in defeat served to heal some of the wounds left by the fierce partisanship of the election. Pike wrote a long *Tribune* article, which was also issued as a pamphlet, defending the motives of the great editor in the recent election. To all those who either attacked or apologized for his candidacy, the Downeaster replied that Greeley "threw himself into the canvass as the determined opponent of a sordid corruption that he believed was disgracing the Republican party and destroying the public morals." Even this tribute to his old friend earned Pike another violent attack in Calais. An irate Republican there scorned the "noisy little throng of political katydids" who had smothered revenue and civil service reform, promised free trade to one group and protection to another, guaranteed civil rights to the freedmen and "free riding" to the Klan, and sworn to maintain the Reconstruction policy as well as hang all the carpetbaggers. The Liberal Republicans, according to this Calais critic, would "hasten the millennium and during a single Presidential term would make Jefferson Davis and Wendell Phillips lie down together, and enable a little child to lead them."[76]

A political pariah in Maine, Pike now forgot that he himself had defended President Grant until Greeley's nomination, and his endorsement by the Democrats, had made bolting seem safe. He had originally ascribed the contemporary corruption and scandals to the "ancient depravity" of man, but

---

[75] *Calais Advertiser*, Oct. 2, 1872; *Calais Times*, Sept. 30, 1872, Pike MSS.

[76] Pike, *Horace Greeley in 1872: His Political Position and Motives in the late Presidential Contest* (New York, 1873). The answer was by T. O. Howe in *Calais Advertiser*, Jan. 7, 1873, Pike MSS. Van Deusen, *Greeley*, pp. 400-424, treats the editor's anticlimactic end.

now and later he increasingly blamed everything on "Grant-ism." His earlier doubts and reservations about much of the attack on the President's administration now changed into fixed hostility. It was in this mood that he went South in 1873 and wrote his book on South Carolina's Reconstruction government.

VIII. *South Carolina:*
The Prostrate State

Fresh from the crushing defeat of the Liberal Republicans, Pike embarked in January, 1873, on his influential visit to South Carolina. A series of his articles in the *Tribune* and the book built around these articles, *The Prostrate State: South Carolina under Negro Government,* bore telling traces of the Downeaster's political frustration and bitterness. Yet many of his contemporaries as well as later historians erroneously regarded him as merely an impartial and experienced Republican observer who happened to go South.

His immediate purpose in making the trip was to write a series for the *Tribune.* Perhaps Pike and Whitelaw Reid, the new editor of Greeley's paper, remembered the highly successful piece on Carolina which the correspondent had done in the spring of 1872. Gathering information from men like Wade Hampton and Senator Sprague, Pike had then written a vivid story of the "deplorable" conditions in the proud Palmetto State. A year before he even visited the South, he had assailed the carpetbaggers, the "great mass of [Negro] ignorance and barbarism," and the Federal troops which supported the Radical state government. In fact, he anticipated in this 1872 article every major theme in *The Prostrate State.*[1]

"I was moved to visit S. Carolina," Pike explains in his notebook, "from the extraordinary circumstances of its political condition." It had been the "birthplace of secession," the

[1] See above pp. 187 ff.

"peculiar home & centre of the rebellion," and was "the only spot under the sun where an ignorant Black Parliament legislated for & governed a cultivated and high spirited white population."[2]   Rhetoric aside, it appears likely that the *Tribune* editor and the Maine journalist regarded the trip from the first as likely to furnish another bill to add to their damning indictment of Grant and his carpetbagger and Negro allies in Carolina.[3]   Fortunately the revealing journal Pike kept while in the South contains not only the germ of his published material, but also many long passages which were transferred, after modifications, into print.

The *Tribune* gave enthusiastic editorial support to Pike's articles.[4]   Other newspapers across the country also publicized the series, although some of them attacked the *Tribune's* "impartial observer."   Frederick Douglass' *National New Era*, for example, assailed the author's tone as "calculated to fire the negro-hating heart to deeds of violence against the black race." "What good THE NEW YORK TRIBUNE expects to work by its thrusts at the struggling colored people we cannot imagine," the leading Negro spokesman declared.   The Pittsburgh *Dispatch* suggested that the *Tribune* "had not yet forgotten the unanimity with which the colored voters supported President Grant through last Autumn's campaign."

From other papers North and South came approval.   The Savannah *Republican* emphasized Pike's background in these words: "Years ago, when abolition was a forlorn hope and its

---

[2] Notebook No. 30, p. 64.

[3] For Reid's attitude toward "Grantism," see Royal Cortissoz, *The Life of Whitelaw Reid* (New York, 1921), I, 195-228, 314-28; and Harry W. Baehr, *The New York Tribune since the Civil War* (New York, 1936), pp. 145-54.

[4] *Tribune*, March 29, 1873.   The first article in Pike's series of seven on "South Carolina Prostrate" appeared on the front page of the *Tribune* of March 29, 1873; the last two articles appeared in the issue of April 19.   The four other *Tribunes* containing the series appeared on April 8, 10, 11, and 12, 1873.   Although the series is datelined from Columbia during late February and early March, the articles were probably written after Pike had returned to the North in late March.   The first four pieces correspond exactly to the first four chapters in *The Prostrate State*, the fifth article to the twelfth chapter, the sixth to the thirteenth, and the seventh and last article to the fourteenth chapter.

open advocates under the ban, Mr. Pike was one of their leaders—he shared in their struggles, he enjoyed their triumphs, and has had no cause, either of interest or ambition, to feel sympathetic toward the Southern people. . . . But he is a man of convictions, and an out-spoken one, and the unutterable horror and loathing, surprise and indignation, with which the actual condition of misgovernment and oppression at the South have inspired him, cannot be silenced. So he has spoken out and told truths which, from his lips and pen, will be listened to by the Northern people—ignorant accomplices in these crimes. . . ." The book inspired the *Charleston News and Courier* to declare, "Not pity, but justice, is all that South Carolina has ever asked or ever will ask." Meantime in the North, papers like the *Sun* and *Herald* saw the Pike series as confirmation of their own worst fears and as support for the attacks on Grant.[5]

The stir created by his articles probably impelled Pike to expand his material, pad it a bit here and there, and give it more permanent form in a book. To get his work published, however, he had to underwrite a large part of the costs, which he easily did through loans from New York friends.[6] Since the preface is dated October, 1873, he probably submitted his manuscript about that time. The New York firm of D. Appleton and Company published *The Prostrate State* early in December, 1873, at a price of one dollar. Copies were also on sale at the *Tribune* office, and advertisements proclaimed "THE BOOK FOR THE DAY" as a work of "keen observation, thorough research, and calm judgment."[7] The total number of sales is not known, but the book received wide publicity and probably sold well. In 1935 a new edition of the book was issued. Professor Henry Steele Commager wrote the introduction for this edition, in which the text is reprinted from the 1873 ver-

[5] These comments along with others reprinted in *Tribune*, April 19, 1873. Also clippings in Pike MSS.

[6] Information in the Whitelaw Reid MSS, courtesy of Professor Jeter Isely.

[7] *Tribune*, Dec. 6, 1873.

sion. Commager praises the "transparent honesty" and "thorough documentation" of Pike's study of South Carolina Reconstruction.[8]

Reviewers in the magazines generally applauded Pike's book. A lengthy notice in the *Literary World* endorsed Pike as one "who, in view of his long and enthusiastic service in the anti-slavery cause, can hardly be accused of color-prejudice."[9]

E. L. Godkin's influential *Nation* found "a great deal of valuable information as to the present condition of South Carolina" in the book. A *Nation* editorial, emblazoned "Socialism in South Carolina," borrowed heavily from Pike in showing that the average of intelligence among the vast majority of Negroes was low—"so low that they are slightly above the levels of animals." Godkin, another virtuous critic of the Grant administration, concluded with a query as to how long it would take to transform the "once 'sovereign State' of South Carolina into a truly loyal, truly Republican, truly African San Domingo."[10]

Reports of the bloody race rioting at Hamburg, South Carolina, in July, 1876, appalled many people all over the country. When discussion of the riot reached the House of Representatives, an incident occurred which suggests another aspect of *The Prostrate State's* early repercussions. A Democratic congressman from New York state assailed the "miserably bad government" which Pike had delineated in his book.

[8] Published by Loring and Mussey (New York, 1935). A Dutch translation, *Zuid-Carolina onder Negerbestuur*, was published in Holland in 1875, doubtless because of the author's diplomatic mission at The Hague during the war. According to a letter from Appleton's (Oct. 25, 1951), a fire in 1904 destroyed many of their records, including those concerning *The Prostrate State*.

[9] *Literary World*, IV (Jan., 1874), 116.

[10] *Nation*, XVIII (April 16, April 30, 1874), 282, 247-48. This editorial brought a stirring protest from "T. W. H." of Rhode Island, presumably Thomas Wentworth Higginson, an abolitionist and befriender of John Brown. The protest led Godkin to admit that his "assertion was too sweeping" and should have referred only to the coastal or Gullah Negroes. But he again insisted on the point that as a legislator the Negro was "merely a horrible failure" (*ibid.*, April 30, 1874, p. 282). A reviewer in the *Atlantic Monthly* (Feb., 1874), endorsed *The Prostrate State*, as did newspapers like the New York *Express* (Jan. 20, 1874), the *St. Louis Republican* (Jan. 20, 1874), the New York *Herald* (Jan. 11, 1874) (other clippings in Pike MSS).

Using the Maine Republican as his authority, the congressman
declared that the book showed how "after the carpet-bag
governments had taken nearly all, there was a worse crew of
robbers called native Africans of South Carolina." These
"provocations" the congressman offered not as justification for
the killing of Negroes in Carolina but merely as extenuating
circumstance. The retort of a Negro congressman from South
Carolina, Robert Smalls, to this attack was, "Have you the
book there of the city of New York?"[11]

Aside from its contemporary impact, *The Prostrate State*
has been much used by historians of the Reconstruction period.
A detailed study of the book's place in historiography is hardly
necessary, but one or two examples will illuminate this aspect.
Claude Bowers extravagantly designates Pike's work "the
'Uncle Tom's Cabin' of the redemption of the South," and he
explains: "Soon thoughtful men throughout the North were
reading the truth [about Reconstruction] which had been
denied them. Democrats had declared it—but here was Republican authority."[12] James Ford Rhodes, long the dean of
American historians and author of what was once the standard
study of post-1850 American history, cites *The Prostrate State*
no less than seventeen times in one chapter, devotes three full
pages to quotations from the book, and describes Pike in the
usual, reassuring words as a "strong anti-slavery man before
the war and a consistent Republican during it."[13] Some South

---

[11] *Congressional Record*, 44th Congress, 1st Session, p. 4707.

[12] *The Tragic Era: The Revolution after Lincoln* (Cambridge, Mass., 1929),
pp. 417-18.

[13] James Ford Rhodes, *History of the United States from the Compromise of 1850
to the Final Restoration of Home Rule at the South in 1877* (New York, 1906), VII,
149, 152-55. The seventeen citations are in chap. xlii. William A. Dunning, another
early authority on the subject, describes *The Prostrate State* as one of the "highly valuable sources of the period" by travelers (*Reconstruction, Political and Economic, 1865-
1877*, New York, 1907, p. 352). E. Merton Coulter, *The South during Reconstruction,
1865-1877* (Baton Rouge, 1947), p. 399, describes Pike's book as the "classic work on
the outrages" of Radical government in South Carolina. The most recent evidence
of the book's continuing influence is in a widely noticed series of articles in the
popular magazine *Life* (Sept. 10, 1956, p. 101), when Pike, though not identified, is
quoted about Reconstruction.

Carolina historians have seized upon Pike as chief witness, one stressing the fact that the "most interesting chronicle of the carpetbag-negro mis-rule" was written by a "dyed-in-the-wool Republican abolitionist."[14] From this it is clear how much influence Pike's supposed party orthodoxy and general background have had with most historians, as well as with his own generation.

This, then, is the position occupied by *The Prostrate State*. But Pike's journal affords the opportunity of a much closer and more instructive look at his visit in the South than does his printed account. By following his movements to some extent, examining the sources of his information, and comparing his own notes and first impressions with what he later published, a new and sharper light is thrown on the book and its author.

Early in the wet, gray morning of January 21, 1873, Pike's train crossed the Potomac. The rolling Virginia countryside he admired, but uncultivated patches of ground and the "old decayed looking town of Fredericksburg" were not so pleasing. Richmond, where he spent several days, offered him his first close look at postwar Southern conditions. The "soft & charming" weather with "no vestiges of ice or snow" probably mellowed the Downeaster; he benignly noted broad shady streets, handsome residences, and "the apparent thrift." He sentimentally sympathized with the "throngs of blacks out after dark" and enjoyed the "jolly countenances of the Negro wenches in the Streets." Even the Richmond newspaper discussions of financial issues struck a happy chord, for Pike detected "a healthy temper in this almost bankrupt State"

[14] Henry T. Thompson, *Ousting the Carpetbagger from South Carolina* (Columbia, 1927), p. 33. William W. Ball in his *State That Forgot: South Carolina's Surrender to Democracy* (Indianapolis, 1932), p. 138, tells a revealing story of the reaction of one adopted Carolinian to *The Prostrate State:* Austrian-born Martin Vorak left word at his hotel-desk to have a porter call him early the next morning. After reading *The Prostrate State* until late in the night, he finished it and fell asleep. When the Negro porter entered to arouse him at dawn the next day, Vorak, yelled, "Get out of here, you tam black rascal, I haf read *Prostrate State*,—I let you know I am vun vite South Caroleenian mineself."

indicated by the conservative newspapers' exhortations that the people should "carry their burdens like men" and reject the evil temptation to repudiate the vast state debt.[15]

During his visit in the lower house of the Virginia Legislature, Pike heard a "colored member ¾ths black" make a lengthy, aggressive, and capable speech against a tax proposal then being considered. The Negro was "listened to with a good deal of interest after it was found he could not be drowned out by rustlings & loud talk," although the "venerable Old Virginia gentlemen on the democratic benches looked on with a mixture of surprize & chagrin at the spectacle of such a successor" to Jefferson and Madison. The "self contained, half saucy half intelligent expression" of a colored senator prompted the observation that the "race has learned that it is not by modesty that their claims are to be advanced."[16]

After interviews with several white Conservative leaders, he left Richmond by train on January 23. Passing into the gently undulating, scrubpine country around the Virginia border, Pike spent an uncomfortably cool night in the little town of Weldon, North Carolina. The journalist kept the passing scene under close observation. He noted the "rawboned & stiff" cows, the ox-pulled cart "of the purest rural origin," and the "almost inviting" cabins perched on sand knolls in the midst of pine-fringed corn fields. Such things as the wages paid to the freedmen interested him, and in Weldon he learned that the male, ex-slave cook received fifteen dollars a month while the chambermaids earned only five. En route to Wilmington, he enviously spotted the timber which flourished in the inaccessible swamps, although on higher ground he thought he "found the Yankee by his tracks." Carloads of lumber, a new steam sawmill, and newly built shacks could only denote, he scribbled, the presence of imported, Northern enterprise.[17]

Pike found Wilmington wearing a shabby, "hopeless

[15] Notebook No. 28, pp. 33-34. [16] Notebook No. 28, p. 35.
[17] Notebook No. 29, pp. 1-3.

aspect," with sandy paths for streets and "a perfect welter of negroes whose nests shockingly disfigure the outskirts." The giant live oaks which kept their brilliant foliage in winter could not compensate for the "garbage of the streets, the wandering swine of the exact wild boar pattern," or the other underfed animals which roamed the roads. Amid such gloom, the visitor discerned a few hopeful signs: property had increased in value, finances flourished, and Wilmington business had doubled since the war. Even more encouraging to him was the fact that the railroads had fallen "into the thrifty hands of Northerners & it is for their interest to exploit the state which they are assiduously doing."[18]

Pike believed that even the Negro population in and around Wilmington had participated in "the general improvement." Some of them, he heard, had bought small pieces of land on the outskirts of the city, and they soon found land values upped by high cotton prices. The journalist heard often of "the thrifty & capable darkey." This led him to predict a "future for the race quite different from that bred from the old pro slavery idea of universal inferiority." Politically too, in this early stage of his journey, Pike approved of what he found; he judged that the Negro-controlled municipal government was conducted "with sense & prudence." The much criticized leagues or clubs which banded the Negroes into an "inexorable partizan association" he credited to the example set by the whites. If the freedmen failed to vote for party nominees, "their old enemy" would triumph. The Downeaster concluded that the "darkey . . . is not so much of a fool as he is of a philosopher in his politics." Such charitable views of the Negro in politics were not repeated in *The Prostrate State*. Pike's description of the situation in Columbia, and in South Carolina as a whole, presented a vastly different picture.[19]

[18] *Ibid.*, pp. 6-9.

[19] Notebook No. 29, pp. 9-10. He arrived in South Carolina during the last week of January, 1873, and apparently remained in Columbia, the capital, until February 20, when he began a tour to Charleston, Savannah, and Augusta. Returning briefly to

With his long years of experience as a Washington political correspondent and his numerous visits to sessions of Parliament during his trips to London, he naturally chose the legislative halls as a focus of interest. If British M. P.'s and peers had made him scornful of Washington senators, how might he regard the members, white or black, of a provincial legislature? Aside from his techniques of observation and independent study, Pike's journal furnishes us with some idea of the sources of his information and impressions. These are impressive neither in their number nor in their character.

The best example of this may be found in the use which Pike made of a casual conversation with a "round-headed, young black man" who chanced on one occasion to be standing beside him on the floor of the South Carolina lower house. In reply to a question from Pike about the white man then speaking, the Negro answered with a reference to the white speaker's scanty brainpower. "My pride of race was incontinently shocked," Pike explains; but he proceeded to converse with his "thick-lipped, wooly-headed" neighbor, pumping him about various members of the legislature. This conversation with an unknown man, which is recorded in the journal practically as it appears in the book, forms the larger part of Chapter V of *The Prostrate State,* which is headed "Sambo as a Critic on [*sic*] the White Man."[20] Apparently this is the only occasion on which Pike gained information from a Negro Carolinian; at least, it is the only one recorded in the journal. But there were a few whites, natives and carpetbaggers, whom he met and talked with.

There are eight instances mentioned in the journal when Pike gained information or opinions from native white Carolinians. A "low-country planter," who also happened to be

---

Columbia on March 20, he departed for Washington either the same or the next day. He spent altogether about two months in the South (*ibid.,* p. 13; Notebook No. 31, pp. 11-20).

[20] Chap. v, pp. 39-43; Notebook No. 29, pp. 18-21.

standing near by, commented on the shock of seeing the freedmen as legislators. This incident found its way into Pike's
book.[21] One of the few Conservative state senators, David R.
Duncan from Spartanburg, informed Pike that the Negro legislators learned the methods of legislation and the rules and
orders "like a flash." Yet Pike did not use this estimate from
a "Bourbon of pure blood" in his book.[22] Another Conservative legislator from Spartanburg, Gabriel Cannon, furnished
him with a couple of items,[23] and a white doorkeeper gave him
statistics on the composition of the legislature and the origins
of some of the Negro members.[24] The four other native white
sources, including a "rigid old secessionist," were unimportant
and need not be listed. The scarcity as well as the conservative
nature of his contacts with white Carolinians should be
clear.[25]

From carpetbaggers, too, the journalist learned some
things. He omitted from the articles and the book any mention
of the female schoolteacher from Vermont who claimed extensive influence as a lobbyist in Columbia. But then he might
well have ruffled many Northern feathers with his journal
references to "blatherskyting parasites" and "Northern Ama-
zons & leeches."[26] A fellow Downeaster who was employed in
the state auditor's office predicted the "Africanization" of the
state to Pike;[27] and Colonel S. A. Pearce, the agent of Rhode
Island's millionaire Senator Sprague, who had railway and
other business interests in South Carolina, told the newspaperman the Sherman version of the burning of Columbia.[28] Two
foreigners, a German ironfounder and an English gardener,

---

[21] *The Prostrate State*, p. 11; Notebook No. 29, p. 14.

[22] Notebook No. 30, p. 17.

[23] Notebook No. 30, pp. 53, 62; for one of these in *The Prostrate State*, see the
story on p. 86 of the Republican congressman, elected by Negro votes, whose prewar
stand on slavery is attacked.

[24] Notebook No. 29, p. 28; *The Prostrate State*, pp. 14-15.

[25] Notebook No. 30, pp. 15-18, 22, 27, 32, 118.

[26] Notebook No. 29, p. 18.

[27] *Ibid.*, p. 22; *The Prostrate State*, pp. 43-44.

[28] Notebook No. 30, p. 33; *The Prostrate State*, pp. 114-15.

complete the list of individuals whom Pike mentions in his notebooks.[29]

The inference cannot be drawn that the journalist, who was generally inquisitive and talkative, spoke with only those persons mentioned here. He undoubtedly failed to name the source for much that he recorded. Still, the failure to seek out either Negro or white Radical leaders suggests an unwillingness even to attempt an impartial survey. Merely observing the manners of legislators and bewailing the lack of decorum was a superficial approach to such a complex problem as "South Carolina under Negro Government."

If Pike was careless or casual in his search for information, were there any preconceived motives or theories which made his task easier? One factor which probably served just this purpose was his animus against the Grant administration. The darker the picture of the South Carolina Reconstruction government, which was yet controlled by the Radicals, the greater the discredit to Grant. And the *Tribune* correspondent perhaps yielded to the desire to strike back at the Radicals who had so recently triumphed over the Liberal Republicans. Strategic omissions as well as alterations seem to corroborate this explanation.

One clearly developed theme in Pike's original journal relates to quiescence and lethargy on the part of the white Carolinians. Commenting on the problem of inducing white immigrants to come to South Carolina, Pike had this to say in his notebook: "The old proprietors own such an overwhelming proportion of the soil that an intelligent combination among them, such as would be formed in six months by Yankees if the land were in their hands, would lead to measures that would restore the just equilibrium of the races and remove the offensive political anomaly that now exists, in a comparatively short period."[30] In the published version,

[29] Notebook No. 29, p. 26; *The Prostrate State*, p. 22; and Notebook No. 30, p. 56; *The Prostrate State*, pp. 100-101.
[30] Notebook No. 30, p. 49.

however, there is no invidious comparison of Carolina planters
and hustling Yankees. Pike merely declares that the whites
have the power, if they would use it, to "remove the offensive
political anomaly that now exists."[31]

Concerning this same topic of immigration, Pike commented
on the defeat of tax-exemption bills designed to attract industry. He privately noted that the legislature, "or at least the
white members of it," were not ready for an agitation of the
subject. "On this, as on all subjects bearing on the present &
future relationships of the races," he wrote, "the whites are
now wholly reticent & reserved, and apparently fearful." When
this same incident is mentioned in his book the explanation is
vastly changed. Referring to the defeat of the tax-exemption
measures, he declared that it merely illustrated how "the
jealousy of the blacks is constant against the white man, and
that they do not favor any influential participation by him in
the government of the State." The Negroes were "willing to
perpetrate the greatest injustices" to prevent white "participation."[32] "Participation," in this case, meant one of the typical
railway-subsidy or tax-exemption schemes which had encountered opposition.

In another place in his notebook Pike credited the great ma-
jorities which the Negroes and their allies wielded in some
counties with producing a feeling of hopelessness among the
whites, creating "the depression & inaction which prevails
among them in such a striking degree." Yet in the published
account this same matter of the counties with a great majority
of Negroes is discussed without any reference at all to white
"depression & inaction."[33] At one point during his stay in
Columbia the visitor noted "an air of mastery among the

[31] *The Prostrate State,* p. 106. Rowland T. Berthoff, "Southern Attitudes toward
Immigration, 1865-1914," *Journal of Southern History,* XVII (Aug., 1951), pp. 328-60,
has interesting material on this matter; also Robert H. Woody, "The Labor and
Immigration Problem of South Carolina during Reconstruction," *Mississippi Valley
Historical Review,* XVIII (Sept., 1931), 195-212.

[32] Notebook No. 30, pp. 6-7; *The Prostrate State,* p. 55.

[33] *Ibid.,* pp. 47-48; *The Prostrate State,* p. 56.

colored people" and expressed surprise at "how reticent the whites are in their dealings with the blacks, & how entirely self contained & self asserting the blacks appear to be." But the published version contains but one short reference to white reticence or fearfulness.[34]

This estimate of the whites' political inactivity takes on added significance in connection with another of Pike's original theories, namely that South Carolina was already, in early 1873, in the hands of her own people, white and colored, and that "there really is nothing within the just scope of federal power that can be done to relieve the State from its anomalous condition."[35] He judged that "any federal administration" which performed only "its legitimate duties" could have no influence on internal affairs in the state. If the whites and blacks would only forge some sort of harmonious union in the state government, "no federal administration will have any call to practice guardianship or meddle in any way with the State's Affairs."[36] According to this line of reasoning, it would be impossible to discredit the Grant administration or the Federal government by revealing any anomalous conditions in South Carolina. But in his book Pike largely followed another tack. The Washington government became, accordingly, the main instrument in supporting the Radicals who governed South Carolina.

"Outside forces" accomplished the changes which South Carolina had experienced during Reconstruction. This became a major tenet of *The Prostrate State*. The "ignoble and incompetent crowd" ruled the state by means of "an alien and borrowed authority only." The Negroes were the humiliating means whereby a "foreign" power forced the native whites to obey. "It is not the rule of intrinsic strength; it is the compulsive power of the Federal authority at Washington. But for that, the forces of civilization would readjust themselves

[34] Notebook No. 30, pp. 44-45; *The Prostrate State*, p. 110.
[35] Notebook No. 30, p. 23.
[36] Notebook No. 30, pp. 20-21.

and overturn the present artificial arrangement."[37]   He expressed his conviction that the whites had to have their relative weight in public affairs, not only in accordance with their numbers but with "the still weightier claims of property, intelligence, and enterprise."   "While the laws of the universe remain," Pike concluded, "these claims must in the end successfully assert themselves.   Not even governments can prevent it.   And it is about time for the Federal Administration to take this reflection to heart."[38]

The net result of his emphasis on Washington's responsibility for Reconstruction in South Carolina was to absolve the local whites; at the same time the local Negroes are pictured as the ignorant dupes, the tools, of Federal power.   Pike emphasized the importance of Federal troops and appointments in South Carolina, and he both recorded and published his observations on that aspect of Carolina affairs.[39]   But the sweeping manner in which he blamed Washington for the continuation of Radical rule, and the fact that this had not been so clear and simple in his notebooks, leads to the conclusion that the desire to damn Grant and the Radicals led him to distort his own findings.[40]

Yet Grant was not the only victim of Pike's dramatic indictment of Carolina Reconstruction.   Even more than the Radicals in Washington, the Negro in Carolina, and by implication the whole race, received the hardest blows and bore the brunt of the Maine journalist's most vitriolic denunciation.   The paradox of the antislavery spokesman with a bias against Negroes has already been discussed.   He frankly admitted that his "pride of race" was profoundly shocked when the

---

[37] *The Prostrate State*, p. 83.

[38] *The Prostrate State*, pp. 54, 57; no notebook source.

[39] Notebook No. 30, pp. 65-67; *The Prostrate State*, pp. 85-88.   See also Simkins and Woody, *South Carolina*, pp. 112-13.

[40] Such would, moreover, suit the general policy of the *Tribune* during 1873 and 1874.   Reconstruction in the South furnished the new editor, Whitelaw Reid, with much of his ammunition in the attack on Grant.   A series on Louisiana and one on Mississippi paralleled Pike's on South Carolina.   For examples see issues of April 9, 1873, Jan. 2, 1874.

young Negro standing beside him on the floor of the House
dared to criticize a white man.[41]

The racist or "white supremacy" note in *The Prostrate
State* can hardly be missed, and it appears that the author
added or greatly strengthened it, possibly unconsciously, in
preparing his material for publication. The examples which
could be cited are numerous, but the following comparison
shows one type of significant change. Commenting in general terms in his journal on the situation in Carolina, Pike
judged: "Looking at its situation & resources, we cannot admit
that S. Carolina is going to stop in its progress. . . ." The same
sentence, in the published version, became: "Looking at her
situation and resources, and the invincible qualities that mark
the Anglo-Saxon race, we cannot admit that she is going to be
arrested in her progress. . . ."[42] In another published passage,
which has no counterpart in the notebooks, Pike exclaimed that
to allow South Carolina to remain in the permanent control of
her "present rulers" would be "a violent presumption against
the manliness, the courage, and the energy of South Carolina
white men." "It would be a testimony against the claims of
Anglo-Saxon blood, and it would be an emphatic testimony to
the decline of public virtue that would be worse than all.
These considerations alone should be sufficient to inspire every
white man in South Carolina with a resolution to achieve a
reform that will bring the State back to its ancient respect-
ability."[43]

Even more damaging to the Negroes than the "Anglo-
Saxon" line was the close identity which Pike gave to ignorance
and corruption, on the one hand, and Negro blood on the
other. The end result of his portrayal of legislative venality
and incapacity is to make them seem inveterate racial charac-
teristics. Yet his original, on-the-spot impressions were dif-

[41] See above, p. 209.
[42] Notebook No. 29, p. 42; *The Prostrate State*, pp. 56-57.
[43] *The Prostrate State*, p. 89.

ferent. On one occasion while witnessing the legislature in action, Pike observed that the art of legislative robbery was as well understood in Carolina as in any Tammany Hall conclave. As proof for this in the notebook he cited the example of a certain white legislator, "the adroitest among the strikers," who angled for bribes from a railway company which desired a charter. But his illustration in *The Prostrate State* for the Tammany parallel is "the colored Representatives in Congress from South Carolina."[44] Another journal statement is: "Sambo dotes on committees. The white man has shown him their uses & how they can be more profitable." But the revised version reads: "Sambo dotes on legislative committees. The struggle to get on those that pay best is amusing."[45]

In giving a racial slant to Carolina corruption, corruption which admittedly existed, Pike had every reason for realizing his injustice.[46] The Liberal Republicans of 1872 had raised their loudest cries against the infamous jobbery they professed to see in Washington. And even in Columbia Pike bemoaned "this corrupt perversion of the objects of government" which was rampant "throughout many other parts of the country." Either "society is rotting all the way through," he reasoned, or else "the villains are too much or too many for the honest men." In this broad context, it is clear that corruption had no racial aspect, unless it be a white one.[47]

Other omissions were damaging to the general picture of freedmen. Concerning their political behavior, for example, Pike originally decided that the only well-grounded complaint that could be made against the Negro was that "his reasoning & his methods are no improvement upon those of a large

[44] Notebook No. 30, p. 62; *The Prostrate State*, p. 46.

[45] Notebook No. 30, p. 5; *The Prostrate State*, p. 109.

[46] In his book he borrowed heavily from the "Report of the Joint Select Committee to Inquire into the Condition of Affairs in the late Insurrectionary States, made to the two Houses of Congress, February 10, 1872" (*The Prostrate State*, chaps. xviii through xxxiii, pp. 122-272). This portion of the book is the least interesting and most colorless part of his narrative. For a more recent discussion of the frauds, etc., see Simkins and Woody, *South Carolina*, pp. 147-85.

[47] Notebook No. 30, p. 39.

majority of white men." He explained the Negro majority of
30,000 in one election as arising from the fact that "Sambo
is fighting for his life, with a deep-seated apprehension of his
enemy." His only weapon was his ballot, and with this he
was bound to "give one blow every time an election comes
round." The white man, on the other hand, might vote or
not "as the humor seizes him." This was the notebook explanation. In his book Pike merely comments that "all the blacks
vote, while the whites do not."[48]

On the subject of the freedman's "ignorance," or "the
blackness of darkness" as he confusingly phrased it, Pike left
out a great deal more than he included. Education is treated
only briefly on about two pages of his book. The conclusion
there is the gloomy one that education of the Negro offers no
remedy for Carolina's dilemma. And race is the reason why
it does not. "The education they [the Negroes] require is the
formation of a race the opposite of the existing race. They
have to be taught not to lie, not to steal, not to be unchaste. To
educate them properly is to revolutionize their whole moral
nature." "Reading and writing" merely lends a cutting edge
to their "moral obtuseness" because Negro education really
means "the moral enlightenment and regeneration of a whole
people debauched and imbruted for ages."[49] A more discouraging estimate could hardly be imagined; the factual basis for it
is not to be found in Pike's journal. As far as can be determined from his notes, he gave no attention to educational
matters while in the South. The free school system, inaugu-
rated by the Radicals in their constitution of 1868, either
escaped the journalist's notice or did not awaken his interest.
As a result, in an area where the Reconstruction governments'
achievement, not only in South Carolina but in most of the
Southern states, is most widely recognized, Pike remained not
only uninformed but outspokenly prejudiced. Where he did

---

[48] Notebook No. 29, p. 19; No. 30, pp. 8-9; *The Prostrate State*, pp. 89-90.
[49] *The Prostrate State*, pp. 62-63.

observe the freedmen at work—in the sun-splashed fields—he found that the Negro made "the best of workers," men and women alike being "vigorous, quick and athletic." The clear but undrawn moral was that the Negro's place was in the field.[50]

Thus Pike presented the South Carolina situation to the nation. In 1873, and since then, "this prominent Republican Abolitionist" from Maine appeared to offer the outsider's objective view of a controversial and crucial issue.[51] Part of the explanation for the book's weakness seems to lie in a tenuous psychological area; Pike, even as a vehement antislavery spokesman, had revealed lack of understanding or sympathy for the human potential of the Negro. This, however, still leaves unexplained the differences between his journal and his published work. Stylistic improvements and other such changes are to be expected. But discrepancies such as have been mentioned reflect more than mere stylizing.

Pike's animus against the Grant administration may account for part of his abusive treatment of the South Carolina Negroes, Grant's Radical allies. Reworking the material for publication in the *Tribune*, he perhaps wished to have his articles conform to the editorial policy of the leading Liberal Republican organ, as well as to find a numerous and receptive audience in the North.

The solution which Pike suggested for the problems besetting South Carolina, was, in reality, no solution at all. The entire nation, and not merely South Carolina, he asserted, had to study and understand the "Negro question," for "it is a question of the predominance and antagonism of races." If it were true that ours was not "a white man's government," should it be "a black man's government"? Then, perhaps recalling earlier moral crusades of the Republicans, Pike

---

[50] *The Prostrate State*, p. 273; Notebook No. 31, pp. 3-9.

[51] This phrase, typical of many descriptions of *The Prostrate State*'s author, is found in Robert G. Rhett, *Charleston, An Epic of Carolina* (Richmond, Va., 1940), p. 283.

admitted: "We only disposed of one phase of the negro question in abolishing slavery. The great perplexity of establishing just relations between the races in the negro States is yet
to be encountered. And it comes upon the country under a
cloud of embarrassments. It has to be settled under the growing urgency . . . of the question whether the great mass of the
black population at the South is not now mentally and morally
unfit for self-government, and whether the progress of events
will not force a modification of the original reconstruction
acts—not based upon race or color or previous condition, but
upon other considerations yet to be evolved and eluci-
dated."[52]

The "other considerations" were never found. When
Democratic rule in South Carolina was restored in 1876, factors
other than the ballot played a part. The Hamburg massacre,
"rifle clubs," and "Red Shirts" with their "shotgun policy"
were among the answers found to the question Pike had treated
three years earlier.[53] While these events shook "the Prostrate
State," Pike was quietly pursuing literary labors in his far-away
Maine home.

[52] *The Prostrate State*, pp. 68-69.
[53] Simkins and Woody, *South Carolina*, pp. 474-513. For a less scholarly view, see
William A. Sheppard, *Red Shirts Remembered: Southern Brigadiers of the Reconstruction
Period* (Atlanta, 1940).

IX. *The Last Years*

A BOUT THE TIME he returned from Europe in 1866 Pike purchased a large, handsome home, known as the Mansion House, which overlooks the St. Croix River at a point about twelve miles below Calais. Originally a tavern in the early nineteenth century, the Mansion House had later been the residence of an affluent shipbuilder. Despite its fine colonial lines, and exceptional setting, Pike purchased the residence cheaply, even for those days. His agent had written that it could be bought for "$3000 in gold or $4000 'Skedadle' money that is greenbacks."[1]

The Pikes spent many pleasant summers at this Mansion House in Maine. He had always enjoyed sailing, and after the war his small sailing craft was much in use. The fishing and hunting were excellent, and Pike and his friends took advantage of that fact. Just as today, well-to-do New Yorkers and Washingtonians in the Gilded Age were happy to retreat to Maine in the summertime, and the Pikes hospitably received their political and journalistic friends.

One important source of pleasure and relaxation for the journalist was "driving." He took as much pride in his horses and turn-outs as any present-day Jaguar owner takes in his machine. Speed fascinated him, so much so that he invariably clocked his trips when riding over the countryside. Residents

[1] Sam G. Pike to Pike, April 4, 1864, Pike MSS; this letter does not specify but presumably the reference is to the Mansion House. The Mansion House still stands as one of the show places of the St. Croix valley.

of the Calais area still relish this aspect of Pike's character since he left them tangible evidence of it: he had twelve stone markers cut from gray granite, and, after measuring twelve miles down the road from Calais to the Mansion House by counting the revolutions of his buggy wheel, this early speed fan and his wife placed a marker at the end of each mile. Thus he could time his progress to and from Calais.[2]

When not enjoying these varied activities, he worked at improving the grounds of the Mansion House, planting trees and laying out paths through the forest along the river bank. Gentlemanly farming took up some time. Like his friends, Greeley and Dana, Pike had the sentimental if not the economic instincts of a farmer; every spring and summer after his return from Europe, he supervised the sowing and harvest of his small grain fields, and he kept some livestock about the place.[3]

Each year when the snow began to fall in Maine, however, the journalist in him triumphed over the farmer, and the Pikes headed for Philadelphia and Washington. This had been his custom since the 1840's and old age did not change it. Pike's interest in political life still drew him to the nation's capital. His editorials for the *Sun* continued through the winter of 1876-77. He remained after 1872 a bitter critic of the administration, and observed with mixed satisfaction and outrage the corruption, graft, and general "low tone" which also marked Grant's second term in office.[4]

[2] H. E. Lamb, "James Shepherd Pike," undated tear sheet from the *Calais Advertiser*. Mr. Lamb kindly furnished this article, along with others of local interest in connection with Pike, and several photographs. Some of the markers may be seen today alongside U. S. Highway 1 between Robbinston and Calais.

[3] For example, see Notebook No. 32, p. 41. George F. Talbot, "James Shepherd Pike," *Collections and Proceedings of the Maine Historical Society*, I (1890), 225-60, has some reminiscences on this personal aspect. Talbot's paper, which was read to the Maine Historical Society in 1885, also contains an appreciation of Pike written by his daughter, Mrs. Mary Caroline Pike Robbins of Hingham, Massachusetts. Mrs. Robbins was a painter and writer; a large number of her watercolors are in the Pike MSS. For a list of her writings, see *History of Town of Hingham, Massachusetts* (Hingham, 1893), I, 222.

[4] *Sun*, Oct. 7, 1875; March 8, 1876; also *Tribune*, March 1, 1875, for another defense of the 1872 bolt.

In the spring of 1876 he was about ready to give up in disgust on the "reform" issue, and he editorially inquired if the country was "debauched and demoralized." Had Americans become "case hardened to political immorality and crime"? But he thought he discerned two possible reasons why apathy reigned. First, the rural Republicans believed that they could "uncouple their train from the Washington engine," and since the "localism of our interior political organization" made them largely self-supporting, their claim of independence from Washington was partially justified. The other, and more characteristic, reason he advanced for the immobility of the "public conscience" was a "profound fear of Democratic ascendancy that is felt by the great mass of decent Republicans."

On this latter point, the veteran journalist proved that his ancient partisanship still blinded him to one of the fundamental political facts of the day: namely the "purification" and rehabilitation of the Democracy which had occurred since the war. Democratic endorsement of Greeley in 1872 had indicated that a majority of the Democratic leaders, at least, had been converted to the new economic dispensation. Pike himself had furnished in *The Prostrate State* an excellent bit of ammunition in the Democratic fight for "redemption" in the Southern states. Yet the habits of a lifetime are not easily dropped, and in 1876, even as those prodigious wavers of the bloody shirt, he could still say: "There is such an apprehension of committing the Government into the hands of those who sought to destroy it, that numbers of honest men would to-day submit to almost any degree of Republican maladministration and wickedness, sooner than vote to give power to the Democrats."[5]

Despite this opaque view of the Democrats, the New Englander continued to attack the Grant administration's Southern policy. He still believed as he had in 1872 that Grant's whole

[5] *Sun,* March 16, 1876.

Southern policy had "been based on party and personal grounds solely, and this is the present fountain of all the troubles down there, from first to last." Forgetting that he himself had originally justified Radical reconstruction on party grounds, he now thought that the whole Southern question had "never been treated from a judicial or statesmanlike point of view"[6]

Louisiana political chaos and violence, accompanied by the intervention of Federal troops, kept the Southern question in the headlines during the winter of 1874-75. Pike calmly viewed the matter in terms of home rule. Was the South to become merely another Ireland? He condemned the national legislators for trying to eradicate certain racial and social evils in the South, since "you cannot legislate virtue into a people nor vice out of them." Sounding much like traditional Southern apologists, he insisted that "outsiders" should be "careful and reserved" in judging Southern matters; to introduce the strong arm of Federal force in order "to settle difficulties and embarrassments growing out of fundamental changes between the races, which would compose themselves if left to time, is unwise and hazardous." The injustices and hardships which would be the Negro's lot under home rule were inevitable, and anyhow, the "progress of all civilization and the amendment of human condition has always been supremely slow."[7]

Thus the former Radical Republican and antislavery champion foreshadowed much of the thinking and rationalizing that lay behind the compromise of 1876-77 when the Republicans finally renounced a large part of their humanitarian mission in the South in exchange for another four years of executive control. Professor C. Vann Woodward has recently written, in his *Reunion and Reaction: The Compromise of 1877 and the End of Reconstruction*, that the bargain, or series of bargains, involved in the settlement of the Hayes-Tilden electoral

[6] *Tribune*, Feb. 23, 1875.
[7] *Tribune*, March 1, 1875; datelined Washington, Feb. 27.

controversy revealed profound changes in the party of Stevens and Sumner. The compromise brought the party that had originated and engineered Radical reconstruction into an alliance with former rebels and slaveholders. The "party of Carpetbaggery" repudiated the carpetbaggers, and the former champions of emancipation and freedmen's rights abandoned the Negro to his former masters.[8]

Pike and some of his Liberal Republican colleagues had been demanding the general equivalent of this policy at least four years earlier. That did not mean, however, that he or many of his contemporaries saw the deeper significance of the compromise when it was settled. The bargain meant, in part, that the "dominant whites" in the South secured political autonomy along with nonintervention in racial matters and a promised future share in the "blessings of the new economic order."[9] All this Pike would have conceded in 1872. Now, not only was he too close to the exciting events of 1876-77 to see the over-all picture, but his alienation from both major political parties gave him something of a plague-on-both-your-houses attitude. Pike's *Sun* editorials in December, 1876, and January, 1877, were filled with indignation at the Republican attempt to "steal" the election by "frauds" in Louisiana, South Carolina, and Florida. For him these were additional manifestations of the corruption which he had so vigorously assailed in 1872 and afterwards. In what was virtually his last important editorial, the Downeaster cried: "It is a pretty crowd, indeed, who are engineering the fortunes of the once noble and triumphant Republican party, but now fallen, fallen, fallen from its high estate."[10] Distracted by his disgust with the election "frauds," he did not realize that a settlement of the Southern question was at hand.

The economic and political factors that lay behind the last

[8] Woodward, *Reunion*, p. 211.
[9] *Ibid.*, p. 246.
[10] *Sun*, Jan. 17, 1877. For the pro-Tilden policy of the *Sun*, see Wilson, *Dana*, pp. 443 ff.

great compromise concerning the Southern Negro were indeed complex; no simple statement of them could possibly suffice. But one social aspect of the development should be emphasized in connection with Pike's case: throughout his long career as a Free Soil Whig, and Antislavery, Radical, and Liberal Republican, he had never been deeply concerned over the lot of the Negro in America. Despite his great hatred for the institution of slavery, his view of the Negro as an inferior being closely resembled the proslavery racial argument. During the 1850's he had contemplated disunion partially because he was indifferent, if not hostile, toward the slaves and fiercely hated the slaveholders. He had fought strenuously to keep the territories free soil in the 1850's not only to keep them from being contaminated by the vile institution of slavery, but also because "just so much of North America as is possible" had to be preserved for the white man.

During the war he had been ready to accept a negotiated peace, partially because of his distress over the financial and military muddle in the North, but also because the slaveholders and their human chattels might thereby be cooped up in a Southern "negro pen." This would be, in his view, one way of "sloughing off" the "mass of barbarism" that filled the South. After the war he accepted Negro suffrage in the Southern states as a politico-economic necessity for the Republican party. Events soon made it clear that the Democrats were not, indeed could not afford to be, economically "heretical" concerning the tariff, the finances, or such matters as the debt and taxes. This fact, along with his disgust at the brazen jobbery that characterized the Grant era, kept him ambivalent toward the two parties from 1872 on. Also from that time on his attitude toward the white Southerners, or at least the conservative, respectable element (like Wade Hampton), changed from his ancient contempt for and vindictiveness towards the "slaveholder." It was probably an unconscious development, but at last Pike had realized that class interests might traverse the Mason-Dixon line.

Happily, Pike spent the last years of his life outside the main currents of national politics, if the torpid administration of President Rutherford B. Hayes may be said to have had currents. The Downeaster was sixty-five years old in 1876, and had only six years to live. He spent these years fruitfully engaged in literary work and, thanks to his activities during that time, he earned the gratitude of historians of later generations. The two books which he published in 1879, *The New Puritan* and *The First Blows of the Civil War*, although vastly different in content, were both labors of love. Perhaps that is why they reflect some of the best that was in Pike's character.[11]

The New Puritan: New England Two Hundred Years Ago is the less important of the two books. The title is misleading, for, as the subtitle reveals, the book is actually an "Account of the Life of Robert Pike [,] the Puritan who Defended the Quakers, Resisted Clerical Domination, and Opposed the Witchcraft Prosecution." Robert Pike, a seventeenth-century ancestor of the Maine journalist, appealed to him as an early defender of toleration and an opponent of the strict rule of the Puritan clergy. The materials for a full biography did not exist; so Pike, working with published and archival material, wove a sketchy life of his atypical Puritan ancestor around the few major events for which evidence was available.

There is some exaggeration of Robert Pike's role, but the little book is useful to the student of seventeenth-century New England. The author modestly admitted in his preface that the book would most likely interest the numerous descendants of Robert Pike, but the first edition, which was probably limited to a small number, sold out quickly and a second was soon

[11] *The New Puritan* (New York: Harper & Brothers, 1879), 244 pp.; *First Blows* (New York: American News Company, 1879), 526 pp.

issued. This proved to be a mistake, and Dana soon reported to his friend that the major part of the second edition was still on the publisher's hands. "I should say that the best thing you can do is to take them," Dana slyly suggested, "and give them to the district school libraries throughout the State of Maine. By such means judiciously directed you may yet elect yourself Governor of the State."[12]

The other book Pike published in the closing years of his life has survived better, for it is a valuable source for the study of the turbulent 1850's. *First Blows of the Civil War* is a collection of what he termed "public records" and private correspondence, the former consisting largely of a selection of his editorials and political letters in the *Tribune* from 1850 to 1860. The private correspondence is a large number of the personal letters addressed to him in the same period, the most numerous and important being from Chase, Dana, Greeley, Fessenden, Gurowski, and others among the political and journalistic group which helped launch the Republican party in the mid-1850's.

In a day when many public men either destroyed or bowdlerized their papers, Pike must be credited with courage in the publication of so much of his correspondence. On the whole he worked honestly in giving his material to posterity. In the letters, for example, most of the omissions are of purely personal references to Mrs. Pike or to the families of his correspondent. Although there is less purification and name-eliminating than was common in the painfully proper (and dull) era, he occasionally toned down some of the abusive passages by eliminating an adjective or an adverb. The spirited Gurowski's letters are among the most interesting, along with Greeley's, but even they would have been improved if Pike had

[12] Dana to Pike, Aug. 23, 1880, Pike MSS. For a review of *The New Puritan,* which both praised and criticized the work, see the *Atlantic Monthly,* XLIV (July, 1879), 125-26. The abolitionist Quaker poet, John Greenleaf Whittier, encouraged Pike to write this book; one of his Quaker ancestors had been among the persecuted Friends defended by Robert Pike in the 1650's. See *The New Puritan,* preface; John G. Whittier, *Narrative and Legendary Poems* (Boston, 1888), pp. 419-21, 435.

included the salutations: the Polish count usually began his letters with "Damn Yankee" or "Dear blundering Yankee."[13]

The editorials and political articles are less valuable than the letters, since the student of the period may go to the newspaper files. With the important exception of his disunionist arguments,[14] Pike included a broad sampling and transcribed his material accurately. As a journalist in the 1850's his stylistic excesses probably helped him become a national figure; as a sophisticated former diplomat and retired free lancer in the 1870's his improved writing taste compelled him to eliminate some of the verbiage and rhetorical flourishes of his early pieces. Regardless of these slight changes, the published editorials and newsletters give a fair indication of the vigorous, slashing style that made Pike a famous correspondent in the 1850's. Like other journalists of his day, he gave his readers partisan polemics rather than factual reports. Yet there was no pretense of detachment, and the aroused, crusading spirit that animated his antislavery Republicanism must have appealed to the vast *Tribune* audience. His hard-hitting and occasionally sarcastic articles were aptly termed "first blows," for he gave no quarter to his opponents in the stormy decade that preceded civil conflict.

First Blows of the Civil War is a book for historians, and it must have annoyed Pike when magazines like the *Nation* derogated his newspaper articles as of no permanent value "except to the future historian, for whom they may throw light upon disputed points." Another of the *Nation's* comments, which testifies admirably about the change that had occurred in the Northern public temper since the Civil War, is the statement that much of the antislavery material was as hard to read as "old sermons."[15] James Ford Rhodes, writing about

---

[13] The originals of the published letters, along with others from the prewar period, are in the Pike MSS.

[14] See above, pp. 18-28.

[15] *Nation*, XXIX (Sept. 25, 1879), 214.

the turn of the century, was the first important student of the period to use the material in *First Blows*. Since his time many of the better histories, monographic and general, include material afforded them by Pike's collection.[16]

There were some contemporaries who appreciated *First Blows of the Civil War* when it appeared. A young *Tribune* writer, David D. Lloyd, gratified the aging Downeaster with a letter which struck a happy note, for the younger man felt about the book and the decade it covered just as did Pike. "It was a great period," he wrote kindly, "and they were large men who moved in it. I suppose the golden age is always a past age; but, in truth, when I consider the flatness and dullness and pure personality of the politics of the present day, I look back with something like longing to the days when there were real, and not manufactured, issues, and principles were at stake between the two parties."[17]

For Pike too the period of the antislavery crusade had become a golden age, and he never satisfactorily adjusted to the crass, materialistic standards that prevailed after the Civil War. He died suddenly on November 24, 1882, at the age of seventy-one, just as he was about to depart on his annual migration from Calais. His will directed that Mrs. Lizzie Ellicott Pike receive the Mansion House, other real estate, and the sum of thirty thousand dollars for her use and disposal. He left the income from about fifty thousand dollars to the other members of his family; his daughter, Mrs. J. H. Robbins, received the largest share but he also included his various nieces and nephews. Following the decease of these legatees, all of the income was to be transferred to four charitable funds which he designated: "the Calais Free Library and Reading Room Fund, the Calais Poor Widows Fund, the Calais Hospital and Free Medicine Fund, and the Calais Fuel Fund."[18]

[16] For Rhodes's use of *First Blows*, see his *History of the United States from the Compromise of 1850* (New York, 1893), II, 178 ff. For later examples, see Isely, *Greeley, passim,* or Potter, *Secession Crisis,* pp. 23 ff.

[17] D. D. Lloyd to Pike, May 12, [1879?], Pike MSS.

[18] Copy of will in Pike MSS.

It is for the Calais Free Library that Pike is best remembered in the pleasant little town where he grew up and from which he never dissociated himself. In addition to the income from the trust fund, he also bequeathed to the city his "homestead property" along the St. Croix river and near the main street of present-day Calais. This property he designated as the site of the public library. A few years after his death Frederick A. Pike and another local citizen, Freeman H. Todd, each added five thousand dollars for the building of a brick library. In 1892 the small, handsome Calais Free Library and Reading Room was opened to the public and is yet enjoyed by residents of the area.[19]

Pike's love of reading thus benefited both him and Calais. The only strange aspect of his generous arrangements for a free local library was a clause in his will which still haunts and harasses the librarian. "I interdict the purchase of all novels for this library," he commanded, "except such as have been published more than ten years, as I do not wish to make it a receptacle of rubbish." Cold comfort the lovers of the latest bestsellers got from James Pike.[20] His personal library is housed in a private section of the building and contains a wide variety of books ranging from *French without a Master in Six Easy Lessons* to Smollett's translation of Voltaire's *Works*.[21]

For his time the Maine journalist was a well-read man. Like so many of his more important contemporaries, he was largely self-educated and apparently his appetite for books increased with age. Despite all his accumulated information from reading and the ability to express himself which he developed and which his writings reveal, he himself realized his

---

[19] Article by H. E. Lamb in *Calais Advertiser*, Sept. 29, [1948?].

[20] Pike will, Pike MSS. Conversations with Miss Edith Beckett, the librarian. Other arrangements have been made for buying new fiction.

[21] There are various editions in his personal collection which appear to be Americana items, such as an 1800 edition of Jefferson's *Notes on Virginia*, first editions of Fanny Butler, Emerson, Irving, and such. There are autographed first editions of some of Henry James, Sr.'s works, since he was a personal friend with whom Pike occasionally corresponded in a light, joking manner.

limitations. From the vantage point of Europe he had decided' that Americans, of all people, were what he called "newspaper educated." He later defended this trait when he argued in the *Sun* that newspapers were the best mode of influencing "the general judgment" and spreading "wide the seeds of truth and knowledge." This was so because of all the media for communicating ideas the press reached the largest number.[22]

But such easy, superficial reasoning did not actually satisfy Pike about his own or his contemporaries' education. It was probably toward the end of his life, when the original anti-slavery dream had become spoiled by the troubled events of Reconstruction and by the accompanying Northern reaction, that he regretfully concluded that Americans, as a rule, "are an unlearned people." The foremost men in the country often worked up from the "ground tier," and they reached manhood without education and usually without having the time to read or study in order to remedy the defect. "They know the present by contact and experience, and rapid instructions," he concluded, "but of the great Past they know little or nothing. It is a great defect."[23] He judged himself as fairly and honestly as could any man. That alone, in any generation, is a difficult but creditable achievement.

[22] *Sun,* March 9, 1876.
[23] Undated memorandum in the Pike MSS.

Bibliography

I. Manuscript Sources

Pike MSS—The Pike manuscripts in the Calais Free Library, Calais, Maine, constitute the backbone of this study. It is a large and rich collection, which is well preserved but disorganized. The principal items are as follows:

a. NOTEBOOKS—From 1861 until his death in 1882, Pike spasmodically kept a notebook or journal in which he wrote many of his ideas, copied his letters, and jotted down memoranda about conversations or his reading. The forty-two small notebooks are written in ink and in pencil; some of the penciled pages have become illegible. My notebook citations refer to a typed transcript of the original volumes, which the Calais Free Library generously allowed the Princeton Library to keep on an extended interlibrary loan. Aside from the drafts of Pike's letters, perhaps the most valuable material is related to his South Carolina visit; much of the original version of *The Prostrate State* is contained in two of the notebooks. A relatively small portion of the material in the notebooks has been included in Professor Harold Davis' M.A. thesis in manuscript at Columbia University, "Notebooks of James S. Pike, 1861-1882."

b. LETTERS—The letters addressed to Pike number in the hundreds and date from 1850 until 1882. The originals of the letters he included in *First Blows*, plus others from the 1850's, are valuable for the study of prominent Republicans like Chase, Greeley, and Fessenden. He apparently did not preserve as many letters after 1860, but there are, nevertheless, a large number from the later period.

c. SCRAPBOOKS—Pike befriended me by making these. In them he pasted his articles and editorials from the *Tribune* and from Dana's *Sun*. There are about a dozen of these "Original Article" scrapbooks, covering the period from 1850 until the late 1870's. Those from the 1850's are particularly interesting, since he marked and edited many of the pieces for publication in *First Blows*. There are also scrapbooks of "Miscellaneous Articles" which contain varied items that interested him as well as clippings from Maine newspapers relating to his state and local political activities. This rich assembly of newspaper material largely obviated the need for an extensive study of newspaper files, except for the *Tribune* in certain periods.

d. MISCELLANEOUS—In addition to the notebooks mentioned above, there are about a dozen or more notebooks relating to varied topics like "English Agriculture," or "Dutch History." Several of these are biographically valuable, such as the personal memoir of his early life which is used in the first chapter and the notebooks which contain Pike's reminiscences about men and events in his early Calais life. Also there are several large envelopes of assorted newspaper clippings, receipts, and business memoranda, and a small collection of photographs. Pike's personal library, which is kept intact in the Calais Free Library, is an interesting collection.

JSP Papers—The James Shepherd Pike Papers in the manuscripts division of the Library of Congress, Washington, D. C., consist mainly of letters from Pike to William Pitt Fessenden. Although some are from the prewar period, most of them were written while Pike was abroad. Some are duplicated in the notebooks, but the collection is especially useful for a Radical slant on domestic politics and foreign policy.

DoS Papers—The Department of State Papers in the National Archives, Washington, D. C., contain transcripts of Seward's despatches to Pike and the original reports from Pike to Seward. Since the published despatches in *Foreign Papers* are highly edited and often unrepresentative, these DoS Papers are indispensable in studying Civil War diplomacy. The "Appointment Papers" in the same section of the National Archives also contain valuable material.

Other papers—The following contain material of slight value:
Salmon P. Chase Papers, Library of Congress
Charles A. Dana Miscellaneous Papers, Library of Congress
Adam de Gurowski Papers, Library of Congress
Elihu B. Washburne, Jr., Papers, Library of Congress

II. PIKE'S PRINTED BOOKS AND PAMPHLETS

Chief Justice Chase. New York, 1873; 18 pp.
Contributions to the Financial Discussion, 1874-1875. New York, 1875; 44 pp.

The Financial Crisis: Its Evils and Their Remedy. New York, 1867; 38 pp.

The Finances, 1867-1878. Privately distributed volume containing his three financial pamphlets.

First Blows of the Civil War. New York, 1879; 526 pp.

Horace Greeley in 1872: His Political Position and Motives in the Late Presidential Contest. New York, 1873; 15 pp.

The New Puritan: New England Two Hundred Years Ago. New York, 1879; 244 pp.

The Prostrate State: South Carolina under Negro Government. New York, 1873; 279 pp.

The Prostrate State: South Carolina under Negro Government. A reprint of the first edition text with a twenty-page introduction by Henry Steele Commager. New York, 1935; 279 pp.

The Restoration of the Currency. New York, 1868; 52 pp.

III. OTHER PRINTED PRIMARY SOURCES

APTHEKER, HERBERT, ed. *A Documentary History of the Negro People in the United States.* New York, 1951.

BIGELOW, JOHN. *Retrospections of an Active Life.* New York, 1909-13. 5 vols.

BEALE, HOWARD K., ed. "The Diary of Edward Bates," *Annual Report* of the American Historical Association, *1930.* Washington, 1933.

Boston Courier, January-May, 1849.

Calais Advertiser, 1872-1873, and scattered earlier issues.

CARLYLE, THOMAS. "Ilias in Nuce," *Macmillan's Magazine,* VIII (August, 1863), 301.

————. "Occasional Discourse on the Negro Question," *Fraser's Magazine,* XL (December, 1849), 670-79.

CHASE, SALMON P. "Diary and Correspondence of Salmon P. Chase," *Annual Report* of the American Historical Association, *1902.* Washington, 1905.

Congressional Globe.

Congressional Directory. . . . Washington, 1861.

CURTIS, GEORGE W., ed. *The Correspondence of John L. Motley.* New York, 1889. 2 vols.

DANA, CHARLES A. *Recollections of the Civil War.* New York, 1898.

FORD, WORTHINGTON C., ed. *A Cycle of Adams Letters.* Boston, 1920. 2 vols.

Gazette and Advertiser (Calais), August, 1836-August, 1838.

GREELEY, HORACE, and JOHN F. CLEVELAND, compilers. *A Political Textbook for 1860.* New York, 1860.

GREELEY, HORACE. *Recollections of a Busy Life.* New York, 1868.

GUROWSKI, ADAM. *Diary.* Boston and Washington, 1862-63. 3 vols.

MILLER, DAVID HUNTER, ed. *Treaties and Other International Acts of the United States of America.* Washington, 1931- . 8 vols.

MOORE, JOHN B. *A Digest of International Law.* Washington, 1906. 8 vols.

NICOLAY, JOHN G., and JOHN HAY, eds. *Complete Works of Abraham Lincoln.* New York, 1905. 12 vols.

Official Records of the Union and Confederate Navies in the War of the Rebellion. Series I, 27 vols., Washington, 1894-1914. Series II, 3 vols., Washington, 1922.

[REED, WILLIAM B.] *The Diplomatic Year: Being a Review of Mr. Seward's Foreign Correspondence of 1862.* Philadelphia, 1863.

———. *Paper Containing a Statement and Vindication of Certain Political Opinions.* Philadelphia, 1862.

———. *A Review of Mr. Seward's Diplomacy.* [Philadelphia ?], 1862.

REID, WHITELAW. *After the War: A Southern Tour.* Cincinnati, 1866.

SCHURZ, CARL. *The Reminiscences of Carl Schurz.* New York, 1907-8. 3 vols.

SEMMES, RAPHAEL. *The Cruise of the Alabama and the Sumter.* New York, 1864.

———. *Memoirs of Service Afloat, During the War Between the States.* Baltimore, 1869.

The Times (London), May-June, 1861.

The Tribune (New York), December, 1860-March, 1861; January-May, 1868; January-May, 1872; January-May, 1873.

UNITED STATES DEPARTMENT OF STATE. *Papers Relating to Foreign Affairs.* Title varies; Washington, 1861- .

WALLACE, SARAH A., and FRANCES E. GILLESPIE, eds. *The Journal of Benjamin Moran.* Chicago, 1848. 2 vols.

WELLES, GIDEON. *Diary of Gideon Welles.* New York, 1911. 3 vols.

IV. SECONDARY BOOKS AND ARTICLES

ADAMS, CHARLES F. *Charles F. Adams.* New York, 1900.

ADAMS, EPHRAIM D. *Great Britain and the American Civil War.* London, 1925. 2 vols.

ADAMS, HENRY. *The Education of Henry Adams.* New York, 1931.

AMICIS, EDMONDO DE. *Holland and its People.* New York, 1888.

BAEHR, HARRY W. *The New York Tribune since the Civil War.* New York, 1936.

BAILEY, THOMAS A. *A Diplomatic History of the American People.* New York, 1940.

———. *The Man in the Street: The Impact of American Public Opinion on Foreign Policy.* New York, 1948.

BALL, WILLIAM W. *The State that Forgot: South Carolina's Surrender to Democracy.* Indianapolis, 1932.

BANCROFT, FREDERIC. *The Life of William H. Seward.* New York, 1900. 2 vols.

BARINGER, WILLIAM E. *A House Dividing: Lincoln as President Elect.* Springfield, Illinois, 1945.

———. *Lincoln's Rise to Power.* Boston, 1937.

BARNES, GILBERT H. *The Antislavery Impulse, 1830-1844.* New York, 1933.

BARRETT, DON C. *The Greenbacks and the Resumption of Specie Payments, 1862-1879.* Cambridge, Mass., 1931.

BEALE, HOWARD K. *The Critical Year: A Study of Andrew Johnson and Reconstruction.* New York, 1930.

———. "The Tariff and Reconstruction," *American Historical Review,* XXXV (January, 1930), 276-94.

BEARD, CHARLES and MARY. *The Rise of American Civilization.* New York, 1934. 2 vols.

BELOFF, MAX. "Great Britain and the American Civil War," *History,* XXXVII (February, 1952), 40-48.

BEMIS, SAMUEL F. *A Diplomatic History of the United States.* New York, 1936.

BERTHOFF, ROWLAND T. "Southern Attitudes toward Immigration, 1865-1914," *Journal of Southern History,* XVII (August, 1951), 328-60.

BEVERIDGE, ALBERT J. *Abraham Lincoln, 1809-1858.* New York, 1928. 2 vols.

BILLINGTON, RAY A. *The Protestant Crusade, 1800-1860.* New York, 1938.

BLAKE, NELSON M. *William Mahone of Virginia.* Richmond, 1935.

BLOK, PETRUS J. *History of the People of the Netherlands.* New York, 1898-1912. 5 vols.

BOWERS, CLAUDE. *The Tragic Era: The Revolution after Lincoln.* Cambridge, Mass., 1929.

CARMAN, HARRY J., and REINHARD H. LUTHIN. *Lincoln and the Patronage.* New York, 1943.

CARROLL, E. MALCOLM. *Origins of the Whig Party.* Durham, 1925.

CHANNING, EDWARD. *A History of the United States.* New York, 1925. 6 vols.

CHILDS, JAMES R. *American Foreign Service.* New York, 1948.

CLAPP, MARGARET. *Forgotten First Citizen: John Bigelow.* Boston, 1947.

CLAY, CASSIUS M. *The Life of Cassius M. Clay.* Cincinnati, 1886. 2 vols.

CLEVEN, N. ANDREW N. "Some Plans for Colonizing Liberated Negro Slaves in Hispanic America," *Journal of Negro History,* XI (1926), 35-49.

COLEMAN, CHARLES H. *The Election of 1868.* New York, 1933.

COLENBRANDER, H. T. *Koloniale Geschiedenis.* The Hague, 1925. 3 vols.

CONWAY, MONCURE D. *Thomas Carlyle.* New York, 1881.

CORTISSOZ, ROYAL. *The Life of Whitelaw Reid.* New York, 1921. 2 vols.

COULTER, E. MERTON. *The South during Reconstruction, 1865-1877.* Baton Rouge, 1947.

CURTIS, FRANCIS. *The Republican Party.* New York, 1904. 2 vols.

DALZELL, GEORGE W. *The Flight from the Flag.* Chapel Hill, 1940.

D'ARCY, WILLIAM. *The Fenian Movement in the United States: 1858-1886.* Washington, 1947.

DAVIS, HAROLD. *An International Community on the St. Croix.* Orono, Maine, 1950.

DENNETT, TYLER. "Seward's Far Eastern Policy," *American Historical Review,* XXVIII (October, 1922), 45-62.

DEWEY, DAVIS R. *Financial History of the United States*. New York, 1928.

DuBois, W. E. B. *Black Reconstruction*. New York, 1935.

DUNNING, WILLIAM A. *Reconstruction, Political and Economic, 1865-1877*. New York, 1907.

EDMUNDSON, GEORGE. *History of Holland*. Cambridge, 1922.

ELLIOTT, CHARLES W. *Winfield Scott: The Soldier and the Man*. New York, 1937.

FAULKNER, HAROLD U. *American Economic History*. New York, 1943.

FESSENDEN, FRANCIS. *Life and Public Services of William Pitt Fessenden*. New York, 1907. 2 vols.

FLEMING, WALTER L. "Deportation and Colonization: An Attempted Solution of the Race Problem," *Studies in Southern History and Politics*. New York, 1914.

FOX, E. L. *The American Colonization Society, 1817-1840*. Baltimore, 1919.

FUESS, CLAUDE M. *Carl Schurz: Reformer*. New York, 1932.

GOSNELL, HARPUR A., ed. *Rebel Raider: Being an Account of Raphael Semmes' Cruise in the C. S. A. Sumter*. Chapel Hill, 1948.

HALE, WILLIAM H. *Horace Greeley: Voice of the People*. New York, 1950.

HAMLIN, CHARLES E. *The Life and Times of Hannibal Hamlin*. Cambridge, Mass., 1899.

HAMMOND, BRAY. "Jackson, Biddle, and the Bank of the United States," *Journal of Economic History*, VII (May, 1947), 1-23.

HARPER, ROBERT S. *Lincoln and the Press*. New York, 1951.

HART, ALBERT B. *Salmon Portland Chase*. New York, 1899.

HATCH, LOUIS C. *Maine: A History*. New York, 1919. 3 vols.

HAYES, CARLTON J. H. *A Generation of Materialism*. New York, 1941.

HESSELTINE, WILLIAM B. *Ulysses S. Grant: Politician*. New York, 1935.

HODDER, FRANK H. "The Genesis of the Kansas-Nebraska Act," *Proceedings* of the Wisconsin State Historical Society, *1912* (1913), 69-86.

ISELY, JETER A. *Horace Greeley and the Republican Party, 1853-1861*. Princeton, 1947.

JARRELL, HAMPTON M. *Wade Hampton and the Negro*. Columbia, S. C., 1949.

JONES, GROSVENOR M. *Government Aid to Merchant Shipping.* Washington, 1925.

JORDAN, DONALDSON, and EDWIN J. PRATT. *Europe and the American Civil War.* New York, 1931.

JOSEPHSON, MATTHEW. *The Politicos, 1865-1896.* New York, 1938.

JULIAN, GEORGE W. *Political Recollections, 1804-1872.* Chicago, 1884.

KERN, JOHN W. "The Presidential Election of 1872, and Its Effect Upon the Democratic Party," unpublished senior thesis, Princeton University.

KIEHL, ERNST J. *Ons Verdrag met Amerika.* The Hague, 1863.

KLOOS, G. J. *De Handelspolitieke Betrekkingen Tusschen Nederland en de Vereenigde Staten van Amerika, 1814-1914.* Amsterdam, n.d.

KNOWLES, L. C. A. *The Economic Development of the British Overseas Empire.* London, 1928.

KNOWLTON, I. C. *Annals of Calais, Maine and St. Stephen, New Brunswick.* Calais, 1875.

KORNGOLD, RALPH. *Two Friends of Man.* Boston, 1950.

LARSON, HENRIETTA M. *Jay Cooke: Private Banker.* Cambridge, Mass., 1936.

LUTHIN, REINHARD H. *The First Lincoln Campaign.* Cambridge, Mass., 1944.

MAN, ALBON P., JR. "Labor Competition and the New York Draft Riots of 1863," *Journal of Negro History,* XXXVI (October, 1951), 375-405.

MILLER, ALPHONSE. *Thaddeus Stevens.* New York, 1939.

MILTON, GEORGE F. *The Age of Hate: Andrew Johnson and the Radicals.* New York, 1930.

———. *The Eve of Conflict: Steven A. Douglas and the Needless War.* Boston, 1934.

MITCHELL, WESLEY C. *A History of the Greenbacks.* Chicago, 1903.

MONAGHAN, JAY. *Diplomat in Carpet Slippers: Abraham Lincoln Deals with Foreign Affairs.* New York, 1945.

MORISON, SAMUEL E., and HENRY S. COMMAGER. *The Growth of the American Republic.* New York, 1942. 2 vols.

MOTT, FRANK L. *American Journalism.* New York, 1950.

NEFF, EMERY. *Carlyle.* New York, 1932.

NEVINS, ALLAN. *Emergence of Lincoln.* New York, 1950. 2 vols.

――――. *American Press Opinion.* New York, 1928.

――――. *Hamilton Fish: The Inner History of the Grant Administration.* New York, 1936.

――――. *Ordeal of the Union.* New York, 1947. 2 vols.

NICOLAY, JOHN G., and JOHN HAY. *Abraham Lincoln: A History.* New York, 1890. 10 vols.

OBERHOLTZER, ELLIS P. *Jay Cooke: Financier of the Civil War.* Philadelphia, 1907. 2 vols.

O'BRIEN, FRANK M. *The Story of the Sun, New York: 1833-1928.* New York, 1928.

PATTERSON, ROBERT T. *Federal Debt-management Policies, 1865-1879.* Durham, N. C., 1954.

PEARSON, CHARLES C. *The Readjuster Movement in Virginia.* New Haven, 1917.

PERKINS, DEXTER. *The Monroe Doctrine, 1826-1867.* Baltimore, 1933.

PIGGOTT, SIR FRANCIS. *The Declaration of Paris.* London, 1919.

PINCHON, EDGCUMB. *Dan Sickles: Hero of Gettysburg and "Yankee King of Spain."* New York, 1945.

POAGE, GEORGE R. *Henry Clay and the Whig Party.* Chapel Hill, 1936.

POORE, BEN PERLEY. "Washington News," *Harper's New Monthly Magazine,* XLVIII (January, 1874), 225-36.

POTTER, DAVID M. *Lincoln and His Party in the Secession Crisis.* New Haven, 1942.

RAMSDELL, CHARLES W. "Lincoln and Fort Sumter," *Journal of Southern History,* III (August, 1937), 259-88.

RANDALL, JAMES G. *The Civil War and Reconstruction.* Boston, 1937.

――――. *Lincoln and the South.* Baton Rouge, 1946.

――――. *Lincoln the President: Springfield to Gettysburg.* New York, 1945. 2 vols.

――――. "When War Came in 1861," *Abraham Lincoln Quarterly,* I (March, 1940), 3-42.

RATNER, SIDNEY. *American Taxation: Its History as a Social Force in Democracy.* New York, 1942.

RAY, PERLEY O. *The Repeal of the Missouri Compromise.* Cleveland, 1909.

RAYBACK, JOSEPH G. "The American Workingmen and the Anti-slavery Crusade," *Journal of Economic History,* III (November, 1943), 152-63.

RHETT, ROBERT G. *Charleston, An Epic of Carolina.* Richmond, 1940.

RHODES, JAMES F. *History of the United States from the Compromise of 1850 to the Final Restoration of Home Rule at the South in 1877.* New York, 1893-1906. 7 vols.

ROBBINS, ROY. *Our Landed Heritage: The Public Domain, 1776-1936.* Princeton, 1942.

ROBERTS, W. ADOLPHE. *Semmes of the Alabama.* New York, 1938.

ROBINSON, WILLIAM M. *The Confederate Privateers.* New Haven, 1928.

ROSEBAULT, CHARLES J. *When Dana Was the Sun.* New York, 1931.

ROSS, EARLE D. *The Liberal Republican Movement.* New York, 1919.

SANDBURG, CARL. *Abraham Lincoln: The War Years.* New York, 1939. 4 Vols.

SHEPPARD, WILLIAM A. *Red Shirts Remembered: Southern Brigadiers of the Reconstruction Period.* Atlanta, 1940.

SHIPPEE, L. B. *Canadian-American Relations, 1849-1874.* New Haven, 1939.

SHUCKERS, J. W. *The Life and Public Services of Salmon Portland Chase.* New York, 1874

SHULTZ, WILLIAM J. *Financial Development of the United States.* New York, 1937.

SIMKINS, FRANCIS B., and ROBERT H. WOODY. *South Carolina during Reconstruction.* Chapel Hill, 1932.

SMITH, WILLIAM C. *The Francis Preston Blair Family in Politics.* New York, 1933. 2 vols.

SPAULDING, ELBRIDGE G. *History of the Legal Tender Paper Money.* Buffalo, 1869.

STODDARD, HENRY L. *Horace Greeley, Printer, Editor, Crusader.* New York, 1946.

STOREY, MOORFIELD. *Charles Sumner.* Boston, 1900.

SWISHER, CARL B. *Roger B. Taney.* New York, 1936.

TALBOT, GEORGE F. "James Shepherd Pike," *Collections and Proceedings of the Maine Historical Society,* I (1890), 225-60.

TAUSSIG, F. W. *The Tariff History of the United States.* New York, 1923.

TAYLOR, AMOS E. "Walker's Financial Mission to London on Behalf of the North, 1863-1864," *Journal of Economic and Business History,* III (February, 1931), 296-320.

TAYLOR, ALRUTHEUS A. *The Negro in South Carolina during the Reconstruction.* Washington, 1924.

THOMPSON, HENRY T. *Ousting the Carpetbagger from South Carolina.* Columbia, S. C., 1927.

TURNER, FREDERICK J. *The United States, 1830-1850: The Nation and Its Sections.* New York, 1935.

TYLER, DAVID B. *Steam Conquers the Atlantic.* New York, 1939.

VAN DEUSEN, GLYNDON G. *Thurlow Weed, Wizard of the Lobby.* Boston, 1947.

————. *Horace Greeley: Nineteenth-Century Crusader.* Philadelphia, 1953.

VERKADE, WILLEM. *Overzicht der Staatkundige Denkbeelden van Johan Rudolph Thorbecke (1798-1872).* Arnhem, 1935.

WARREN, CHARLES. *The Supreme Court in United States History.* Boston, 1922.

WEISBERGER, BERNARD A. *Reporters for the Union.* Boston, 1953.

WESLEY, CHARLES H. "Lincoln's Plan for Colonizing the Emancipated Negroes," *Journal of Negro History,* IV (1919), 7-21.

WESTERMAN, J. C. *The Netherlands and the United States: Their Relations in the Beginning of the Nineteenth Century.* The Hague, 1935.

WHITE, HORACE. *The Life of Lyman Trumbull.* New York, 1913.

WHITTIER, JOHN G. *Narrative and Legendary Poems.* Boston, 1888.

WILLIAMS, KENNETH P. *Lincoln Finds a General.* New York, 1949. 2 vols.

WILLIAMS, T. HARRY. *Lincoln and the Radicals.* Madison, Wis., 1941.

WILSON, JAMES H. *Life of Charles A. Dana.* New York, 1907.

WOOD, CHARLES W. *Through Holland.* London, 1877.

WOODY, ROBERT H. "The Labor and Immigration Problem of South Carolina during Reconstruction," *Mississippi Valley Historical Review,* XVIII (September, 1931), 195-212.

WOODWARD, C. VANN. *Reunion and Reaction: The Compromise of 1877 and the End of Reconstruction.* New York, 1951.

Index